SUPERNATURAL STORIES FOR BOYS

SUPERNATURAL STORIES FOR BOYS

Illustrated by REG GRAY

HAMLYN
LONDON · NEW YORK · SYDNEY · TORONTO

ACKNOWLEDGEMENTS

The publishers wish to express their thanks to Fleetway Publications Ltd for permission to include 'Diable Rouge', 'The Whispering House', 'The Ancestor Who Returned', 'The Phantom of Cursitor Fields' and 'One Foggy Night' in this collection.

First published 1968

Second impression 1971

Third impression 1972

Published by THE HAMLYN PUBLISHING GROUP LIMITED

London · New York · Sydney · Toronto

Hamlyn House, Feltham, Middlesex, England

ISBN 0 601 07073 9

Printed in Czechoslovakia by Naše Vojsko, Prague

51089/3

CONTENTS

Page

DIABLE ROUGE—THE RED DEVIL PHANTOM 7
by Christopher Kay

THE PREY 22
by Ted Cowan

DEATH AFTER LIFE 39
by Bill Swallow

THE WHISPERING HOUSE 49
by Jeffrey Gaunt

THE ANCESTOR WHO RETURNED 180
by James Garnett

THE GOLDEN AMULET 196
by Sydney Philips

THE PHANTOM OF CURSITOR FIELDS 213
by Henry Pope

THE BLACK CAT 318
by Edgar Allan Poe

ONE FOGGY NIGHT 326
by Dan Wallis

THE GREEN FEATHER 343
by Sydney Philips

'Diable Rouge' – the Red Devil Phantom

by CHRISTOPHER KAY

It was quiet in the barn. The last rays of the setting sun shone in through the doorway, revealing the workbench, the tools, and tyres, which had taken the place of farming implements and bales of hay.

On an upturned petrol tin sat Jim Duncan, testing the spokes of a racing car's wheel, and leaning against the bench behind him was old Sam Johnson, a grey-haired mechanic. The man was staring thoughtfully through the doorway and along the highway which ran straight through the French village, disappearing in the distance.

'It's about time Ben was back!' he muttered.

Jim made no answer as he continued his work, but his ears were strained for the first sound of an approaching racing car. Somewhere along that highway his brother Ben was at the wheel of a powerful sports car, making his last practice run before the start of what was likely to prove the greatest motor race that Europe had ever seen.

It was a race over a special three hundred and fifty mile circuit near Paris, and when the cars left the line Jim would be at his brother's side, acting as mechanic. Winning the race meant a lot to Ben; his was the only British car that had been entered, and it was one he had built himself.

There was a long silence, while the dusk deepened and the fields beyond the village became dim under gathering purple shadows. Then the grey-haired man spoke again.

'I told him to be sure and get back before dark,' he said, 'because—because that road's haunted!'

'What do you mean?' Jim asked, lookong at him sharply.

'This road forms part of the course,' Sam replied. 'And it's the same road that was used when this race was run thirty years ago, when the 'Diable Rouge' was driving. That name means the Red Devil, and it's one they gave to Karl Zimmer—and a devil he was, too!'

He turned slowly from his contemplation of the long highway, facing the sinewy young fellow. Jim was frowning now, wondering what the old mechanic would say next.

'I've been working with racing cars for the last forty years,' the man said. 'I was here when they ran the last race on this circuit, over thirty years ago, and do you know why they never held it again? It was because there were so many smashes, and because the Red Devil was killed within a mile of the finish. He had led for almost all the way, but he crashed within sight of the end—and it's he who haunts this road!'

He went silent for a moment, then went on.

'He's supposed to be seen at nights racing through the dark, just as he raced so long ago,' the mechanic said. 'There are mysterious accidents happening all the time down this road, and the people who live beside it won't drive their cars over it at night. That's why I shan't rest until Ben's safely back again.'

Jim drew a long breath. He knew old Sam well, and knew that he was not the sort of man to worry without cause. But this was the first that Jim had ever heard about the highway being the haunt of a spectral driver and a ghostly racing car.

He knew Ben was late. It was two hours since he had started with the car. They had been working on it all the afternoon, and Jim would have been riding with him now—since he was to be mechanic in the race—but Ben had chosen one really skilled in engineering to accompany him, just to make absolutely sure that there was nothing more to be done to make the car ready.

This was the first time that Ben had entered for a really big race. Jim had driven in races several times, but he lacked Ben's skill with a car, although Ben had assured him that one day he would be a fine driver. That was why he was to ride with the machine in this race, in order that he might get accustomed to really high speeds.

The two stood by the doorway, waiting and watching. The barn formed their headquarters, and they slept in the loft above the car. It was the only accommodation left in the village, because all the rest was occupied by rival machines and their crews.

If Ben could win it meant earning a fortune. He would drive to win, Jim knew that, but everything was against him. He had entered the race last, and would take last position at the start. Everything had to be found from his own resources, and if he failed he would be beaten and financially broken.

The fading sunshine vanished from the sky, and the darkness came with a rush. The purple shadows in the fields turned to a deeper hue. Lights sprang up in the quiet village, and then suddenly the two heard the blaring thunder of an approaching car.

'Here's Ben!' Jim exclaimed.

He recognised the sound of the car. It carried no lights, so that he could not mark its approach, but it was coming out of the darkness at terrific speed—at a pace which was dangerous in the gloom. Jim's heart seemed to stand sill as he listened; then, watching the road, he saw the car appear.

It was in the very centre, bursting out of the dark, with red flame stabbing from the exhaust, appearing to light the road behind. It came with a tremendous rush, then the engine note died and the car slowed, rushing towards the front of the barn, skidding again and again under the brakes before it stopped.

Jim and Sam ran towards it, and through the gloom the young mechanic could see that his brother was pale, and so was his companion. They made no answer to Sam's questions as they climbed slowly out, for both to stand looking back up the road.

'Is anything wrong?' Jim asked.

'No.' And Ben turned to him. 'The car's fine—perfect. It's never been faster.'

His voice was quiet, subdued. Much of the ruddy bronze had gone from his face, and, somehow, his eyes seemed very dark. When he unbuckled the strap of his helmet his fingers were quivering.

'Run the car inside,' he said. 'We'll clean everything up ready for the official inspection tomorrow, then we'll make final arrangements for the race.'

Ben's tone was short now. As he turned from Jim his glance met that of the mechanic who had travelled with him on this last practice dash, but each immediately avoided the other's glance and a few moments later all were busy running the racing car into the old barn.

When Jim switched on the lights which had been rigged from batteries, he noticed that Sam was looking at Ben curiously with something searching in his gaze, but he made no comment, and they started work on the car. It had to be made ready for inspection, and there would now be no more practice before the race.

There was much to be done, and it was late when Jim turned in. He mounted the ladder to the loft where blankets were stretched out on masses of hay, forming a soft and fragrant bed. He left Ben and Sam below, bending over a map of the course, making arrangements for the replenishment depot which was to be set up half-way round the one-lap, three hundred and fifty mile race; at this depot the car would stop for more fuel. The other mechanic had gone off into the village about some small matter.

Soon Jim had rolled himself up in his blankets, and he lay there listening to the voices of the two as they talked below. Somehow sleep would not come to him, and presently he noticed that the two had grown silent. He could hear the crackling of paper as Ben folded up the map, then Sam's voice came.

'You saw something tonight, didn't you?' he asked. 'What happened on that last run?'

'We were held up by plug trouble,' Ben replied. 'That's why we were late back.'

'Plug trouble didn't make you turn pale,' Sam said slowly. 'You saw—something!'

Again there was silence; then the mechanic spoke once more, his tone insistent now.

'Did you see the ghost?' he breathed.

Ben must have nodded, because Jim heard the grey-haired mechanic draw a sudden breath; then he spoke quickly on.

'I guessed it!' he exclaimed. 'That's why I didn't want you to remain out too long. What happened? Did he chase you?'

'Yes!' Ben answered, and his voice shook. 'I was never so scared in my life. The Red Devil seemed to come up behind me, when we were about seven miles away. His car was enormous, and it seemed to shine in the dark. I could see him—with his eyes burning behind his goggles. He was bent over the wheel, glaring at us!

'An old car he had—like those they used before the war. I couldn't hear it. I could hear nothing except our own machine; but he was close behind us, trying to pass—and you know how the legend goes. If the Red Devil chases you he tries to get by, and if he can pass he sends you off the road. That's the cause of all the accidents the French people talk about.'

'Thank Heaven that you kept ahead!' Sam breathed.

'I thought he'd got us!' Ben said swiftly. 'Twice he almost came level. My mechanic was shouting, and the car was moving as it's never moved before. I don't know how I kept in front, but I managed it; then we saw the lights of the village ahead, and the Red Devil vanished.'

The two were quiet for what seemed an age. Jim was sitting up now, listening with straining ears, yet hardly believing what he heard.

'I've never believed in anything like this befor,' Ben said slowly, 'but I do now. The Red Devil haunts that road; and I've got a feeling that he'll be watching the race tomorrow.'

'Ay, he'll be watching,' Sam replied grimly. 'He'll be watching, and he'll be waiting, and there'll be more than one who'll see him, even though the race is run in broad daylight.'

* * *

Jim tried to steady the wild beating of his heart as he stood by the roaring sports car. The bellowing of other machines was in his ears, for the cars were lining up in readiness for the start of the great race.

Oil smoke hovered all around him, pierced by the sunlight, which picked out the sleek, green colour of the British machine. It was low-built, very grim in its lines, and it had the appearance of being tremendously fast. Ben was bending over the side of the cockpit, keeping the engine running so that it warmed up. Beyond were their rivals, each machine the centre of a group of white-overalled men, anxiously examining their cars, and making certain that all was ready.

The burning sunshine caught the faces of spectators who had assembled, and they were packed along the edge of the tree-lined road which ran away ahead, vanishing in a pin-point over the distant horizon. For much more than three hundred miles that road ran on in a giant circle through towns and villages, across rivers and hilly heights. In half an hour the forty waiting machines would start, commencing a race like that of thirty years before. Soon they would be hurtling along the road down which the Red Devil, Karl Zimmer, had rushed so desperately, and over which his phantom shape still drove.

Ben suddenly switched off the engine and straightened up, glancing around at the other machines as Sam reappeared with the other mechanic, bringing spare goggles and tools whitch they stowed away.

'Well, you'll soon be off!' Sam panted, as he wiped the back of his hand across his forehead. 'As soon as you've gone, me and my mate will make a dash for the plane. We'll fly straight through to Poitiers, and we'll be waiting for you there when you stop to replenish. After that we'll fly back, and you'll see us on the finishing line when you arrive—the winner!'

'I'll do my best to win,' Ben said. 'This race means a lot to all of us.'

The start was only a few minutes away now.

Sam shook hands with Ben and then with Jim, wishing them luck, and the two climbed into the car. As he did so, Jim glanced past the spectators, and between the houses he could see the airfield just outside the village. Here there waited more than a dozen planes, which would take to the air the moment the cars left. One of them would carry their two mechanics on to the replenishment depot at half-distance, and it had been specially chartered for this purpose by Ben.

The road was cleared. Engines roared once more, and the rows of cars stood bellowing impatiently. Jim tightened the belt of his overalls, settling down in the seat beside his brother, and he saw Ben smile at him. He shouted something, but it was lost in the uproar.

A minute slid away; then the starter appeared at the side of the road, only just visible through the clouds of grey-blue exhaust smoke. The flag went up, and the bellowing of the waiting machines increased. Ben slid into gear while his right shoe eased the accelerator down.

Jim's gaze was glued to the flag. He saw Ben watching it as it was held high, poised for an instant, and then slashed down.

The whole mass of cars surged forward. Ben's car leaped away, jerked—and then its engine went dead!

It stopped, just as the Red Devil's car had stopped thirty years before!

Jim saw all the others getting away, howling down the road, leaving a smoke cloud behing them as they jostled and fought for leadership along the highway; then Sam and his companion had come running to where the green car stood alone at the start with a stalled engine.

They thrust on the tail. The car rolled forward. Ben let up the clutch and the engine fired. Next instant they were off, two hundred yards behind the rest, but with the rear wheels spinning for grip on the road, engine booming and exhaust roaring as the car leaped away in pursuit of the others.

'It's all right!' Ben called. 'We'll get by them. Being delayed will give them a chance to spread out, and passing them will be easy. We've a long way to go, and I'll take it steady at first.'

They were last for a dozen miles, then Ben began to open up. Jim could see three cars immediately ahead, and they rushed down on them, with Ben pulling out to the side of the road as he came to their tails. The rear wheels of the three cars flung back stones; grit and dust beat across the radiator in a stinging hail; then they were level and passing.

Jim saw the other drivers. He had a glimpse of huddled mechanics, then they were left behind, and Ben set himself to overtake another car which showed ahead.

A corner came up as they overtook the other car, and Ben held his speed, shooting past it before he used his brakes. They fairly leaped into the turn, the steering-wheel was locked over, and then they were sliding round, with the dust skating from their tyres. Another swift bend, then the road opened up once more, and Ben's foot went hard down on the throttle again.

That was four cars they had passed, and Jim kept count of them. In order to win, they had to get by thirty-five more machines; only then would they be in the lead.

Steadily now, Ben set himself to overtake the machines ahead, and there were ten behind them when, roaring through a bend, Jim had a glimpse of a car half upside-down at the side of the road, with a crowd rushing towards the wreck.

It was a blue French machine. It was smoking, and one wheel was still spinning, while flames were starting to lick from under the bonnet. In an instant, it had been left behind, but Jim knew that he had seen only the first crash in the long race. The second came on the very edge of a town, just as Ben roared up overtake the car.

The driver of the machine ahead applied his brakes to take the turn into the town, when a front tyre burst. Jim saw the car lurch, flinging into a broadside skid—blocking the road! Instantly Ben drew to the far side of the highway, brakes shrieking. The other driver tried to straighten out, only for his car to mount the footpath.

Next instant, it caught the front of a house which edged the path, and the sound that the impact made was like that of an explosion. The car bucked away from the wall, and for one instant Jim thought that it would strike them. But it missed and fell behind, while Ben carried on through the corner, kicking the throttle open to its limit once more.

On they thundered, overtaking car after car, always with Jim keeping count. The green machine was enormously fast as it raced over the sunlit roads, and they were twenty miles from the half-distance point, where they had to stop for more petrol, when they had put thirty of the rival machines behind them, and they passed five more before the town of Poitiers showed in the distance.

At its edge was the village where Sam had set up the replenishment depot, and Jim shouted as he picked it out. He saw the fuel beside the road, the tools that had been spread out, the spare wheels and the two men waving their arms. The car stopped; instantly Jim leaped out and began work.

Oil, water, and petrol were flung in, and the four wheels were changed, while Sam shouted to Ben, telling him how the race was going.

'You're sixth!' he called. 'There cars immediately ahead have gone through in a bunch. Giulio, the Italian, is leading —but you'll catch him!'

The work was done. The two leaped into the car again, and the watching crowd cheered them off. Through the town they swept and into open country again, and it was then that Jim sighted the three bunched machines in front. They closed on them gradually. The three were duelling together, each striving to leave the rest behind, and Ben had to pull to the very side of the road to get by.

He passed them, one after the other, each time with a bellowing roar as the thunder of the cars merged, and the smooth metal sides all but touched. When the three machines lay behind in the choking dust Jim knew that but two cars lay between themselves and leadership of the race.

Now Ben's pace increased. Fifty miles and more sped under the thrashing wheels, and they then saw the German car that held second place. It was like a white blur on the road, and it lay very far ahead, but they overtook it, although they were no more than a hundred miles from the finish by the time that they did get past. Once, however, the dust cloud which it raised was left behind, they saw another cloud in front and knew that it was Giulio, the Italian who led the race.

Ben's face set. His eyes glittered behind his goggles, and now he drove as he had never done before. Gradually he closed down, and as they sped into a village he shot to the Italian's tail. Here the road surface was loose. The leading car's rear wheels shot a volley of stones back at the British machine. They smashed on the front and along the side of the car as Ben pulled out to pass, and, suddenly, the green car swerved dangerously.

For one moment Jim thought they would leave the road. Their wheels skidded as they bit against the grass, then Ben regained control and the brakes went on. Jim looked at him, and saw blood on his brother's face. He had been hit by one of the flying stones, and he slumped back in his seat as the machine stopped.

'Are you hurt?' Jim gasped.

His brother made an effort to speak, and his voice came hoarsely.

'Take over—drive on!' he gasped.

Jim scrambled from his seat. He could not tell how much Ben was hurt, but as he ran around to the other side of the car he saw his brother changing places, tearing away his goggles and dabbing weakly at his brow with his hand. The blow had half stunned him, and he was in no condition to drive on. All Jim could do was to take over and do his best.

He slid into the vacated seat, and as his hands dropped behind the wheel he saw that the red car had halted on the road far ahead. On those loose stones it had punctured a tyre; the Italian and the mechanic were making a racing change, and they had almost completed the work by the time that Jim went forward.

His heart was thudding in his chest now, as the engine responded to his touch on the throttle. He knew that they had only to pass the car ahead to take the lead, and if only he could drive well enough they might yet win.

They roared on, and he saw the Italian crew climbing back to their cockpit. They were looking back when the green car rushed level—and passed! Jim was in the lead—but could he hold it? Could he drive fast enough to withstand the challenge of the experienced driver behind him?

Jim did not know how far they now had to go, and he called to his brother. Ben answered faintly from his seat, and Jim dared a glance at him. Ben was holding his head, but he was alert now, and gradually recovering. Jim could see enough to learn that the stone had smashed his goggles and had cut one eyebrow; he would not be able to drive, whatever happened, now, because blood was trickling from his wound, masking his sight.

All Jim could do was to roar on. He took a bend in the road and the car skidded a little, but he straightened safely. He glanced in his rear-view mirror, and saw the Italian coming up behind, although he was still some distance away. For all that, he was gaining, and Jim's foot went hard down. A brief straight ended in another village, and he thundered through it, the crowds cheering him on. For miles he held the lead, and then the strain began to tell. He slowed, and he heard Ben shouting for him to keep the throttle open.

But Jim was not used to driving for so long at such speed. It took toll of his nerve and strength. He knew that he was near the finish now, but he felt that he could not withstand the strain much longer. The hammering and jolting that he had undergone in the earlier part of the race had tired him, but he knew that he must do his best. At any moment Giulio might overtake and pass him. He glanced in the rear-view mirror, and then a gasp of horror left his parched lips.

Another car was on his tail, and his heart seemed to stand still, because it was not Giulio, the Italian driver.

It was a red car, but it was altogether bigger, and there was something strange about it as it loomed through the dust-cloud. Jim dared another glance, and all the blood drained from his face, for he recognised the driver of the machine behind him.

It was the Diable Rouge—the Red Devil!

It was the phantom which had pursued his brother, and now it was pursuing him!

Jim dared not look behind again. His foot ranned the throttle pedal to its limit, and he went through a bend ahead as fast as ever Ben could have done. His foot never eased on the throttle, as he flung the car on—while the shadowy shape appeared to creep up at one side, grimly determined to pass.

At that Jim called on every last ounce of nerve and strength, and the phantom of the road faded behind, only to draw almost level again. Jim could see eyes glittering behind dark goggles, but he could hear no sound above the thunder of his own machine.

And now the spectral shape behind him made a last effort to pass. From the corner of his eye, Jim saw the red and glistening shape coming up, edging nearer and nearer, while he went down the descent with the throttle rammed to its limit—and suddenly recognised the corner at the bottom as the one where the Red Devil had crashed.

The spectral shape was forcing him to go too fast—hoping that he, too, would find disaster in the same spot!

The spectral car came nearer—forcing Jim to a faster speed

Jim did not ease his speed. He held his pace until the last possible moment and he was almost on the turn when he made use of his brakes. He felt the car skid into the corner. He juggled with the steering-wheel, fighting the skids. He straightened the car and sent it on through the turn to where great crowds were waiting at the finish.

And now, the red spectre was no longer behind him. It had vanished.

Mechanically he drove on. He saw the finishing line and the winner's flag falling as he passed it. He saw Sam rushing to meet the car; then he put on the brakes and stopped.

Ben's injury was not serious and he soon recovered. He was full of praise for the way in which his brother had driven over the last miles.

'We'd have lost, if it hadn't been for you,' he said.

'I didn't win,' Jim answered. 'It was the Diable Rouge who won—he was chasing us until we got to the corner where he crashed.'

That evening, when the crowd had gone, Jim Duncan took the laurel wreath which had been placed over the Duncan Special's bonnet and he set it on the stone which marked the resting-place of Karl Zimmer, the Diable Rouge.

He placed it there in tribute to a man who had been a fine driver, and in thanks for the strange part that the ghostly form had played in the big race.

And now men travel at night over the long French road, for the spectre of the highway has gone.

No one has seen it since Jim Duncan won his first big race.

The Prey

by TED COWAN

In the evening light—such light as a leaden-grey sky shot with scud would permit—the road stretched out in sombre, meandering ceaselessness. Dusty verges vanished into grass, storm-lit grass, that writhed snakelike in an eddying wind. Rain was in the air and its chill bite stung the eyes.

'Twenty-three miles from Cromer. We should have stopped there,' Gil Martin said, hammering his miserably fickle cycle lamp which had a particular aversion to lighting. 'Confound this lamp! I wish I'd slung it and bought a dynamo hub.'

Two companions, pedalling behind him and with little interest in the vagaries of cycle lamps, hunched deeper into their capes and looked anxiously at the ominous merging of sky, road and shadowed hedgerows. The wind crawled deeper into blackthorn, poplars and creaking elm trees, a tattered confetti of leaves dancing before hissing tyres.

It had been fine and sunlit at their departure some two long hours previously. Since then they had turned and side-tracked, taking time to gaze at various intriguing views of the Broads. That was until the swift and surprising deterioration in wether had trapped them.

'It's going to thundering well *bucket!*' Reg Denby was definite. 'Blasted weather. It's the third time we've been caught out this week.'

Toddy, last of the trio and the nearest to twenty, grinned to himself while using gears to advantage. The joint cycling holiday, far from uneventful, would make an amusing topic for dull moments in the future. He at least had escaped from even a puncture, and his self-congratulation eased the discomfort of the wind.

'We'll make for Ovelton. I've an address for lodgings there. Mrs Burt passed it on,' Gill shouted back over his shoulder. He found a left turn, took it—and caught the wind broadside, and straightened out with certain words old Mrs Burt would not have approved of.

'Feeling better?' Reg asked unwisely. 'Your rear lamp's not working. You'd better stop and kick it like you did the last time.'

Gil's reply was lost in a sudden sobbing gust of wind that engulfed the cawing of flighting rooks seeking sanctuary. The ominous hue of the sky darkened a shade, while fresh showers of leaves descended to stick tackily to capes and entwine between wheel spokes.

A new urgency forced the trio to increase speed, no spare breath available speech. The rain started slowly, then the drops pattered through overhanging boughs to become lances of water. Rivulets poured from capes and soaked into trousers or danced back just as coldly from the road. The riders wavered, swaying from side to side as if to avoid the misery already surrounding them. Two dynamo lamps cut sickly swathes through the gloom.

It was Reg Denby who first noticed something wrong in the road surface, namely that dark asphalt seemed to have disintegrated into deep ruts of originally hard mud. The cycle jolted and jarred over what might well have been a cyclo-cross course chosen by some non-cycling sadist. Gil's front lamp, after coming on briefly, jolted from its bracket and, after sudden application of brakes, brought all three disgrunted victims to a halt.

'Very clever, Gil. You nearly had me over the handlebars. It's not your day,' Reg breathed heavily. 'As a matter of interest, where are we? You do know, of course? I mean, we're not lost or anything ridiculous like that?'

'Gil uses a map. He memorises it,' Toddy said hopefully. Toddy was the loyal kind. 'Don't you remember what he said about map-reading? You know, that time you lost us where the T-road seemed to go the wrong way.'

Gil did not answer. He was on hands and knees, recovering his lamp from a ditch abundant in nettles.

He finally rose, gazed all around and impressed his comrades by how he appeared to be taking in all landmarks. Rain coursed down his face and he dropped a handkerchief while trying to get the worst from his eyes.

'Yes, I know. We're lost!' The thought cheered him. 'We're on the wrong road, in the wrong place, at the wrong time. And I've left the map at Mrs Burt's. I can tell we're wrong because this isn't a second class road or a third class—it's a perishing cart track in the heart of a rain-beaten wilderness. We *are* lost!'

'That's what I thought,' Reg said. 'I knew the signs. Remind me to let you go as pathfinder again. You've chosen the peach of a time.'

Gil chuckled, and Toddy found himself following.

'We'll remember our holiday. Could happen to anyone,' Gil said. 'Look here, our best bet is to keep moving and stop at the first place that looks as if it'll provide bed-and-breakfast.'

'There'll be dozens of'em. Like we haven't seen so much as a cottage in the last hour,' Reg answered. 'For Pete's sake refit that lamp and get riding. I don't fancy trees when lightning starts doing its stuff.'

They fumbled, rearranged capes and set off along the track which oozed at each pedal-thrust.

'No bird sings!' Gil called, determined to brighten the

occasion. A sense of guilt was the cause. 'Into the great unknown. Yell out if you ride into the Broads.'

Again silence followed. Trees and shrubs lashed and twisted as the wind-carried rain mounted in savagery. A bough cracked and fell splintering behind them. Then the first real fork of lightning cut skies in two and left coloured lights dancing before half-closed eyes. The crash to follow made Toddy cry out, flinching involuntarily. The air was electrified and heavy with the taint of ozone.

'It isn't fooling. We're in for it!' Reg exclaimed, when his ears had ceased ringing. 'We can't ride on in this. Gil, stop, you idiot.'

They all stopped. Another flash revealed an old finger-post which seemed to leap from the shadows beneath tossing boughs.

'Go back. Read it!' Gil directed Toddy. 'You're nearest. Go on, you be clever for a change.'

Toddy propped his bike against a dripping poplar and retreated into the murk where the finger-post had merged to invisibility. Another glaring flash silhouetted them both.

'Ye Hunters!' Toddy yelled, 'Ye Hunters or something.'

He advanced towards them, a cape-draped figure in a halo of rebounding rain.

'Sounds like a pub. Not like a place name—we hope,' Gil said, struggling to remount. 'We'll try them for bed-and-breakfast. Anyway, it'll be shelter.'

'Come on! Don't hang about talking,' Reg said sharply, 'let's head for cover. I don't fancy being outside longer than we can help.'

They swayed away again, Toddy leading the single-file procession. Trees closed about them, while the storm darkness grew to night intensity, the wind sounding like some mad train in a tunnel. The track was little more than a footpath, then a light showed clearly from near where osiers flailed.

It winked out cheerfully, an oasis of comfort in a desert of sobbing, roaring darkness.

'A pub! Ye olde inne,' Gil exclaimed with enthusiasm. 'It'd hardly be a mock Tudor tea-house. Not in this forsaken hole.'

The lightning's blaze and the accompanying clap came together. It robbed them of breath and destroyed Gil's attempt at encouraging humour. Around the lights, which could only glow from windows, the surrounding structure sprang into being and vanished again, a photographic impression which died almost as soon as it came.

'You're right, Gil! An inn—hotel—half-timbered,' Toddy called from ahead of them. 'We're in luck.'

'Half-timbered? Didn't look like it to me,' Reg answered from the darkness behind.

'Queen Elizabeth slept here,' Gil called. 'Go on, keep pedalling. It doesn't matter a hoot about timbers. A dry room and some food are what we have to worry about.'

They glimpsed iron gates swinging against supports shrouded by foliage. The wind veered to behind them. Wet masses of tangled boughs bent aside from their path. Rain made the impression a blurred series of sensations. They only halted when they heard gravel crunching under their tyres. Dynamo lamps faded and dismounting figures were swallowed by darkness. Only Gil's inefficient lamp spread its yellow glow over a matter of two feet at the most.

'Where's the house then? The pub—or what-have-you?' Reg asked sharply. 'We saw its lighted windows. Where are they now?'

'Hanged if I know!' Gil's detached lamp flickered as he turned it about him. 'Perhaps someone switched off.'

'At this hour? Folk don't turn in at seven o'clock!'

Red sounded puzzled and vaguely uneasy. It was Toddy who walked ahead and suddenly gave a shout that brought them both to him. Above them the vague shape of the house loomed in contrast to the rest of the background. They stared at it, their eyes growing accustomed to the variations in shade.

'It's not a pub. It's all dark—not a light,' Gil stared up at it. 'Who mentioned Tudor style? Toddy, is this what you saw?'

'I don't know. This seems all brick. I saw timbers—white plaster. You know the kind of thing. Perhaps there are two houses. This is bigger—'

Toddy broke off, for the storm wind tore at them viciously, its buffeting carrying them almost off their feet. The rain came with it, finding its way beneath theie capes at the neck and reminding them of what they hoped to escape. Shelter was a matter of urgency, and further discussion died a natural death.

'We'll knock! Someone ought to take pity on us.' Gil had to shout to make himself heard. 'There's a porch here. Leave your bikes!'

They followed him blindly, stumbling into each other. Reg hit his leg on a pedal and the fierceness of the pain made him halt. He glanced up, a grey light piercing the sky's sombre blanket. For an instant he saw an inn-sign swinging over his head. Its shrill squeak grated before being swamped by the wind.

The buffeting eased. They were within the large porch, gazing back in some relief at the merciless rain which rebounded in a white hare from flooded gravel. Toddy felt himself start as he heard Gil knock on a door. The sound boomed back uncannily, reminding them of the now grumbling thunder. They had left their cycles, Gil retaining his lamp.

'It's open!' Gil's voice rose a trifle. 'The front door's open. Should we go in?'

'Yes—explain later.' Toddy pushed the two of them ahead

of him. 'You're good at talking. Anyway we don't look like burglars. You can't do more than knock.'

The storm fell behind them, its sounds strangely distant. Gil's lamp flickered across bare walls and damp boards of an equally bare floor. They were in a hall. The smell rushing to greet them held that cold 'emptiness' with a tinge of decay that Toddy was the first to recognise. He laughed and the hollow echoes laughed back.

'It's derelict! An empty house! Isn't it typical?'

'Shut up!' Reg said.

The echoed laughter had been unpleasant and his own tones held a rasp which he himself recognised. The sickly light from the lamp was as unpleasant as the distant odour of fungus. He wondered how it would sound if he suggested they were to leave and move on.

The crash of thunder sent every wall shuddering about them. Lightning glared lividly, reflecting from ugly moist balls of decay on the floor. A shadow swept in, a second thunderous crash startling them. A pale oblong vanished; the front door had slammed.

'Made me jump,' Gil exclaimed shakily. 'Wind must have caught it.'

He moved across to the door, Reg striding to clutch at the ring handle which rocked in the light of the lamp. They gripped together, but the door withstood their joint efforts. A warped frame held it securely, the damp oak not giving so much as a fraction.

'Jammed?' Toddy tried to make the question casual.

'Well and truly. Still, we're under cover. Bit of a joke really.' Reg revealed none of the panic that made his stomach start crawling within him. 'Might as well explore. Let's find a room with a grate and then think about starting a fire.'

The idea was applauded, though Toddy's mind was still on the inn sign he had seen and heard swinging. It worried him, for the sign held nothing in common with the type of dwelling his senses now recognised. The house they were in—it was a house—was old and horribly ordinary. He wished he had not thought of 'horrible'. It was wrong; the wrong word in the wrong house, at the wrong time.

He shook his head and, clenching both hands, forced himself to a matter-of-fact set of actions. Toddy stripped off the wet cape, his example reminding his friends they were in the same plight. Gil stood adjusting the lamp, his anxiety to keep it operational showing in the too nervous haste of his fingers. He led the way, and their footfalls echoed from empty spaces, the island of light keeping back the flood-tide of dark.

The storm was distant. They glimpsed it several times through dusty panes of glass across which a green film of bacteria crept from the leprous, rotted window frames. Several windows were boarded and the air in these rooms made them abandon them fast. One room led into another, and a sudden unpleasant realisation made Gil catch his breath.

'I think we're circling,' he said, 'I can't find how to return to the front door. Silly isn't it?'

No one answered him. From the depths of the unknown house a breath of air stirred. Reg found his own breath coming faster. He had heard something, heard a movement like heavy feet dragging. A door slammed somewhere away in the vastness. Gill spun around, the lamp throwing weird shadows across peeling walls.

An inn sign creaked. They glimpsed it as it twisted in the wind beyond a window. Toddy darted to the panes and gazed out.

'Creeper tendrils,' he said, aware that everyone was regarding him very closely. 'Stupid, dam' place. Probably full of rats. There'll be plenty of them in this neighbourhood.'

'Here, I've found the other door,' Reg called, dragging back a rotting partition. 'This way! I think it leads us back

 'The front door! It's disappeared!'

to the hall. Let's follow this way and see where it leads us.'

They moved out. What they saw reawoke the earlier glimmerings of panic, for the hall was not the one by which they had entered. At least, where the front door had been was now a blank wall.

'Must be a wing. You know, a kind of duplicate of the other part,' Gil said quickly—too quickly. 'Ghastly smell. Dry rot or . . .'

'Fungus,' Reg exclaimed harshly. 'We're beginning to make a thing of this, aren't we? For heaven's sake let's get organised—and stop whispering.'

'Who's whispering?' Toddy wished he had kept silent. 'I mean, it's the air movement. The whole place is vibrating in the storm.'

The tension mounted. There *was* something wrong about the house; each of them felt it. It wasn't what they saw, heard or imagined, it was more of a feeling. The atmosphere seemed to be closing tighter about them. A clattering made them look up.

A piece of wood had fallen. It rolled from stair to stair down a staircase; a staircase only revealed when Gil moved his lamp swiftly to an area which darkness had formerly concealed.

'Let's try up here!' he said, without knowing quite why he said it, 'Are you scared or something?'

He strode forward and mounted the stairs, glad to hear the swiftness of their footfalls behind him. They reached a landing and passed beyond into a large room overlooking the gravel drive along which they had arrived. The light from the large window, each pane intact, seemed cheerily bright after the shadows of the lower interior. Even the storm sky was cheering. Toddy wiped his brow in sudden relief.

'That's better. Good, there's a fireplace. There ought to be enough rubbish in this old dump to start a bit of a fire.'

'O. K., you look around. Any dead wood will do,' Gil said, producing some matches. He knelt by the grate which was half filled with discoloured soot. 'Strip off some wall-paper, if it actually needs stripping. Most of it's hanging by itself.'

The lamp was placed on the floor, beside a metal fender that rust had encrusted. A beetle scurried from beneath it as the heavy fender moved beneath the disgusted thrust of Gil's foot. Minutes later a flame flickered, fed by oddments they gained from a hurried search. The flames grew, glowing ruddily on the walls which exuded moisture. It became a matter of urgency to keep the blaze going, and Gil counted the last few pieces of wood.

'Try to find some more. There's a room next to this. You go, Toddy.'

'Can I have the lamp?'

Gil hesitated only a moment. He nodded, and Toddy took the lamp, and slowly made for the door.

'Hurry, must keep the old fire going,' Gil prompted.

Toddy's cry rang through the room and brought Reg, white-faced, tearing after him.

'I've found a four-poster bed!' Toddy was calling. 'In the room next door.'

He met them outside, only a few yards from the room in which the feeble fire crackled. He pointed to where his lamp cast its glow over a second room almost identical.

'My grief, did you have to shout like that?' Reg asked shakily. 'We thought . . . I thought . . .' He broke off.

'What four-poster bed?' Gil was staring into the lamplight. 'Have you flipped?'

Toddy turned and looked again. His lips worked, his tongue moving over them wetly. The room was empty. Broken floorboards lay where rot and time had displaced them. He had seen the bed though, seen it with its drapes agleam in the lamplight. He had noticed how the shadow covered all of one wall.

'Get that wood for the fire,' Gil said quietly, moving to gather new fragments. 'Here, give me a hand, Reg. Toddy, just hold the lamp still!'

He was sweating. He could feel it running down his back while a primitive chill began to tear away at all reasoning. He did not doubt Toddy; that was why he was frightened. Yet he dared not believe him. It would not take much more to snap self-control.

They hurried back to the fire room and fed wood hastily on to flickering embers. The flames danced anew and, next door, a door closed very distinctly. Toddy crouched by the small blaze; he was shivering.

'That bed,' he said, 'I saw it. Gil, there—there was a body under its covers.' He pressed a handkerchief to his mouth. 'I feel sick.'

Gil sucked in breath. He poked the fire with his foot and watched sparks shower up the chimney. He dared not look at Reg. In fact, he dared not turn round.

They could all hear it. Their own door—and they never remembered the room having a door—was closing. It had closed! The fire flickered from the quiet movement. Then there was the click of a heavy key being turned.

Reg was the first to move. He crossed to the door, saw it was without a handle. It was old; too for old the house. From below them the air whispered, whispered through corridors like something unspeakable chuckling. Gil leaned across and gripped Toddy's arm.

'That other room. It WAS empty when we saw it. But I belive you.' He had to say something. Terror was rising now, for something in the house was nearing a climax. If ever before they had experienced a meeting with evil, they certainly were experiencing it now.

'You know it's our turn next, don't you?' Toddy, eyes very bright, stared as if hypnotised. 'That body in the four-poster bed. I—'

Gil moved like lightning, his hand cracking across the white cheek.

Toddy sat up with a jerk. He blinked surprisedly and stared at Gil in amazement. He seemed like someone who had come out of a trance.

'What?' he started, then stopped for he could see how Gil and Reg were both looking. He did not want to know any more.

'We've got to get out. Get out of here—fast!' Gil said.

Reg nodded. Both noticed that the fire, though still with fuel, was burning lower. A choking, heavy atmosphere made the room and its walls seem to close in about them. They clutched involuntarily at their collars to loosen them, while smoke from the smouldering fire writhed out suffocatingly into the room. It was like the pressure of some pillow against them, yet the normal smoke smell had been replaced by an age-old odour of dust.

At the same time the house stirred with faint sounds below, the shuffling they had heard once before. It was hard to say what was imagined and what was real, for their heads swam and breathing was difficult. Light came from outside the window, and Toddy's soundless gesture made them look at one peeling wall.

'Bars!' Gil said thickly, and reeled to the window. Shadows like the bars of some hideous cage scarred the peeling whiteness of the wall. It was as if some huge cage held them as victims—held them trapped and waiting—but for *what*?

Gil tried the window, but there was no sash or casement; just a frame for the many panes which glittered with condensation now forming inside. He tried to think clearly, but the suffocating air stifled thoughts even more than it stifled his breathing. He heard swift footfalls behind him; something very heavy was dragged.

'Gil, get back!' Reg's voice was vibrant with urgency. 'Come on, Toddy—now. Together!'

Gil, still clutching his collar to loosen it, moved aside. He had a vague impression of Reg and Toddy carrying the heavy iron fender between them. There was a blurred, indistinct movement, then fender crashed against window; the detonation of shattering glass and splintering wood jerked him back to reality again.

The whole window with frame smashed from the brickwork; it fell outside, the storm air rushing cold and fresh into the room. Rain beat on their faces, while storm sounds swelled back to as they remembered them. The nightmarish atmosphere of the room was dispelled by cleansing elements, those elements they had once sought to escape.

'Climb out!' The voice sounded like Toddy's. 'You first, Gil! Wake up, man—for pity's sake!'

Gil scrambled through the yawning aperture, plaster falling in powder around him. Sturdy creeper skinned his hands as he gripped. Within seconds three forms were struggling down the wind-beaten creeper which dragged on the dark frontal brisks of the old three-storey house. Their combined weight was a danger that never occurred to them; their only thought was escape. Gil jumped directly he reckoned he could hit the ground safely, and the jarring impact of sodden gravel was not only painless but a relief.

Water splashed as two more figures descended. They gazed up at the gaping window above and, in the storm light, saw fire smoke or dust writhing eerily. It formed a shape, at least as far as Gil was concerned, and that brief glimpse only spurred him to running the faster. Capes had been left behind, but the freshness of the cold rain had a wonderful normality Gil would never forget.

'The cycles,' he shouted. 'We left them on the porch!'

They dragged the bikes free and, scooting, lunged in the direction of the path they had arrived by. But now the foliage swung to impede them; long tendrils and boughs lashed across them. A blackthorn grazed Gil from his ear to his chin.

Thunder rolled again. It seemed to Gil that the house must be moving behing them, that it hunted them. He could not believe that it had any intention of letting them go. They crashed their path through dripping masses of greenery, regardless of pain and discomfort. They reached the iron gates, which the strong wind now began to dislodge from where they were wedged back.

One gate fell. It tore from rusted hinges and, with a tortured squealing, seemed to try to hurl itself bodily upon them. But by a miracle the lashing movement of a bough deflected it, held it suspended for a moment in space. The three cyclists were through; they were out on the rutted track. Together they turned, sensing that some crisis was over. The heavens ripped in two as lightning blinded them, silhouetting trees in its garish brilliance. They glimpsed a half-timbered structure—white plaster and an inn sign swinging crazily. It was one storey only; that much Gil noted before the scene changed.

The crash was deafening. As they plunged blindly into the storm they had a last glimpse of the house—the house as they recalled it—burning where the lightning had struck it. A chimney had fallen, demolishing one roof and splitting brickwork like some gaping wound. 'The Fall of the House of Usher', Gil thought, having a vivid memory of Poe's famous story. He rode on furiously, following the tail-lights of his two friends ahead.

It was one o'clock in the morning when they reached the first village. The storm had blown itself out, and a bright moon reflected from the mirror wetness of roofs. Gil, without a front lamp, found himself thinking of what he would say if he encountered a policeman. He was beginning to react normally, but only just.

Perhaps it was then that luck helped them, luck in the shape of an old countryman returning to a small cottage not many yards from them. A chance word led to conversation, and conversation led to some hint of their misfortunes, the final outcome being the bed-and-breakfast they so desperately required.

Nex morning, seated at a small table where eggs and bacon gave a homely fragrance, the trio gave their host as much of an account of their experience as they thought he would believe. Gil, Reg and Toddy added the odd touch, though playing down the element of terror. What kind of house was it? Who had owned it? Did it have a history? they inquired.

The replies formed an anti-climax. The house, although old, had no eerie or abnormal history. It had been owned by the Weir family until being more or less abandoned about a decade ago. No one would buy it, but the ground was still up for sale.

'Mark you, it wasn't like the old inn,' their host told them, smiling. 'Aye, that's a real bit of local history. You see, the house was built on where this old in once stood. In the eighteenth century it was. The story goes that rich wayfarers who called at the inn were murdered for their valuables. Bad old times, them.'

He looked up quickly, aware of the way his audience had tensed.

'How were they murdered?' Gil asked, and gripped his cup tihgter. He could guess the answer.

'Smothered, I believe. Something to do with a four-poster bed. One or two inns like that in Britain then. Being a traveller could be dangerous, very dangerous.'

'Any idea what the inn was called?' Toddy asked.

Their host pondered, lit his pipe and called to the motherly soul responsible for the breakfast.

'Something to do with "Hunters" perhaps?' Toddy said.

'That's right, lad. I think it was,' came a voice from the kitchen. 'I remember my grandfather telling us about it. Used to scare us when I was a girl.'

Gil, Reg and Toddy looked at each other. They paid their account and went out into the warm sunshine. As they cycled along, no one spoke of their strange experiences of the night before. Finally Gil had the courage to speak.

'Had we stayed in, we'd have been buried under the rubble,' Gil said simply. 'Crushed or suffocated. I——' He stopped dead, terribly aware of his words.

The "Hunters"—inn of murder and ill repute—every detail of their host's account came back to him. Gil recalled the wraith of smoke he had seen at the window when he had looked back. He mentioned the episode.

'Looked like a man, if that's what you mean,' Reg answered. 'I thought of an inn-keeper. Just an impression. I was pretty scared at that time.'

They cycled away, each one having his own thoughts to occupy him.

Finally, Toddy spoke in his direct way, summing up the terrifying thought which was in all their minds.

'We were the Hunters' prey. But we escaped.'

Death after Life

by BILL SWALLOW

A milky haze enveloped the B. E. A. Vanguard as it dipped through the cloud shelf above Edinburgh. Peter Lloyd stared thoughtfully through the dripping window as the bright sunlight which had been with the plane all the way from London gave way to a steady drizzle on the run-in to Edinburgh's trim little airport.

For the hundredth time he wondered what had made him decide to come to Scotland for a holiday. He had made the decision months before, and as he had waded through the travel handouts, with their glossy pictures of great kilted Highlanders and Edinburgh Castle, he had become aware of an intense excitement—an unnatural tightening of the stomach muscles. Why, he did not know. Madrid, Oslo, Naples, he had been to these and many other places on previous holidays, but never had he felt the same sense of drama as when he had planned this trip to Britain's northern tip. He had never explored Britain fully—as far as he knew.

As far as he knew. Those five words carried the full load of the mystery of Peter Lloyd. Two years previously he had woken up one afternoon to find himself in a bed in London's Charing Cross Hospital. He had been discovered lying spread-eagled on a Bayswater pavement—60 feet underneath an open fifth-floor window.

'I saw him fall, guv—an' I ran to get you right away!'

Those were the words of the hapless road-sweeper who had seen the plunge and called the ambulance.

Incredibly, amazed doctors at the hospital had found no injuries—no marks, even—on his unconscious body. He had slept for two and a half days, and when he awoke had no knowledge of who he was and what he had been doing in—and out—of a Bayswater flat. He had attempted to investigate, of course, but his only discovery was a strange coincidence ... *The woman who occupied the fifth-floor flat had had a son fall to his death from the very same window two years earlier.* Peter would have liked to find something more out about this fall, but as the woman had moved from the flat the day before Peter's accident, and had left no forwarding address, he had to abandon even this slender lead.

Saddened, 18-year-old Peter had found a bedsitter in Hammersmith, a reasonable job in an architect's office, and had tried to forget about the whole thing.

The months passed, he found new interests, and eventually his obsession with the mystery of his past fell into a small niche at the back of his mind.

Until now.

Ever since he had first planned the trip to Scotland, he had felt the whole ghastly story looming over him again. He couldn't get it out of his mind. The last fall from the window had been fatal, and he couldn't help feeling that his accident was going to prove fatal, too.

These, then, were the thoughts of Peter Lloyd as he stepped off the airport bus in Prince's Street, Edinburgh. Lugging his leather grip in one hand and his overcoat in the other, Peter made for the small private hotel in Waverley Street where he had booked to stay for the night. His plans after that were not really settled.

He had vaguely thought of getting a train to Glasgow early in the morning, and then catching the morning flight to Inverness from Prestwick airport, and returning to Glasgow by train a week or so later. He had just finished reading *John Macnab* and rather fancied exploring for himself the wild moorland that John Buchan so faithfully described.

The next morning he arrived in Glasgow bright and early and went directly to a travel agent.

'Good morning. I'd like to get a plane up to Inverness sometime today.'

'Well, sir, there's the morning flight at 9.15, but you'll have to rush to catch that one. At this time of the year the next one isn't until tomorrow.' The travel agent's clerk started to peer closely at the timetable, as though he thought that hard-enough staring might miraculously produce a specially-chartered jet leaving at 11 o'clock. It didn't however, and he closed the book with a soft sigh. By that time Peter was vaulting into a taxi on the pavement outside.

The driver was young, the roads were clear and the traffic lights were favourable, but even so the Viscount was lifting off the runway and winging round to the north and Inverness by the time the cab raced into the airport.

Peter was annoyed at missing that flight. He would have been more annoyed still had he foreseen the ghastly, supernatural discovery which would result from it.

What now? It was still early, and Peter felt he should get away from Glasgow. He couldn't remember ever visiting the city before, but there was something oppressively familiar about its grey, rain-soaked streets. He wandered along to the station and peered up at a map showing the network of railway lines stretching out from the great city. His eyes settled on the Clydebank line, which went west from Glasgow to Dumbarton, and then curved round to the north, cutting between the two great lochs of Lomond and Long, finishing up many miles to the north at Fort William.

Bright early-afternoon sun sent a film of steam rising from

the rain-soaked platforms of Dumbarton station, promising that the day should end better than it started. The small diesel pulling Peter Lloyd's train thumped slowly out of the station, clattering over the points and then turning gradually to the right to join the track to the Western Highlands. Peter sat in the first carriage, a single ticket to Fort William in his top pocket and a worried frown on his face. The train was half an hour out of Dumbarton before he stopped staring at the floor and looked out of the window. It seemed as though every travel brochure he had ever read had burst into life. The sun shone, the heather smelt lovely and the old farmer in the opposite corner just had to be a direct descendant of Robbie Burns. But still Peter wore his frown. Something was wrong, he knew that; but what it was he did not know. A sickening feeling of doom was implanting itself on him—getting stronger with each mile the little diesel took.

Eventually the train stopped.

'Arrochar and Tarbet!' called the porter, station-master and taxi-driver of that little station as he walked down the single platform.

Two people got out, and before a minute had passed the train was moving slowly away. Then, the most inexplicable thing happened. With a sudden 'Whooop!', Peter leapt up from his seat, grabbed his grip, shoved past the ancient farmer to get to the door, and vaulted out on to the platform. He came to rest against a refuse bin at the very end of the platform, half-standing, half-lying. His bag lay burst beside him, toothbrush and towels spilled out on to the platform. He wasn't hurt, but there again, he could never remember feeling pain as the result of any of the numerous small accidents he had had over the last two years or so.

'Och! Ye young foool!' The station-master was standing above him. 'I dinna want death on ma hands—and you seem to be doing your best to provide me with it!' he raged on.

'Ye shoulda waited until the next station—it's but a few miles farther on!'

'I'm all right,' grinned Peter, rising to his feet and brushing down his clothes.

'What the hell did I do *that* for?' he thought to himself. 'I was going to Fort William, wasn't I? What did I leap off *here* for?'

'Oh, well, nothing ventured, nothing gained,' he said out loud, hoping to brush away the cheery little railwayman's suspicions as to his sanity. With that he picked up his belongings, handed over the ticket and trudged out of the station towards Arrochar village.

'I should be able to get some bed and breakfast in the village,' he muttered to the station-master as he left.

But as he walked, the cold chill he had felt before began to steal over him again, striking its strange icy fingers ever farther into his heart with every step he took. If only he knew what was causing it! By the time he reached the edge of the village he was sweating profusely, and his feeling of impending doom was stronger than ever. What had driven him off the train near this tiny Scottish fishing village—and what was waiting for him when he got there?

He walked on. He couldn't turn back now. Like a runaway convict, he skirted close to the verge, now and again darting into the low ditch at its side as a car came along. Soon he came to a dip in the road, a long curve, and before him lay the high street—and the only street—of Arrochar. Peter stared down it. It seemed strange that this pleasant village should strike such strange thoughts into his mind—but strike them it did.

He crossed the road and walked to a pub on the loch edge. Welcoming lights twinkled in the growing dusk, and the forecourt was filled with the cars of early-evening customers. Peter felt as though he needed a drink. He had seen a nice cottage with a 'Bed and Breakfast' sign it the window; that and the thought of a nerve-steadying whisky lifted some of the weird dread from him. And so, with a near-cheerful jaunt, he threaded his way between the cars in front of the saloon-bar entrance.

Right against the door was a green mini-van. Something made him look twice at that humble vehicle as he passed, and he couldn't help but notice the front number plate.

'Oh, my God!' he cried, staggering back as he saw it. Those icy fingers closed back down on him. 6196 SC—that was the number of the van, and the effect it had on him seemed most ominous.

'Large whisky, please,' he gasped as he threw himself on to a high stool at one end of the comfortable bar.

'Yes, sir,' said the barman, adding as he returned with the drink, 'You all right, sir? You look as though you've seen a ghost.'

'Yes—no—yes—quite all right, thank you. I say—do you know who owns the mini outside the door?'

'The green van, you mean, sir?'

'Yes.'

'Why—that's young Iain McCarter's. He's had it getting on for a couple of years, now.'

'Oh, thanks.'

Peter was disappointed. Such had been the shock that the van had given him that he had felt the name of the owner would have provided a clue to his mystery. He had never heard of Iain McCarter.

'Did I hear my name being mentioned in vain?' said a friendly voice at Peter's shoulder.

'No, Iain—young gentleman's just askin' about your van,' said the barman.

'Oh, ah? Why—do you want to make me an offer?' he said, turning hopefully to Peter. 'It would be a very good buy for you, 1963, thirty thousand miles, good condition . . .!'

'No, no, no,' smiled Peter. 'I don't want to buy—I just want to know something about it. Do you know who was the previous owner?'

'Fellow who lived the other side of Tarbet—didn't know him myself. I bought the car from his mother. I'm told that he was killed and that his mother was getting rid of some of his things—the van was one of them.'

'Do you know anybody who *did* know him?'

'Yes, there's a crowd of fellows that comes in here later—'bout closing time, usually. They used to be his closest friends, from what I know.'

Peter left the pub then. He went to the cottage advertising bed and breakfast and fixed up for the night. He then went for a walk and at 10 o'clock returned to the pub. The saloon bar was packed now. At one end of the bar stood a group of six or seven young men and a couple of girls. Although his job had given Peter a fair degree of confidence in meeting strangers, for some unaccountable reason the thought of walking over and introducing himself to that small group of open-faced youngsters filled him with horror. That icy hand was pressing on him again!

He walked over to the bar, pale and unsteady, his mouth dry. He didn't feel like another whisky, and so ordered a pint of bitter. The solid feel of the heavy glass in his hand steadied him up in a surprising way. He looked around the room, the warm and friedly room, and again that feeling of familiarity which he had experienced in Glasgow swept over him. It was as though he had been there before.

On a quick impulse, he half-drained the glass and marched stiffly across the room towards the group of chattering youngsters. He could hear their conversation now. They were talking about pop records. The only pop record which Peter could think of was one called 'It's Now or Never'. He paused behind the youth nearest to him and touched him gently on the shoulder. The youth turned, smiled.

'Hello, Pet—' he said. That was all he said, for the next second he turned ashen, took a step back and hit his head against the brick edge of the mantelpiece. Peter watched helplessly as he crashed to the ground.

Nobody went to his aid. They were all staring at Peter, mouths open, jaws wide, eyes staring. None spoke, although several of them looked as though they were trying to.

'What the hell *is* all this,' snapped Peter. 'Why are you all staring at me?'

'I—I—*Peter!*' stuttered someone at last.

'How do you know my name?' cut in Peter, whirling round on the speaker.

'We should do,' said one of the girls. 'We've been friends since we were so-high, haven't we?'

'We thought you were dead, Pete,' said someone on Peter's right.

'We heard that you had had an accident a couple of years ago—been killed,' continued another of the group.

'*What?*'

'Well that's what your mother said, anyway.'

'My mother? What do you mean? You know my mother? Where is she?' The questions poured out of Peter just like a waterfall. He gripped the other's shoulder in excitement. At last he was getting somewhere!

Other side of Tarbet. You mean you haven't seen—'

'Never mind that,' cut in Peter harshly, 'what do you know about this accident I'm supposed to have had? Tell me about it!'

'Well, I—' the pale-faced youth was only stopped from running by Peter's steel grip on his shoulder. 'Well, we were told you were in your mother's flat in London—Bayswater

The beer glass crashed to the floor from the ghostly hands

I think—and, well, they said that you *fell*—fell from the window—and were killed. And—well—that's all. Of course,' he added with a nervous laugh, 'it can't have been true, otherwise, Ha! Ha!, you would have to be a *ghost*, wouldn't you? Ha! Ha!'

Peter didn't share his laughter. He wasn't *there* to share his laughter. For a split-second his beer glass hovered in the space where he had been holding it, then it crashed down to the tile-flagged floor.

That last joking sentence had meant the end of the ghost of Peter Lloyd—killed three years before in a 60-foot fall . . .

The Whispering House

by JEFFREY GAUNT

The House on the Moors

'Mr Raynor to see you, sir.'

Jacob Markham, publisher, looked up from his desk.

'Yes, show him in,' he said.

The secretary withdrew to usher into the room a tall, slim, ascetic-looking young man in his early thirties. The visitor was wearing a long, dark overcoat over a good, but untidy, lounge suit.

'Good-morning, Raynor, how are you?' said Jacob Markham, rising and shaking hands. 'Sit down, will you?'

Clive Raynor seated himself, stretching out his long legs. After a few generalities, Jacob Markham said:

'Now, about this new book of yours. Have you any idea yet as to plot or setting?'

'No,' confessed Raynor, 'I'm afraid I haven't.'

Jacob Markham looked slightly perturbed.

'I don't want to hurry you, Raynor,' he said, 'but time's getting on. I want you in my spring list. Haven't you any ideas at all?'

'Not one worth going ahead with,' replied Raynor. Then he added, with a laugh: 'But don't worry. I'm going North to-night and I'll get down to work right away.'

'Going North, eh?' said the publisher. 'Whereabouts are you going?'

'Northumberland,' replied Raynor. 'I've bought a house

up there. I saw it quite by chance in the summer and liked it at once. Broom Manor, it's called, and it was going dirt cheap.'

'What the devil d'you want to saddle yourself with a manor for?' demanded Jacob Markham gruffly. 'A single fellow like you. You'll have to staff the place with servants, I suppose—'

'Not at all,' cut in Raynor, with a smile. 'The servant question is already settled. There's a housekeeper and her niece already in residence, and I'm keeping them on. I won't need any servants beyond them. I don't intend opening up the whole of the house.'

'Then why buy it?' put in the publisher.

'Because the place rather fascinated me,' replied Raynor. 'Also, as I've told you, it was going dirt cheap. It stands entirely alone about a mile from the little moorland village of Tarn. It's an ideal place for a writer.'

'Going dirt cheap means that it's in a pretty bad state of repair, I suppose?' remarked the publisher.

'On the contrary, its in an excellent state of repair,' replied Raynor. He hesitated a moment, then went on: 'The reason it was going so cheaply was that the lawyers who managed the estate couldn't find a purchaser for it. Until I came along, nobody would so much as look at the place.'

'Why was that?' asked Jacob Markham.

Raynor shrugged his ahoulders.

'It appears that the house has a pretty bad reputation,' he said. 'It was built some considerable time ago, and, according to local gossip, it has brought ill-luck to every family who has occupied it. A shocking tragedy occurred there about twenty years ago. A Major Burton, his wife, and two children were occupying the house. The major, who was drinking heavily, either had a brainstorm or else suddenly went mad. He murdered his wife, children, and then hanged himself.

Since then the house has stood empty except for the housekeeper whomI've mentioned. She's been kept on by the trustees of the place.'

'And that's your idea of an ideal place in which to write, is it?' commented Jacob Markham dryly. 'It wouldn't appeal to me, I know. However, if it suits you, that's all that matters, I suppose. I only hope you'll find some inspiration there, and get down to work. Your last book didn't do so well as we hoped, you know.'

My next one'll make your fortune,' said Raynor, rising with a laugh. I can write at Broom Manor, and write well. I felt that the moment I saw the place.'

Little did he realise what truth he was speaking.

Little did he realise the manor's profound *evil*, either . . .

He left London the next morning. A fine autumnal afternoon was merging into dusk when eventually a slow local train deposited him and his luggage on the platform at Firfield, the nearest station to the manor.

The driver of the taxi which took him up to the manor was a leathery-faced, well-known local character known as Old Jimmy.

'So you're the new owner of the manor, are ye?' said Jimmy, as he and Raynor bowled along the quiet country road. 'You're a writer chap, I hear. I suppose ye'll be having lots of parties and things like that.'

'No, I intend to live very quietly,' replied Raynor, inwardly amused at the bluntness of Old Jimmy.

'Ah weel, ye'll find it quiet enough in arl conscience,' said Jimmy. 'I'm only hoping things'll turn oot arl reet for ye.'

'What d'you mean?' asked Raynor.

'I mean the hoose,' replied Jimmy. 'Naebody's had any luck in that hoose ever since it was built. Look at poor Major Burton, him what had it last. He was as nice a man as ever ye could meet when first he comed here. So was his wife. She was a real lady, wi' a smile and a pleasant word for everybody. But I see'd the change in her and him after they'd been at the manor a bit. Ay, I did that!'

'What sort of change?' asked Raynor curiously.

'They both got aaful quiet like and stopped entertaining and didn't come oot much,' replied Jimmy.

Raynor made no comment, and Jimmy went on:

'And the bairns, poor things! There was two of 'em. Bonnie little things they were when first they comed here, full of life and fun. But after a bit they got white and thin and frightened-looking, and folks could see that there was summat very much amiss. Then comed that tar'ble night when the major murdered the lot o' them and hanged hisself. But I never blamed him like some folks did. I blamed the hoose. It was the hoose what got him doon in the end, poor chap!'

'How do you mean, the house got him down in the end?' demanded Raynor.

'I mean that hoose is nae good, mister,' replied Jimmy earnestly. 'If ye'd come to me afore ye bought it I'd ha' telt ye so. So would lots of folks around these parts. There's hooses what are lucky and others what are unlucky, and Broom Manor's one of the unlucky ones, so I'm telling ye. Anyway, yonder she lies!'

He pointed through the dusk towards Broom Manor, standing lonely and aloof amidst a clump of firs some distance back from the road. The setting sun had left golden streaks across the sky, and against these the gaunt outline of the house was silhouetted darkly.

'You're keeping Hannah Moffat and her niece on as housekeeper and servant, I hear,' said Jimmy as the vehicle turned in at the gates of a winding, ill-kept drive.

'Yes,' said Raynor, then added: 'She's a very capable woman, I understand.'

'Oh, ay, she's capable enough, I ha' nae doot,' said Jimmy.

'Her and the lass are perfectly fine people, I suppose.'

Something in his tone caused Raynor to look at him sharply. But Jimmy's lips were tightly compressed, nor did he speak again until he pulled up outside the poticoed entrance of the front door.

'Weel, here we are,' he said. 'I'll take your luggage in for ye.'

The Tightening of the Screw

To anyone else but Raynor, Broom Manor, viewed in the now deepening dusk, might well have looked a gloomy and forbidding place. It was a big, rambling house built of stone with bay windows on the ground floor. All the front windows were in darkness, and the house had about it an air of cold and aloof detachment as though visitors weren't welcome.

But Raynor felt nothing of this. The house was his, and, as he looked at it, he felt as strangely and supernaturally drawn towards the place as he had when first he had seen it in the summer.

The front door had opened, and Hannah Moffat, the housekeeper, was standing there. Her gaunt and angular figure was silhouetted against the yellow glimmer of an oil-lamp in the wide hallway behind her. She way a hard-faced woman dressed in sombre black.

'Good evening,' she said to Raynor. 'I hope you have had a pleasant journey.'

Her voice was like her face, hard and mannish. Raynor noticed that she spoke no word to Jimmy as he carried the luggage into the hall, nor did Jimmy speak to her. Waiting until Jimmy had collected his fare and gone, the woman closed the door and turned to Raynor.

'I have set your tea in the dining-room,' she said.

A small tablecloth had been laid at one end of the large table. As Raynor crossed to the miserable fire and spread out his hands to the feeble warmth he heard a light step in the doorway behind him.

Straightening up, he turned from the fire. A girl carrying a laden tea-tray was entering the room. As he looked at her Raynor's eyes widened in astonishment, for the girl was possessed of an amazing and extraordinary beauty.

Taking an involuntary step towards her, he said:

'Good evening! Please allow me!'

He made as though to relieve her of the tray. But the girl set it down on the table. Her movements were cool and entirely self-possessed.

'If you want any more hot water or anything will you please ring?' she said.

Her voice was quiet and well-modulated with a certain fascinating trace of huskiness in it. At least, Clive Raynor thought it fascinating.

'Wait a moment,' he begged, as she moved towards the door. 'Might I ask who you are?'

'I am Miss Moffat's niece,' replied the girl.

'You mean you're the niece who lives here with her?' demanded Raynor, in astonishment.

'Yes.'

Raynor stared at the girl. Not for a moment had he imagined that the grim and hard-faced Hannah Moffat could have a niece anything so bewitching as this. As a matter of fact, he had never given the woman's niece a thought until now.

'What is your name?' he asked.

'Diana,' answered the girl.

She quietted the room, quietly closing the door behing her. Left to himself, Raynor stood staring at the door for a moment. Then, turning away, he pulled up a chair to the table and seated himself at it to enjoy his tea in solitude.

By the time he had finished tea the fire had burned up into a cheerful, crackling blaze which, in spite of the lamplight, cast flickering, dancing shadows about the room.

Not a sound came from outside. Not a sound could be heard in the house save the occasional fall of a coal on the hearth. The intense stillness was so real and heavy as to be almost oppressive.

Raynor found himself thinking about the previous owner of the house, the late Major Burton, and that unhappy gentleman's ill-fated family.

It was strange to think that that once happy family had sat gathered round this very table; strange to think that this room had once echoed to childish glee and laughter, silenced now for ever in the darkness of the grave.

Through the blue haze of his cigarette smoke Raynor's gaze travelled slowly round the room with its flickering, dancing shadows. Did ever the ghosts of those two poor little children come back here to play and romp awhile? He wondered

The thought filled him with a gentle melancholy. He stared about him as though he half-expected to see them somewhere in the shadows.

A sudden faint rustle behind him caused him to start violently. Turning his head, he half-rose to his feet, his hand gripping convulsively on the back of his chair.

But it was only his housekeeper. The woman was standing behind him with two letters in her hand. Why the devil hadn't she knocked? What a fright she'd given him!

'These letters have just come for you by the evening delivery,' said the woman.

She handed them to Raynor and left the room, closing the door behind her. Resuming his seat at the table, Raynor opened his letters. One was from his Aunt Bertha, who lived at Whitley Bay. She wrote:

'My Dear Boy,—By this time, I expect you will be in your new house. I will come over on Thursday and stay with you a few days and help you to settle in. I will give you all the news when I see you. When is your next book coming out?

Your affectionate
Aunt Bertha.'

Well, that was all right, thought Raynor, returning the letter to its envelope. His Aunt Bertha was a decent old scout, if a trifle strait-laced and a bit old-fashoined in her views. She was very rich and was Raynor's godmother.

Raynor's other letter was nothing like so pleasant. It was from a firm of moneylenders in London, and was terse and to the point:

'Dear Sir,—Unless we receive within seven days from date your cheque for three thousand pounds in settlement of your account with us, we will take proceedings for recovery of same without further nitice.

Yours faithfully,
James Lewis.'

Crumpling the letter in his hand, Raynor rose and crossed to the fire. Throwing it into the flames, he stood with brooding eyes, watching it burn.

Where the devil was he to get three thousand pounds within seven days? He thought helplessly. If it had been three hundred pounds, or some such sum, he might have approached Aunt Bertha, or got an advance on his book.

But three thousand pounds was a different matter altogether.

With a shrug of his shoulders he decided to try to dismiss the matter from his mind for the time being. He wasn't going to have his first night at the manor spoiled by worrying about James Lewis and his three thousand pounds.

Moving to the side of the hearth, he pulled the old-fashioned bell and stood listening to the jangling echoes dying faintly away somewhere in the rear premises.

In response to the ring, the girl Diana appeared in the doorway.

'I'd like to have a look over the house,' said Raynor pleasantly.

'Very well,' said the girl.

Moving to the table, she picked up the tray and carried it from the room. From the fireplace Raynor watched her.

'If you are ready,' said the girl, 'we'll take the upstairs rooms first.'

'Yes, all right,' said Raynor. He followed her up the stairs.

His own bedroom was on the first floor. It was a large front room, well furnished and with a big, old-fashioned four-poster bed. A fire had been lighted in the grate, the curtains were drawn across the windows, and a bowl of golden chrysanthemums stood on a small table by the curtained window.

'Quite nice,' said Raynor, looking about him, but taking care to avoid the girl's eyes. 'I suppose I've got you to thank for the flowers?'

'Yes, I gathered them from the garden,' said the girl. Then she added: 'This is the room in which Mrs Burton was murdered.'

Raynor wheeled on her.

'What the devil d'you mean by telling me that?' he burst out violently. 'Why mention it?'

'I thought you might like to know,' answered the girl coolly. 'If I didn't tell you, somebody else probably would. Would you prefer to have some other room?'

'No,' said Raynor brusquely. 'I'll stay here!'

He turned away, ashamed of his outburst. But he was conscious, also, of another emotion. He felt now that he loathed this girl. Good heavens, he asked himself furiously, what sort of a creature was she that she could speak so calmly and unfeelingly of such a very dreadful, brutal murder?

She was standing close beside Raynor. He could see her through the mirror of the dressing-table. She was looking at him, a faint, mocking smile on her lips. And in that moment the veil was torn from Raynor's eyes, and he saw her for what she really was. The girl was evil.

He stood appalled at the discovery, and so shocked that he felt more than a little frightened.

The girl was watching him intently. As she saw the expression on his face her eyes hardened for one fleeting instant. Then as he turned and looked at her, her eyes softened, and she smiled, displaying pearly teeth. And in her smile was such a wondrous sweetness that it seemed to Raynor as though his thoughts of but a moment ago could have been nothing but the disordered phantasms of his own imagination.

He passed a hand across his brow. A hand that was trembling—and his brow was damp with cold sweat.

'I'm sorry I upset you by telling you about poor Mrs Burton,' said the girl contritely. 'Please forgive me. I shouldn't have mentioned it.'

'That's all right!' said Raynor unsteadily. 'I was a fool to flare up the way I ded.'

Abruptly they dropped the subject.

'Shall I show you the other rooms?' she asked. 'Aunt and I have separate bedrooms on the floor above. The rest of the rooms up there are shut up.'

'Then I won't trouble to go up,' said Raynor.

He followed the girl downstairs. Next to the dining-room was a comfortable morning-room which he'd decided to convert into a study. The dining-room would suit him admirably for the time being, he told the girl. He would use the dining-room as a living-room.

'You'll want to see the kitchen, I suppose?' said the girl when she had shown him round the ground floor.

'Yes, I may as well take a look at it,' said Raynor.

He followed the girl along a passageway and into the kitchen. Hannah Moffat was sitting there in an old-fashioned, basket-work armchair. She turned her head and looked at Raynor as he entered. But she made no effort to rise.

He saw that she had a visitor, a ragged old crone of a woman, who was sitting hunched over the glowing kitchen range, a short, backened clay pipe between her toothless gums.

Taking her blackened clay from her mouth, the gipsy turned her little wizened face, and looked at him with watery eyes.

'Why, this'll be the new maister hissel',' she leered. 'Welcome to Broom Manor, me bonnie lad!'

Confound the hag and her impertinence, thought Raynor angrily.

'Who the devil might you be?' he snapped.

'Me? Why, I'm owld Meg fra' Morpeth!' cried the bundle of rags shrilly. 'I'm Mistress Hannah's friend. Cross me hand wi' silver, me bonnie lad, and I'll tell ye the future and what your fortune's gan' to be!'

'Get out of here!' said Raynor sharply. 'Go on, clear off!'

Hannah Moffat rose. Her eyes were hard and angry.

'You have no right to order her out!' she said harshly. 'I can entertain whom I like in my own kitchen!'

The Gipsy's Curse

So it had come, thought Raynor, a show-down between him and Hannah Moffat. It had been inevitable from the first, of course. He had known that, but he hadn't expected it to come quite so quickly.

Well, it was all the better that it had come this early in their relationship. The pair of them would now discover where exactly they stood.

Raynor was furiously angry, with an anger quite foreign to his nature. It was curious how he had changed since he had left London and come to this strange old house. *It was at though the building itself was having an effect on him.*

'I've told that woman there to get out, and she'll get out!' he said sharply. 'If you've any objections, you can pack your bag and get out with her!'

Hannah Moffat's face was pale with passion. Her thin-lipped mouth was tightly compressed, and she was breathing audibly through her nostrils. The girl had set the lamp down on the heavy kitchen table, and was standing watching the scene with a cold, amused interest.

'Am I to understand that I am not to be allowed to entertain my own friends?' demanded Hannah Moffat harshly.

'Not without my permission,' retorted Raynor.

The woman's hands clenched. Her eyes were blazing.

'I have known Meg for thirty years and more,' she grated. 'She is welcome in every house in these parts!'

'She is not welcome in this house,' returned Raynor.

He was experiencing a strange, vindictive enjoyment. He felt so supremely master of the situation.

'What have you got against Meg?' demanded Hannah Moffat, her voice quivering with passion.

'Nothing except her impertinence, and the fact that I don't desire her in my house,' said Raynor. 'Probably she did not intend to be impertinent. That does not matter. I have told her to get out—and she'll get out!'

By a visible effort, Hannah Moffat kept control of herself.

'So that's the sort of man you are, is it?' she grated.

'Yes, it is!' shouted Raynor, who was annoyed as much by her tone as her words. 'What's more, I'm not going to bandy words with you. I consider the question settled.'

Old Meg had risen from her chair.

'Dinna let me get ye into trouble,' she cried shrilly, stowing her pipe away somewhere in the voluminous folds of her ragged skirt. 'I'll gan like I've been telled to gan, and I'll never darken the doors o' this hoose again!'

She turned her little rage-contorted face towards Raynor.

'As for ye,' she spat venomously, 'I wouldn't be in your shoes for all the money i' the world! Ay, ye can stand there looking very grand, my fine gentleman, but if ye could see what the future holds in store for ye your stomach would crawl wi' fear, and, if ye'd the courage to do it, ye'd end your life this very night!

Her voice rose to a shrill, cracked scream:

'There's been murder done in this hoose afore, and there'll be murder done again and by your hand. The mark o' Cain is plain on your brow for them what ha' the gift to see it. For twenty years, ever since owld Burton died, I've fortelled your coming. And noo you're here. Ye think the hoose belangs to ye and that you're maister o' it. But that's where you're wrang, ye fool. It's ye who belang to the hoose, and the hoose is maister of ye, as one day ye'll find out. It'll drag ye doon, it'll ruin ye and cast ye into the deepest pit o' hell—that's as sartin as you're standing there, my fine gentleman, and one day ye'll see my words come true!'

She turned and shuffled towards the door.

'And noo I'll gan,' she mumbled. 'Good-night to ye, Mistress Hannah, and to ye, Diana, me pretty love!'

The door closed behind her and she was gone into the night. Raynor, left alone in the kitchen with Hannah Moffat and the girl, said angrily:

'Garrulous old hag! What the devil was she talking about?'

Neither the woman nor the girl answered him.

He turned on his heel and quitted the kitchen. Returning

'. . . there'll be murder done again and by your hand.'

to the dining-room, he lighted a cigarette and flung himself into an armchair by the fire.

What a rotten start all this was to his stay at the manor, he thought miserably. First that letter from the moneylenders, then this row with Hannah Moffat and the vicious, bitter words of the old gipsy.

What was it the hag had said?

'The mark of Cain is on your brow. You belong to the house and the house is master of you . . .'

What the devil had she meant by that? It was all rot, of course. But was it? thought Raynor, uneasily. There was a shred of truth in her words in so far as he really did feel as though he belonged here. He had felt it the very firts time he had seen the house in the summer. The place had fascinated him. It still did fascinate him. He was glad to be here in spite of the upsets he had experienced that evening.

Yet he was not himself. His mind was uneasy, nervous, troubled. It had been very unlike him to fly into a rage as he had done in the kitchen. Usually he was easy-going and tolerant. He couldn't remember when last he had been so roused as he had been that night. What was causing this change—this change for *worse*—in him? He would soon realise . . .

Murder

Clive Raynor sat late that night in front of the dining-room fire. Hannah Moffat and her niece had long since retired, but Raynor was conscious of a curious disinclination to move from the room.

How still and silent the house was, he thought, as he sat there by the fire. Not a sound disturbed the intense, brooding hush. Solemn and oppressive, it enfolded the lonely house like a heavy, sombre pall. Yet he belonged here. He knew that. He could sense it in the very atmosphere of the room, which seemed to enfold him in a warm, protective embrace.

Protective?

Queer that that word should have come into his mind, thought Raynor. From what could he, Clive Raynor, need protection? From James Lewis and his demand for three thousand pounds, perhaps.

Yes, by heavens, he could do with some protection from Mr Levis and his threats, thought Raynor.

He wondered how he could raise the money, for it would have to be raised somehow. It would be hopeless to ask Aunt Bertha, of course. In her old-fashioned way she looked upon speculation on the Stock Exchange as gambling, and she was dead against gambling in any shape or form.

Yet she was very rich, and he, Raynor, was her heir. She'd always promised him that. Apart from a few charitable bequests, he would come in for all her money when she'd gone.

There was no chance of her going for a long time yet. though, reflected Raynor. She was old and walked with a stick, but her ticker was sound. Unless she had a serious illness or something she was good for a number of years yet,

And James Lewis had given him but seven days!

He stirred at length, flicking the end of his cigarette into the dying embers of the fire. Rising, he lighted his candle and turned out the lamp. As he moved towards the door in order to go up to his bedroom, he fancied he heard, somewhere in the house, a deep sigh.

He paused, listening intently, but the sound was not repeated.

'Wind in the chimney!' he muttered.

But there was no wind. He knew that. The night was calm and still. It was as though the house itself had sighed.

The thought caused Raynor no uneasiness as he ascended the stairs to his room. On the contrary it was a flight of fancy which brought a faint smile to his lips.

The next day was Thursday, and Aunt Bertha arrived for lunch. She was a white-haired, frail-looking woman, approaching seventy years of age.

Raynor spent the afternoon showing her round, but he felt she wasn't as impressed with the place as he'd have liked her to be.

'I'm sorry to see you don't like the place, aunt,' said Raynor eventually. '*Why* don't you like the house?'

Aunt Bertha hesitated before replying. Then she said:

'I'm not a fanciful woman, as you know, but there is something very unpleasant about this house. I felt it the moment I arrived. It's the atmosphere of the place, Clive. It makes me shudder. I feel there is something uncanny about it. Didn't a dreadful tragedy take place here some years ago?'

'Yes, but that can't have left any impression on the house, surely?' protested Raynor. 'Personally, I think the place has rather a pleasant atmosphere.'

'Then you're evidently not so susceptible to atmosphere as I am,' said Aunt Bertha grimly. 'I couldn't live in a house like this. It would make me ill.'

'You're not going to curtail your visit, I hope?' exclaimed Raynor, in alarm.

'No, I shall stay over the week-end as I planned,' said Aunt Bertha. 'But if you can find a purchaser for the house, do so. I would sell it, Clive, if I were you.'

'Very well, aunt, I'll think about it,' promised Raynor.

He did think about it over the week-end, but in a manner undreamt of by Aunt Bertha. For the thought, the dread, in the mind of Clive Raynor was that unless he settled with James Lewis that gentleman would not hesitate to seize the house and sell it over his head.

The very thought of losing the manor brought a chill of fear and dismay to Raynor's heart, for with every hour of every day he found himself becoming more and more attached to the place.

On that Thursday night and on the two following nights he sat for hours in the dining-room long after Aunt Bertha, the girl, and Hannah Moffat had retired to their beds.

He sat there in the firelight, not reading, not writing, just content to let his thoughts drift on in the hushed and brooding stillness.

And strange thoughts they were for one of normally such a pleasant mind as Clive Raynor. Thoughts of Mr James Lewis, and how, by hook or by crook, he could settle with him. Thoughts of the strange but beautiful Diana. He was glad he had come here to this quiet old house. In its eery and unnatural solitude, far from the turmoil and bustle of cities, he was beginning for the first time in his life to see things in their right perspective and to allot to them their proper values.

On the Sunday night at nine-thirty, following his usual custom, he went up to Aunt Bertha's bedroom to bid her good-night.

Her door was standing ajar, and he pushed it open. The old lady was sitting up waiting for him, as she always did. She was seated in an armchair in front of the fire, her back to the door. She was wearing her nightdress, dressing-gown, and slippers. On a small table by the side of her chair stood an empty glass which had contained the hot milk she always took before retiring.

She made no movement as Raynor stood a moment watching her from the doorway. Her white head with its old-fashioned curlers was drooped forward on her chest. It looked to Raynor as though she slept.

He moved forward as though to wake her, then slowly

drew back. His eyes travelled from her lined and peaceful face down her old, quilted dressing-gown to the hem of her old-fashioned but warm and sensible flannelette nightdress.

Raynor stood motionless. She was sitting very close to the fire. If a live coal had fallen from the grate whilst she slept it might easily have set fire to her nightdress. The material was highly inflammable. So was the quilted dressing-gown. Both would have burned swiftly with undoubtedly fatal consequences.

Raynor's hands clenched. His heart had commenced to pound sickeningly. In the firelight his handsome, ascetic face looked all of a sudden strained and wolfish.

There was no one in the house but himself, his aunt, and Hannah Moffat. He knew that. The girl was out somewhere, for it was Hannah who had brought in the supper that evening. The woman would now be sitting in her kitchen.

Slowly and with infinite stealth Raynor's hand moved towards the breast pocket of his jacket Then he froze. The old lady had stirred, sighing in her sleep.

But she did not awaken. The moments passed as Raynor stood there, rigid and motionless. Then from his pocket he silently withdrew an old letter. He glanced at it in the firelight. It was an account from James Lewis.

With trembling fingers, but without a sound, Raynor folded the paper into a spill. Then stealthily he stooped to the fire and held the end of the spill to the glowing coals. It flared into flame.

Turning, Raynor moved the flame along the hem of the old lady's nightdress. The material flared into a blaze, but already Raynor had gone, flinging the spill into the fire and fleeing on silent, frenzied feet from the room.

He sped down the carpeted stairs two at a time. Before he had time to reach the bottom, scream upon scream was coming from Aunt Bertha's room.

Two bounds took Raynor to the door of the dining-room. He whirled in the doorway, staring back up the darkened stairs. A sudden yellow shaft of light along the passageway showed him that the kitchen door had opened. From upstairs were coming those dreadful shrieks.

'My heavens, what's happened?' cried Raynor hoarsely.

Bounding for the stairs, he raced swiftly up them, followed by the hurrying figure of Hannah Moffat.

The Old Woman's Warning

It was a ghastly sight which met Raynor's eyes as he burst into Aunt Bertha's bedroom. The old lady was lying on the floor half-way between her chair and the door. Her nightdress and dressing-gown had been burned almost completely away. Only a few smouldering wisps remained beside her crumpled, still body.

Hannah Moffat spoke, rustling swiftly forward from the doorway, her face pale in the yellow illumination of a lamp standing on a bedside table.

'She's caught on fire, poor thing,' she said tersely. 'She must have been sitting over the fire. Help me lift her on to the bed.'

Between them, she and Raynor lifted Aunt Bertha's body on to the bed.

He went down to the dining-room. He didn't drink as a rule, but he felt he needed a drink now. He splashed himself out a generous brandy-and-soda and drank it off.

As he set down his glass Hannah Moffat came into the room.

'This'll mean an inquest,' she said.

'Yes, I suppose it will,' agreed Raynor jerkily.

The woman withdrew. Left to himself, Raynor lighted a cigarette with fingers which still trembled a little.

So it was all over, he reflected, throwing the match into the fire. Aunt Bertha was dead—and it was he who had killed her. When he had gone upstairs to say good-night to her the thought of killing her had never been in his mind. He could swear to that on his most sacred oath.

It was when he had seen her sitting there asleep in front of the fire that temptation had seized him. And he had yielded to that temptation. He, Clive Raynor, was now a murderer.

With a sudden, violent start he remembered the words of the old gipsy woman. What was it the hag had said?

'The mark of Cain is on your brow—'

Merciful heavens! The hag had known! She had known him then for what he was, yet he had not known it himself—never dreamt of it himself.

Would the hag connect him with the death of his aunt? he asked himself in sudden panic. She might. But what would it matter if she did? A moment's reflection showed him the absurdity of such a fear.

What a silly old fool his aunt was, he thought, talking such utter rot about the house. There was nothing evil at all about the place. It was a grand old house—a warm, comforting, homely old house.

If it wasn't warm and comforting, why was it that he, Raynor, was feeling neither horror nor remorse for the crime he had committed that night? On the contrary he was feeling now only quiet satisfaction at a job well done. Little did Raynor realize that the evil, supernatural power of this dark and brooding house was already changing his character from good to evil.

The inquest would pass off as a mere formality; then would come the funeral, and after that he'd find himself in possession of Aunt Bertha's fortune.

He could snap his fingers at James Lewis now. The old thing upstairs must be worth anything from fifty to a hundred thousand pounds, he was sure, if she was worth a halfpenny.

And it was all his, save for a few minor bequests to charity, reflected Raynor. He fell dreamily to wondering what he should do with the money. Travel? No; he was quite happy here. Cars? No; he couldn't be bothered with cars. Entertaining? No; he didn't want a pack of stupid people cluttering up the house. It was his house. He wanted it to himself.

Raynor stirred at length and went up to bed. In spite of the events of the night and the presence of death in the house, he slept soundly until Hannah Moffat brought him his morning cup of tea.

After breakfast he walked into Tarn. There were telegrams to be sent acquainting his relatives with Aunt Bertha's sudden death.

The Knock at the Door

The inquest was held next day. It passed off without incident, as Raynor had anticipated it would. He gave his evidence and Hannah Moffat gave hers. Both had heard the old lady scream, they said, and both had run up to the bedroom to find her lying on the floor terribly burned.

Dr MacTavish then gave formal medical evidence, and a verdict of 'Accidental Death' was returned. The coroner wound up with a few words of sympathy for Mr Raynor and the rest of the deceased's relatives, and the whole affair was over.

The funeral took place the following afternoon at Whitley Bay. Clive Raynor, in sombre black, was one of the principal mourners.

He ruturned to Broom Manor for the night, then went into Newcastle the next morning, where he had an interview with Grimmett, Grimes & Grimmett, Aunt Bertha's lawyers.

With the exception of a few small bequests to charity, he found himself the old lady's sole heir. He had inherited a fortune of ninety thousand pounds.

It was evening when he got back to the manor. He found a letter waiting for him from Jacob Markham, his publisher. It read:

'My dear Raynor,—I am wondering if you have yet made a start on your next book. This really is becoming very urgent if I am to bring it out in the spring. Please drop me a line letting me know what the position is.

I trust by now that you are comfortably settled in Broom Manor, and that you like it as much as you anticipated.

Yours sincerely,
Jacob Markham.'

Raynor put the letter aside. There was really no need for him to write at all now, he reflected. He was financially independent. No longer need he rely for his livelihood upon the royalties from his books.

But he wanted to write. He felt the urge to write mounting in him most strongly. He'd make a start that very night, he told himself, hanged if he wouldn't!

Now that the inquest and funeral were over, he vould get on with the job without fear of interruption. What's more, he'd got a plot—the most amazing plot imaginable. His book would be a masterpiece, a sensation. It would far outstrip anything he had yet written.

The urge to get it down on paper was surging through him with a tremendous, irresistible force. With a sudden quick movement he flung his cigarette into the fire and crossed swiftly to the table.

Seating himself, he picked up his pen and drew a sheet of paper towards him. Quickly he wrote the title:

'THE WHISPERING HOUSE'

For the next two hours nothing broke the stillness of the

room save the faint, swift scratch of Raynor's pen as it raced across the paper.

Sheet after sheet he filled with his small, fine caligraphy, and steadily the pile of finished manuscript grew.

He named his hero Claude Royston. The name was very similar to his own. That didn't matter. It was, in fact, an integral part of his plan of the story.

Royston was an author like himself. In the things he did, in his dealings with his fellow-men, he imagined he was being decent and honourable and following the traditions of the Old School Tie.

Then, one day, whilst on holiday, Royston saw a house. It was a fine old country house, standing lonely and aloof miles from anywhere. Its name was Graylings. Royston fell in love with the house at once, as he might have fallen in love with some woman.

He bought Graylings, and, shaking the dust of London from off his feet, he went to live there. From the first he was amazingly happy. He felt that after many wanderings he had at last come home. The old house seemed to enfold him in a warm embrace. To Royston the house was not just a mere structure of stones and mortar, of laths and plaster. It lived. It had a soul.

What was more, in the quietude of the lonely house there came to Royston a keener perception and appreciation of the values of things. He saw himself for the prig he'd been. He saw quite clearly that Honour and Decency were false gods which led one along narrow, barren paths, with little or no reward at the end.

And it was the house which taught him this. That was the wonderful part of it all. When he sat alone in the evenings the dear old house seemed to enfold him in its warm embrace and whisper to him that there was no sin, that the soul of man must be free and untrammelled to act as it would.

Royston listened eagerly, ardently, and, having listened, he burst the bounds of man-made conventions and became himself. In his new-found freedom his soul expanded gloriously and he became a man above men—a superman.

Royston was not alone in the house. He had a housekeeper and her daughter to look after him. The daughter was a lovely girl, a dark-eyed mystic beauty. Her mother was a hard-faced hag who hated Royston and resented his presence in the house.

Royston became infatuated with the lovely girl. But at the moment he had something else to think about. He was desperately pressed for money. He had to find the sum of five thousand pounds or else have Graylings sold over his head.

A rich aunt came so stay with him. Royston was her sole heir. In his new-found freedom of soul he saw how foolish it would be to wait for maybe years before he inherited her money. He wanted money now, and he wanted it urgently. The sensible thing to do, therefore, was to take it from where it was waiting for him.

So he killed his aunt. He murdered her one night as she sat asleep in front of her bedroom fire. It was all so ridiculously simple. He set fire to her night-dress as she sat there, then fled from the room. She was burned to death.

Royston was never suspected, and he inherited her fortune. And he had the house to thank for it all. Dear old house, he thought, his guide, philosopher, his own familiar friend.

Clive Raynor's pen raced on. He scarcely knew what he was writing. The words were pouring from his pen in an endless spate.

The inquest and funeral were over, he wrote.

It was night, and Royston was sitting alone, writing, in the dining-room. There came a sudden knock at the door. It opened, and his housekeeper entered the room. What a hard-faced hag she looked at that moment, thought Royston.

'I don't wish to interrupt your writing,' said the woman harslhly, 'but I would like a word with you—'

Raynor started violently, his pen causing a splutter of ink on the paper. A sudden knock had come on the dining-room door. The door opened and Hannah Moffat came into the room.

'I don't wish to interrupt your writing,' she said harshly, 'bur I would like a word with you.'

Raynor stared at her. Then with dilated eyes, he looked down at what he had just written.

Merciful heavens, he thought, the chill fingers of fear gripping at his heart, the woman had voiced the very words he had just set down.

Raynor looked up again at Hannah Moffat. She had closed the door and advanced a little into the room.

'Well, what is it you want?' he demanded sharply.

'You have come in for your aunt's money,' said the woman. 'I understand it is a lot.'

'What the devil has that got to do with you?' demanded Raynor angrily.

'You killed her!' said Hannah Moffat.

There was a moment of tense silence. The woman stood motionless, watching Raynor. The blood had drained from his face, leaving it ghastly in its sudden pallor.

Then, thrusting back his chair, Raynor blundered to his fcct.

'Damn you!' he choked. 'What the devil d'you mean by that?'

'You know what I mean,' said the woman calmly. 'You were up in her bedroom just before she died. It was you who killed her by setting fire to her night attire.'

'It was not!' shouted Raynor, his face convulsed with fear and fury. 'What the devil d'you mean by these lies, curse you? Why are you making these accusation?'

'They are not lies,' returned the woman. 'I can prove it!'

Raynor glared at her, his fists clenched, his shoulders hunched. Merciful heavens, what did the hag know? He asked himself in panic.

'You say you can prove it,' he burst out hoarsely. '*How* can you prove it?'

'I will tell you,' said the woman harshly. 'At a quarter-past nine on Sunday night I took your aunt's nightly glass of hot milk up to her room. She was tired and drowsy. I attended to the fire and swept up the hearth. Do you understand that? I swept up the hearth. I then came downstairs to the kitchen. The time then was just on half-past nine. I know that because I looked at the clock, as I was expecting Diana and Bob Fergus in for supper. A few minutes later I heard your aunt scream. I followed you upstairs, and you know how we found her. We lifted her on to the bed and you ran for a doctor. Whilst you were away I crossed to the fire to see if it was a live coal which had fallen and set fire to her night attire. There was neither a coal nor a cinder on the hearth. It was as clean as I had left it a few minutes before, except for a charred paper spill which was not completely burned.'

Raynor's heart missed a beat, and his stomach crawled with sudden, deathly fear. He could have sworn he had flung the spill into the fire. But in his mad and frantic haste to get away he had not stayed to look.

The spill must either have hit the coals in the grate and fallen back on to the hearth, or else have hit the grate itself.

'I examined the spill,' continued the woman in her hard voice. 'It was an account addressed to you from a man named James Lewis in London. When you folded the spill and lighted it you held the bill-heading part of it in your fingers. The rest of it was burned, including the amount.'

'Yes, go on!' choked Raynor. 'This is interesting!'

The woman paid no heed whatsoever to the interruption.

'It was that spill which set fire to your aunt's night attire,' she continued, 'and it was you who had the spill up there in the bedroom during the short time which elapsed between my coming downstairs and your aunt screaming. Nothing else but the spill could have set your aunt's night attire on fire, for, as I've told you, there was neither a coal nor a cinder on the hearth.'

'Is that so?' grated Raynor. 'Why the devil you don't apply for a job at Scotland Yard, I don't know. But it's quite apparent to me,' he went on savagely, 'that for some reason or other you're determined to accuse me of a foul and gorrible crime. What's your game, confound you? What d'you expect to gain by it?'

'I want a thousand pounds,' said the woman evenly.

Raynor glared at her, his eyes blazing.

'So that's it, is it?' he burst out furiously. 'Blackmail!'

'You can call it what you like,' returned the woman, 'but I want a thousand pounds.'

'Then you,ll not get it!' shouted Raynor. 'Not a ha'penny! Get out of here, you hag! Get out and get your bag packed. Do you hear?'

'Yes,' said the woman, 'I hear. And I'll go. I'm going to the police.'

She turned and moved towards the door. Raynor glared after her, his hands clenched, his face murderous with fear and fury.

'Wait!' he choked.

The woman turned. 'Yes?' she said.

'You're going to the police with this story of the spill?' demanded Raynor thickly. 'You're going to accuse me of murder?'

'I am!'

'They'll want do know why you didn't accuse me before

the inquest,' snarled Raynor. 'What'll you say to that, you hag?'

'I will say that I didn't know what to do for the best,' replied the woman. 'I will tell them that on thinking it over I have come to the conclusion they should know all the facts involved.'

'What are the facts?' grated Raynor.

'The hearth which I swept, the spill which I found there a few minutes later, the fact that you were your aunt's heir and that you owed money to James Lewis, a moneylender,' said the woman.

'Moneylender?' repeated Raynor harshly. 'How the devil d'you know that?'

'I was on his bill heading,' replied the woman. 'Beneath his name were the words "Loans with or without security". I know what that means. The man's a moneylender. How much you owed him I don't know; that part of the paper was burnt. But the police can easily find out!'

Yes, by heavens, thought Raynor, in panic, the police could very easily find out! And what they'd find was that he owed James Lewis three thousand pounds, and that he was being rigorously pressed for repayment.

The circumstances of his aunt's death would at once appear decidedly fishy to the official mind, praticularly in view of the story this hag Hannah Moffat would tell.

He looked at the woman.

'Where is this spill you're talking about?' he demanded harshly.

'It's in a safe place,' replied the woman.

By an effort Raynor kept control of himself.

'Listen to me!' he grated. 'I admit I owed James Lewis money, but what I'll never admit is that I had anything to do with my aunt's death. I swear on my most sacred oath that I am as innocent of that as you are. But, by force of certain devilish circumstances over which I had no control, some sort of case might be made out against me. You've been clever enough to see that, and you've marshalled your facts in a manner which proves you to be a wicked, spiteful, and unscrupulous woman. The result is, however, that I must either buy your silence, or else defy you and find myself involved in a foul and horrible scandal which, no matter how it ends, will mean my ruin. As I've no wish to be ruined, it looks as though I must buy your silence. How much do you want?'

'A thousand pounds,' repeated the woman.

'But it won't end at that,' said Raynor.

The woman made no response.

Only by a supreme effort did Raynor refrain from hurling himself at her throat and choking the miserable life out of her.

'Will you give me until morning to think it over?' he demanded, his voice quivering with suppressed passion.

The woman eyed him carefully.

'You're not thinking of bolting?' she asked.

'Bolting? No!' snarled Raynor. 'Where the devil d'you think I could bolt to?'

'No; that's true,' assented the woman. 'You wouldn't get very far. Very well, then, you can have until morning. But I warn you—if you refuse, or attempt any underhand business, it'll be the worse for you!'

'Underhand business?' jeered Raynor savagely. 'That's good, coming from you! Get out of here—curse you!'

Without a word, but with a faint, triumphant smile on her thin lips, the woman turned and left the room, quietly closing the door behind her.

Raynor crossed to the sideboard and splashed himself out a drink. As he stood leaning against the sideboard, his glass in his hand, he saw his sheets of manuscript on the table.

With a stifled exclamation he downed his drink at a gulp

and crossed to the table. Picking up the topmost sheet, stained with a splutter of ink, he read the words he had been writing when Hannah Moffat had knocked at the door.

'There came a sudden knock at the door. It opened and his housekeeper entered the room.'

'I don't wish to interrupt your writing,' said the woman harshly, 'but I would like a word with you . . .'

Gad, how queer this was! thought Raynor. In his story he had penned the very words his own housekeeper had used a few moments later. He had, in fact, foretold the whole incident.

The story was an account of his own life at Broom Manor. Although he had given fictitious names to himself, his chracters, and the house, the story was a true and authentic record of his thoughts, feelings, and actions since he had come to Broom Manor. By some incredible miracle the house was giving him the power to look into his own evil future!

Raynor knew this. He made no attempt to delude himself otherwise. But he also knew what he had written had been inspired.

And in the story he had got ahead of events here at Broom Manor. That was the astounding thing about it. In his manuscript he had foretold that Hannah Moffat would knock at the dining-room door.

If she had not interrupted him at that point in the story, thought Raynor, would he have gone on to describe what actually did happen after the woman came into the room? Would he have had his hero, Claude Royston, blackmailed by that gentleman's hag of a housekeeper?

Raynor didn't know. He hadn't the slightest idea what he had been going to do with his hero's housekeeper. He didn't even know why, in his manuscript, he had brought the woman into the dining-room at all.

If he went on, would he find a way out of the devilish mess

he was in? Would he find that Claude Royston, the hero of the story, solved his difficulties in a manner in which he, the author, could solve them in actual life?

It might be worth trying, thought Raynor, in mounting excitement. It would be a queer, bizarre and magical experiment.

With a swift movement Raynor pulled his chair up to the table. Seating himself, he picked up his pen.

Slowly at first, but with ever-increasing speed, he wrote.

An hour passed, and then another, but still his pen raced on. It was long past midnight now. Behind him the fire sank lower and lower in the grate, and the embers became cold and grey.

At length he paused. The silvery chimes of a clock on the mantelpiece behind him struck the hour of three. Raynor put down his pen. Picking up the sheets of manuscript covered with his small, fine writing, he shuffled them together.

Leaning back in his chair, he read them one by one. As he did so the faint, triumphant shadow of a smile came to his lips.

In this story of his he had found the answer to his own problem. As his hero, Claude Royston, of Graylings, dealt with the matter of blackmail, so would he—the human shadow of that fictional man of evil—deal with it. Hannah Moffat was doomed!

The Second Victim

By nine o'clock next morning, Raynor had breakfasted down in the dining-room. His first act after breakfast was to take a handful of cigarettes from his cigarette-box and throw them into the back of the fire. Waiting until they had been consumed in the flames, he sat down and read the morning paper until nine-thirty. His mind was clear, his emotions calm.

He then rose and went along to the kitchen. Hannah Moffat and Diana were there. The woman was cleaning up the kitchen. The girl was washing the dishes.

'Who cleans the windows in this house?' demanded Raynor.

The woman eyed him sharply. She was obviously surprised at the question.

'We do,' she said curtly.

'Then you might get on and do it,' said Raynor. 'They need it badly, I consider.'

Very evident was the effort by which the woman bit back the angry retort which sprang to her lips.

'It'll be seen to,' she said grimly.

Raynor turned to the girl.

'I'd like to speak to you,' he said, then added: 'in the dining-room.'

He turned on his heel and went back to the dining-room, where he took up his position with his back to the fire. Some minutes elapsed before the girl appeared. Raynor wondered what she and the woman were talking about. The woman must naturally be curious to know what it was he wanted to speak to Diana about.

When the girl came into the room, Raynor noted that she had discarded her washing-up apron.

'Yes?' she said inquiringly, standing beside the door.

'Close the door,' ordered Raynor.

The girl did so.

'I'm out of cigarettes,' said Raynor pleasantly. 'I worked late last night on my new book—into the early hours of the morning, in fact, and I smoked every cigarette I had. Will you go into Firfield and get me a box?'

'Yes, of course!' assented the girl readily.

'Will you go now?' asked Raynor. 'I want to get on writing again, and I'm simply dying for a cigarette. You won't get the sort I want in Tarn, I'm afraid. You'll have to go into Firfield, but you've got a bike, haven't you?'

'Yes,' said the girl. 'I'll go and get them for you now. What sort do you want?'

Raynor told her and, some fifteen minutes later, from the dining-room window, he saw the girl riding down the drive on her bike. It would take her fully an hour, he reckoned, to get to Firfield and back.

Going into the morning-room which he had intended using as a study, he returned to the dining-room with a heavy, cylindrical ebony ruler. Closing the door, he gripped the ruler by one end and stood a few moments thoughtfully trying the balance of it. Then, crossing to the fireplace, he pulled the old-fashioned bell.

Before the last jangling echoes had died away in the kitchen, Raynor had retraced his steps swiftly to the door and taken up his stand behind it, the heavy ruler in his hand.

Tense and motionless, his mouth dry and his heart pounding, he heard Hannah Moffat come along the hallway towards the door. The handle turned, the door opened, and the woman came into the room.

In that same instant Raynor sprang forward, the ebony ruler whipping up to smash down with sickening force on the back of the woman's head. There was every atom of Raynor's strength behind the blow and, with a groan, the woman crumpled to the carpet, to lie a still and huddled heap.

He was working entirely according to plan, of course. Every act and every word of his since breakfast had been entirely according to plan—the identical plan by means of which Claude Royston, the hero of his story, had got rid of the hag of a housekeeper who had been blackmailing him.

Raynor stooped over the huddled form of Hannah Moffat. Turning her over on her back, Raynor seized her by the armpits. Then, exerting all his strength, he proceeded to drag her from the room through the hall and up the stairs.

The woman was heavy, a dead weight. Raynor's arms ached beneath the strain and his breath began to come in laboured gasps. But he got her up on to the second floor and into the first back bedroom near the head of the staircase.

Leaving her lying on the floor, he sped down to his own bedroom. Whipping off his jacket, he pulled on a pair of gloves and raced down to the kitchen.

Half-filling a bucket with hot water, he flung in a piece of soap, then hunted quickly around for a wash-leather. He found one hanging on a nail by the kitchen sink.

Carrying the bucket of water and the wash-leather, he hastened upstairs again to the bedroom in which Hannah Moffat was lying.

The woman was lying just as he had left her and it seemed to Raynor that she must indeed be dead. He had certainly caught her a frightful crack with the ruler, the same as had Claude Royston in the story.

Claude had felled *his* housekeeper to the floor and hadn't known whether the blackmailing hag was dead or not, for the simple reason that he hadn't had time to look.

Moments had been as precious to Claude of the story as they were to Raynor who had created him.

Continuing to act in exactly the same manner as had Claude, Raynor opened the bedroom window and looked out. Directly below him lay a flagged courtyard. Beyond that were the garden and wooded grounds at the rear of the manor, from the boundaries of which flat ground stretched away towards the rising moorland.

Not a soul was to be seen anywhere, and not a sound disturbed the stillness of the quiet autumnal morning.

Closing the window, Raynor set quickly to work. Dipping the wash-leather into the bucket, he cleaned the inside of the window. In spite of the need for haste, he took care to make a good job of it, as good a job of it as a woman like Hannah Moffat would have made.

Then, opening the window again, he took another careful look round. Satisfied that no one was about, he sat himself on the sill with his legs inside the room and quickly cleaned the lower part of the window on the outside.

That done, he slid back into the room. Placing the wet wash-leather on the floor beside the bucket, he stooped and seized the limp form of Hannah Moffat. Dragging her to the open window, he took another careful survey of the courtyard below and the surrounding grounds and countryside.

Not a soul was to be seen anywhere. Turning his attention to the woman again, Raynor lifted her up so that her shoulders rested heavily against the sill.

There was nothing he was forgetting. Lifting her still higher, and supporting her with one arm around her, he seized first one of her hands and then the other and pressed her fingers against the window-sashes.

'Plenty of finger-prints there!' he panted.

Lowering the woman so that her head and shoulders sagged over the sill, he gripped her round the middle and thrust her half out of the window. Swiftly transferring his grip to her ankles, he braced himself to take the strain, then pushed her right out so that she hung head-downwards over the courtyard, prevented from falling only by Raynor's grip on her ankles.

Next instant he let her go and she went plunging down and down to the flagged courtyard below. To Raynor's ears came a dull thud as she struck the flags. For a moment he dared not look. Then poking his head cautiously out of the window, he looked down.

The woman was lying a crumpled heap far below. From the window she looked like a heap of black clothes, thought Raynor, save for one arm which was grotesquely outflung.

Well, if she hadn't been dead before, she was certainly dead now, thought Raynor with grim satisfaction. And serve her right, the had, she and her demands for a thousand pounds!

Withdrawing his head into the room, Raynor picked up the wet wash-leather. Leaning out of the window again, he dropped it down to the courtyard. It fell some little distance away from thc woman.

Withdrawing his head once again into the room, Raynor straightened up and took a good look round. No, there was nothing he had missed. Everything had gone according to plan right down to the smallest detail.

Excellent, thought Raynor with quiet exultation. He'd done the whole job well within the time limit at his disposal. The girl couldn't possibly get back from Firfield before eleven o'clock at the very earliest. She might even be later than that. She would be if she stopped in Firfield to make any purchase of her own, which was more than likely, reflected Raynor.

A sudden, prolonged, jangling peal on the old-fashioned front door bell cut in on Raynor's thoughts.

'Now who the devil can that be?' he ejaculated, considerably startled.

Pulling himself together, and adjusting his tie, Raynor waited a few moments. Then quitting the room, he stepped briskly to the front door and opened it.

His visitors were a small, stoutish gentleman and a girl. The stout little gentleman had a ruddy complexion, vivid blue eyes, and a white moustache. He was wearing plus fours with cap to match and carried an ash walking-stick. The girl was an extremely good-looking blonde in well-tailored tweeds which fitted perfectly her full but splendid figure.

'Mr Raynor?' demanded the small gentleman.

'Yes,' said Raynor pleasantly.

'I am Colonel Blakeney, of Hollerton Hall,' said his visitor, producing a card. 'A neighbour of yours. This is my daughter Edith. I heard you'd taken this place, so I thought we'd call on you and start to get acquainted, don't you know. H'mph!'

'I'm delighted to meet you,' said Raynor, with a smile. 'It's exceedingly nice of you to call. Will you come in?'

'No—no, perhaps we're disturbing you!' protested the colonel. 'Just leave a card, that's all we intended to do. Neighbourly act, don't you know. Confoundedly lonely place this, if you don't know abybody. Glad if you'll come to dinner some evening.'

'Thank you very much; I should like to immensely,' said Raynor. 'But please do come in! You're not disturbing me at all, I assure you!'

'Well, just for a minute, then,' said the colonel. 'Come on, Edith!'

Closing the front door when they had entered, Raynor led the way into the dining-room.

'I must apologise for your being kept waiting when you rang,' he said. 'I have only a very small domestic staff here—a woman and her niece. The girl is out, and I think the woman must be busy upstairs somewhere. May I offer you a drink?'

The colonel took a whisky-and-soda, the girl a sherry.

'Well, here's to your very good health, sir!' said the colonel, raising his glass. 'You're one of these writing fellows, I understand?'

'Yes, I do a little,' admitted Raynor, with a smile.

'I've read all your books!' put in the girl.

Raynor looked at her. Their eyes met, and she smiled.

'Yes, that's right; she's read your books,' said the colonel. 'Ever since she heard you were coming here she's been getting 'em from the library. Seems to like 'em, as well. I don't read much in that line myself except the sporting magazines and a few biographies. We'd have called on you before, but we heard about your poor aunt and didn't like to intrude. Shocking affair—shocking. Must have upset you dradfully.'

'It did,' said Raynor quietly.

'And you'd hardly even got settled in either,' went on the colonel. 'A pretty ghastly sort of house-warming that was! Hurrh!'

He broke off, coughing and going a rich peony colour, conscious of having committed a most frightful *faux pas*. House-warming, indeed. In view of the nature of the poor old lady's death, house-warming was just about the most unfortunate phrase he could possibly have used.

'D'you do any hunting?' he went on hastily to cover his embarrassment. 'Can give you a mount any time you like. Fine hunting country this! Three times a week ane occasionally more. Edith hunts regularly. Grand rider. Beats me!'

'I should like an occasional day out very much when I get settled down,' began Raynor. 'In fact, I've been looking forward to it—'

Cutting in on his words came a sudden, shrill, terrified yell from the direction of the kitchen.

'Mistor, mistor, where are ye? Owld Hannah's fallen oot o' the winder!'

'Good gad, what's that?' ejaculated the colonel, starting so violently that he spilled most of the contents of his glass.

Raynor knew what it was, all right. The errand-boy from the village had found Hannah Moffat. His booted feet came rushing along the hallway, and his shrill, terrified voice yelled at the foot of the stairs:

'Mistor, mistor, come at once! Owld Hannah's dead! She's lying oot there in the yard!'

Raynor bounded to the dining-room door and whipped it open. Standing in the hall was the errand-boy, with a red muffler knotted round his neck. His face was vhite, his eyes staring. At the sight of Raynor, he blubbered:

'Oh, mistor, owld Hannah's dead! She's lying oot there in the yard! She's fallen oot o' the winder. There's a wash-clowt lying there aside her!'

With a well-simulated exclamation of dismay, Raynor dashed along the hallway, through the kitchen, and out into the courtyard, with the startled colonel following at his heels.

Hannah Moffat was lying where she had fallen, a twisted, crumpled heap. She was quite dead. She appeared to have fallen full on her head, which had received terrible injuries. A few paces away, mute testimony to the nature of the tragedy, lay the wet wash-leather.

'Good gad, poor woman!' ejaculated the colonel in shocked tones, when he and Raynor had examined the body and satisfied themselves that Hannah Moffat was beyond all human aid. 'I wonder how it happened?'

Raynor had stepped back and was looking up at the windows. Directly above the body, high up on the second floor, a window was open from the bottom—the window which he himself had opened.

'She must have fallen from up there, by the look of it!' he said unsteadily.

The colonel joined him and stared up.

'Yes, that's it,' he agreed. 'She probably came over giddy or something like that, poor thing! Stupid practice, sitting outside windows to clean 'em—very stupid practice. Won't allow it in my house!'

Lowering his stare from the window, he looked at Raynor and said in a guarded voice:

'There's no chance of her having put herself out, d'you think?'

'Good heavens, no!' exclaimed Raynor, genuinely taken aback by the suggestion. 'She was a most sensible and level-headed woman!'

'Yes, so I should have thought,' said the colonel. 'So I should have thought. I've often seen her about. Queer sort of woman—very reserved. Didn't associate with any of the villagers, I understand. Still, one's got to look at a thing like this from every angle, you know. I'm on the bench—chairman of the local magistrates over at Firfield—and I've seen some queer things in my time. Deuced queer things!'

He became suddenly aware that his daughter, pale of face, was standing watching the scene with the scared-looking errand-boy.

'Edith, you go indoors!' he ordered sharply. 'This is no place for a girl!'

Obediently, the girl withdrew and the colonel turned to Raynor again.

'You are looking shaken, Raynor,' said the gentleman sympathetically. 'This shocking affair has upset you. Come on, let's get the poor woman covered up, then come indoors and have a drink—it'll do you good; then we might have a look at that room upstaris.'

'Well, it proves what everybody around here's laways said,' began the colonel conversationally, when Raynor had helped him to a whisky-and-soda. 'There's a confounded hoodoo on this house—'

'Stop it!' cut in Raynor harshly.

The colonel started, looking at him in surprise. Then his ruddy-complexioned face took on a deeper hue, and he said, a trifle stiffly:

'I'm sorry—very sorry—if my remark upset you. I withdraw it, of course—withdraw it unreservedly.'

Raynor was leaning against the sideboard, a glass of brandy in his hand.

'No, it's all right; I'm sorry,' he said wearily. 'But I'm sick and tired of people telling me there's a curse on this house. Not,' he added, with an unhappy attempt at a laugh, 'that it isn't beginning to look like it. But it's my house, and I had so looked forward to coming here. I had expected to be so happy.'

'Yes, of course,' said the colonel gruffly. 'It' s rotten for you

—beastly. But, all the same, it does seem that this house—'

'Father!' cut in Edith warningly.

'Yes—h'm—yes, of course, m'dear!' exclaimed the colonel pulling up short; then, to cover his confusion he had recourse to his handkerchief and busied himself with much blowing of his nose.

'Well, what about having a look at that room upstairs?' he suggested, stuffing his handkerchief away when he had recovered.

'Yes, very well,' assented Raynor.

Edith remained in the dining-room, whilst Raynor piloted her father up to the little back bedroom on the second floor.

The bucket of water was still standing on the floor by the window where Raynor had left it.

'Yes, it's clear enough what happened,' said the colonel, stepping to the window and examining it closely. 'She'd cleaned the inside, poor thing, then was busy with the outside!'

He poked his head out of the window and looked down.

'Hollo, there's Podger down there!' he exclaimed. Then, raising his voice, he bawled: 'Hi, Podger, come up here!'

Raynor looked out of the window. A stout policeman was standing by the rug-covered body, staring up at the window. His bicycle was propped against the wall by the rear door.

'This is Mr Raynor, Podger,' said the colonel by way of introduction when the policeman had climbed the stairs. Then he went on: 'You can see for yourself what happened. The woman was obviously cleaning the window when she slipped and fell.'

Raynor said nothing. He was thinking what a stroke of luck it had been for him, this officious little chairman of the local magistrates having called on him as he had done that morning.

In the story he was writing, Raynor had not got this far. But soon he would get down to work again—and then his pen would be racing ahead of the facts in the same supernatural way that it had done before, even predicting the future.

Then Raynor thought of Diana, and the amusement died in his heart. So far as he was concerned, she was the unknown quantity. What would she say if, and when, a statement was required from her, as it probably would be?

No matter what she said, she could fasten no guilt on him, he assured himself again. Even if she knew about the attempt at blackmail on the part of Hannah Moffat, and confessed to it, that was no proof that he had killed the woman. There was not the slightest proof anywhere that he'd had anything to do with the woman's death. He'd been much too clever for that.

The Book of Evil

Constable Podger, notebook in hand, had moved to the window with the colonel.

'You see, the inside's been washed, and she was evidently washing the outside,' Colonel Blakeney was explaining. 'That's when she must have fallen.'

'Yes, sir,' said the constable, writing carefully in his notebook with a stub of pencil. He turned to Raynor. 'Whould you be in the house when it happened, sir?' he asked.

'Yes, I haven't been out at all this morning,' said Raynor. 'Since about ten o'clock I've been sitting in the dining-room, writing.'

The constable wrote this down.

'When did you last see the deceased alive, sir?' he asked.

'Between about half-past-nine and a quarter-to-ten,' answered Raynor. 'I went into the kitchen to speak to her and her niece. I mentioned to her then that I'd like the windows cleaned.'

'Ah, then she must ha' started doing it, like,' observed the constable, noting it down in his book. 'Did you hear a cry or anything like that, sir, when you were sitting down there writing?' he went on.

'No, nothing,' answered Raynor. 'The first I knew of the tragedy was when the errand-boy from the village came running into the house crying that Miss Moffat was lying dead in the courtyard.'

'Well, I think that's all we can do up here, sir, until Sergeant Anstruther and Doctor MacTavish get here,' he said closing his notebook. 'I telephoned for them, and they should be here any minute now. In the meantime,' he went on, turning to Raynor, 'I think maybe I ought to have a word with the deceased's niece.'

'She's in the house somewhere,' said Raynor. 'If you care to go downstairs to the morning-room or the kitchen, I'll find her and send her down to you.'

He knew that the bedrooms of Diana and Hannah Moffat were on this floor, although he had never been into either room since his arrival at the manor.

Waiting until Colonel Blakeney and the constable were descending the stairs, Raynor proceeded to look into the other bedrooms.

He found Hannah Moffat's room almost at once. He knew it was her bedroom by the garments hanging behind the door. It was a small, severely furnished room, with a single bed standing against one wall.

Closing the door, Raynor opened the next one. He saw at a glance that this room was Diana's, for although the girl was not in the room, her coat was lying flung across the foot of the bed.

The room was furnished similarly to that which had been occupied by Hannah Moffat, but with the addition of a small bookcase standing against one wall.

Impelled by curiosity, Raynor stepped into the room

and crossed to the bookcase. He was wondering what type of literature the girl favoured, for he was a staunch believer that the axiom, 'Show me a man's books and you show me his character,' was equally applicable to the opposite sex.

But as he stared at the titles of the few well-thumbed volumes in the little bookcase, Raynor's eyes narrowed in astonishment. For not only were the books exceedingly rare volumes, they were strange reading indeed for a girl twenty years of age.

There was Scharnlorst's infamous *Analysis of Evil*, Orme's masterpiece of sadistic horror, *Torment of the Soul*, Pidowsky's vile *Rites of the Beast*, Fraser's fifteenth-century *Black Worship*, and the madman Vaux's revolting *Lodestone of Hell*.

There were other volumes of a similar nature, some of them unknown to Raynor, but he knew enough of them to know that together they must have cost a small fortune.

Where had the girl got them from, he wondered. That she read them was evident, or they wouldn't be in her bedroom.

Raynor's thoughts flashed back to his first night at the manor when, through the mirror of his dressing-table, in one swift, illuminating moment he had glimpsed the girl for what she really was.

He had thought her evil then—had known her to be evil then, but he had thrust the thought from him. But now he was confronted with the truth of it, for only a mind that was evil could browse and feed on the content of these volumes.

Strangely enough, reflected Raynor, the thought did not repel him; instead, he found himself smiling. Now that he had received this second illuminating insight into the girl's mind, she had become more interesting to him than ever.

He must have a talk with her about these volumes, he decided, and find out what she thought of them. It would be interesting to discover her reactions to them. There would be plenty of opportunities to talk between him and her, now that Hannah Moffat had gone.

The thought of Hannah Moffat brought Raynor to himself with a jerk. He'd better get downstairs, he reflected, and, quitting the room, he hurried down to the kitchen. He found Diana there, standing alone by the kitchen table. She glanced at him with no sign of distress.

'They're all out there at the back,' said the girl calmly. 'Sergeant Anstruther, Dr MacTavish, Colonel Blakeney, and the policeman from the village.'

Raynor looked at her closely. She seemed quite composed, and returned his stare unwaveringly.

'Podger wanted a statement from you,' he said. 'Have you given him one?'

'Yes,' said the girl.

Raynor's heart missed a beat.

'What did you tell him?' he demanded, striving desperately to keep his voice steady.

'Just what I knew,' returned the girl.

The words 'And how much was that?' leapt to Raynor's lips; but he bit them back. He must not, dare not, appear too eager to know what the girl had said. If only he had the slightest idea how much she herself knew, he would know whether or not he was in danger. But he hadn't any idea how much she knew, nor dared he ask her.

He waited a moment, hoping desperately that she might go on to say something which would, at least, give him some indication as to what she had said to the constable. But, moving from the table towards the fire, all the girl said was:

'I've left your cigarettes in the dining-room.'

He would get nothing more out of her. Raynor could see that, and in his heart he cursed her. Then, pulling himself together, he walked out through the rear door to the courtyard.

By the nature of his reception from the little group which was around the body, he told himself, he would know whether the girl's evidence had turned suspicion towards him.

There was nothing in Raynor's reception to cause him any undue anxiety. Little Dr MacTavish gave him a friendly nod, and Colonel Blakeney introduced him to Sergeant Anstruther, a lean-faced and efficient-looking officer, saying:

'This is Mr Raynor, Sergeant. Raynor—Sergeant Anstruther!'

'How d'you do, sir?' said the sergeant.

He turned to Dr MacTavish, who had straightened up from the body.

'Death was instantaneous, and is quite compatible with a fall from the window up there,' said the doctor. 'Her skull and neck are broken, and her right arm, together with several ribs. There are also severe internal injuries caused by the fall. You can have her taken inside.'

The little doctor had picked up his hat.

'Well, I'll be gett'ng along,' he said.

'The inquest will be some time tomorrow,' said Sergeant Anstruther. 'I'll let you know the time later. I've seen Constable Podger's notes, and they seem to cover everything, so I won't trouble you any further now, sir. I can only say I'm very sorry you've had two such tragedies here during the short time you've been in residence.'

'Thank you,' said Raynor quietly.

He accompanied the party to the front door, where Constable Podger was waiting with his bicycle.

'Well, I'll be seeing you to-morrow, Raynor,' said the colonel, squeezing his hand. 'And, remember, you're coming over to dinner some night. Come over to-night, if you like. It'll cheer you up. You're always welcome—more than welcome!'

'Thank you!' said Raynor. 'It's very kind of you indeed. But I'll wait until all this is over before I visit you.'

He shook hands with Edith. She gave his fingers a faint pressure.

'I'm so sorry,' she said in a low voice.

Raynor inclined his head over her hand. But as he watched her and her father walking down the drive after Dr MacTavish's car had gone, there was a peculiar look in his eyes, a look which none of his friends of his London days would have recognised.

He stood watching until a bend in the drive hid her and her father from view. Then, turning on his heel, he re-entered the house, closing the door behind him.

Back in the dining-room, Raynor stood a few minutes plunged in thought. Then, moving to the fireplace, he rang the bell.

In response to the ring, Diana appeared. Raynor looked at her curiously as she stood in the doorway waiting inquiringly. She looked as calm and composed as though nothing had happened.

'I'm very, very sorry indeed about this dreadful affair, Diana,' said Raynor.

The girl made no response. Confound her, thought Raynor irritably, why didn't she say something.

'I must say, you don't seem unduly distressed about it!' he snapped.

'I don't wear my heart on my sleeve,' returned the girl.

'Are you sure you've got one to wear anywhere?' grated Raynor.

The girl looked at him in cold contempt, then turned to go.

'No wait!' begged Raynor 'I'm sorry I said that. I didn't mean it. This rotten affair's upset me. Listen, Diana. I want to ask you something.'

'What is it!' inquired the girl, pausing in the doorway.

'When you asked me how it happened, I told you, and all you said was "I understand". What exactly did you mean by that? *What* did you understand?'

'I understood that she had fallen from the window,' replied the girl.

'But, good heavens, girl, weren't you shocked at all?' burst out Raynor.

The girl studied him intently for a moment.

'Yes, I was very shocked when I went upstairs and looked in the room from which she'd fallen,' she said.

Raynor's heart missed a beat.

'What d'you mean?' he demanded hoarsely.

'I mean that for the first time in twenty years aunt had taken up the wrong bucket with which to wash the windows,' said the girl.

Then, closing the door quietly behind her, she was gone without another word.

The Grip of Fear

Incapable of movement, his face deathly, Clive Raynor — the basically fine man now turned into a raging menace by his supernatural surroundings — stood glaring at the closed door.

The girl knew. Merciful heavens, she knew! Her remark about the bucket proved that. If it didn't mean she knew, why had she said it?

Raynor's heart, which had seemed to cease beating for the moment, commenced to pound sickeningly.

Had she told the police about the bucket? he asked himself in terror. If she had, what did it prove? Nothing. It couldn't prove anything. The woman could easily have taken the wrong bucket up. One bucket was as good as another. But after twenty years, to take the wrong bucket. It might well prove a strong link in a chain of evidence against him, thought Raynor, with stark fear at his heart.

He strove desperately to get a grip on himself. He had to reason this thing out, to think coherently. There was no use giving way to panic.

He crossed to the sideboard. With trembling fingers he splashed himself out a drink. He was drinking more lately than he'd ever done in his life before, he thought. But, by heavens, he needed it.

He downed a stiff brandy at a gulp. The raw spirit served to steady him. Now about this bucket. The girl might suspect something, obviously did suspect something, but she couldn't prove anything.

She hadn't seen him kill Hannah Moffat. Nobody had seen him kill the hag. The only evidence against him must of necessity be circumstantial evidence, and the very flimsiest of circumstantial evidence at that — the question of a wrong bucket.

Again, unless the girl knew of the blackmail and had told the police about it, there could be no possible motive held against him for the killing of Hannah Moffat. But *did* the girl know? Had she told?

Mounting panic threatened to grip Raynor again. Desperately he fought it back. He had to think clearly at all costs. His very life might depend upon it, probably *did* depend upon it.

He turned to the sideboard to pour himself another drink. As he did so he halted in his tracks, for there had come a knock at the door. It opened, and Diana appeared with the tray to set his lunch. She looked curiously at Raynor as she set down the tray.

'What's the matter?' she asked. 'Aren't you well?'

With an effort, Raynor tried to force himself to speak naturally.

'Well?' he repeated hoarsely. 'No, I'm not well. I'm damned upset about this rotten affair this morning, and the extraordinary way in which you're acting. Looking at you, no one would ever think your poor aunt was lying dead upstairs.'

'If you want me to burst into tears, I'm afraid I can't oblige,' said the girl. 'I'm not the crying sort.'

'I know you're not the crying sort,' burst out Raynor savagely, 'and I don't want you to burst into tears. I want to know what you meant by your remark that your aunt had taken up the wrong bucket with which to wash the windows!'

The girl looked at him in either well-simulated or else genuine surprise — Raynor couldn't be sure which. Then she laughed shortly.

'Well, if that's all that's worrying you,' she said, 'it did seem rather peculiar to me that after twenty years of using the right bucket, she should use the wrong bucket this morning.'

'Does it matter what confounded bucket she used?' grated Raynor.

'No, not at all.'

'Then what are you making such a confounded song about it for?'

'I'm not making a song about it — it's you who're making a song about it.'

Raynor steadied himself before he put his next question.

'Did you tell the police about this wrong bucket?' he asked, striving desperately to make his voice sound casual.

'No, of course not,' answered the birl. 'Why should I?'

Raynor's relief was so immense that he was afraid it must show in his face. He turned to the fire and stirred the coals with the poker.

'This isn't exactly the time to talk about new arrangements,' he said, 'but I'd like you to stay on here, Diana, and take your aunt's place as housekeeper. You can get in any extra help you want, of course. I'll leave everything to you. Will you stay?'

The girl looked at him steadily.

'Yes,' she said, 'I would like to stay.'

'That's fine!' exclaimed Raynor heartily.

He meant it, for he was certain by now that the girl knew nothing about the blackmail nor suspected anything about the deaths of his Aunt Bertha and Hannah Moffat. That being the case, there was nothing to fear from her.

'I don't think we'll require any extra help,' went on the girl. 'It's not as though you had the whole house opened up. I can look after the place quite well myself.'

'That'll suit me better than ever,' said Raynor. 'I don't want a lot of servants cluttering up the place.'

The girl smiled cryptically.

'No,' she said, 'neither do I.'

The Madness of Raynor

After lunch Raynor took his stick and went for a walk. He had scarcely been out of the house since he arrived, and he was feeling the need of exercise. Moreover, he thought a good brisk tramp across the moors would serve to clear his brain of the doubts and fears, not only of the past hours, but also of the past few day.

He walked in the opposite direction to Tarn, heading out across the lonely moors.

The grey, autumnal afternoon was calm and still. Around him lay the silent moorland, stretching away towards where, far in the distance, it merged with the purple hills of Cheviot. Not a sound disturbed the hushed and brooding stillness save now and again the cry of a peewit and the occasional mournful cry of some gull gracefully winging its way inland from the sea.

But in the solitude of those silent spaces there came no peace to the mind of Clive Raynor. Instead, with every footstep he took from the manor, he began to feel in his heart amounting horror at the things he had done during the past few days.

Could it be possible, he asked himself aghast, that he, Clive Raynor, was a double murderer, with the blood of two women on his hands?

Yes, it was true, and the knowledge appalled him, sickened him with fear and remorse.

Yet less than a fortnight ago he had been as other men — decent, honourable, and respected — a popular member of his clubs, a welcome guest at the houses of his friends.

But what would they think of him now, those friends, if they knew him for the monster he really was? Wouldn't they shrink from him in scorn and loathing? Yes, indeed, they would.

By his own hand he had made himself what he now was — a pariah and an outcast fit only for the gallows.

With a groan which was near to a whimper of fear, Raynor hurried on. But fast as he hurried he could not shake off those torturing devils of terror and remorse which pursued him.

Unable to bear it any longer, he turned at length and headed for home, hurrying, hurrying, ever faster until, on nearing the manor, he almost broke into a run.

His face drawn and haggard, striving desperately to keep the demon of thought at bay, he hurried up the fir-lined drive and let himself into the house.

Leaving his cap and stick in the hall stand, he went into the dining-room. Afternoon was merging into dusk, and in the firelight flickering shadows danced fantastically on walls and ceiling.

Flinging himself into an armchair by the fire, Raynor stretched out his long legs to the blaze and sat staring with unseeing eyes into the glowing heart of the burning coals.

And as he sat there his fears and terrors gradually left him as though smoothed away by a gentle, soothing hand, and there came to him a strange peace and calm of ming.

No longer was he frightened, no longer did he know remorse for the things he had done. The warm, intimate atmosphere of the room seemed to enfold him in a protective embrace, and he was himself again, secure and at peace in his beloved house. It was as though the building provided an excuse for his wickedness.

He tried to analyse his emotions. Why was it he had felt so frightened out there on the silent moors, so sick with terror and remorse? Why was it that, back here in the old house, he felt so calm, so safe, and so content?

Perhaps it was in those moments that, for the first time, some inkling of the dreadful truth came to Clive Raynor. Perhaps, deep down in his mind, there stirred the unborn thought that the house, being evil, condoned evil and folded to itself those whom it would destroy.

But if that thought did stir in Raynor he was conscious of it for no more than one short instant of time, then it was gone, erased from his mind as though it had never been there.

Lighting a cigarette, he left the room and strolled towards the kitchen.

But as he pushed open the kitchen door he halted, a quick frown of anger on his face. For sitting in the kitchen with Diana was Bob Fergus, a suitor of hers.

At the sight of Raynor, the stoutish young farmer rose uncertainly. He looked awkward and embarrassed, as though he half expected to be kicked out.

'It's all right, Bob, sit down,' said the girl coolly.

'I'd like to speak to you, Diana,' said Raynor, harshly. Swinging on his heel, he returned to the dining-room. A few moments later the girl appeared.

'Yes?' she said.

Insane, unreasoning fury seized Raynor in its grip.

'I don't want that fellow hanging about the place!' burst out Raynor savagely.

The girl's eyes hardened.

'I'll certainly ask him to go if you insist on it,' she said. 'It's your house. But if he goes, I go. There's always a home for me at Shawcross Banks. In fact, he wants me to leave here now.'

Only by a supreme effort did Raynor keep a grip on himself.

'Wants you to leave here?' he grated, his face livid with passion. 'Why?'

'He is afraid of what happens to people who live in this house,' she faltered, 'and . . . he thinks you act strangely.'

A red mist floated in front of Raynor's eyes. He hated Fergus.

He rushed towards the door, but with arms outflung, the girl barred his path.

'You'll leave him alone!' she said sharply.

Raynor's only answer was a curse. Seizing her, he tried to hurl her aside. Then he began to shake her furoiusly.

'Bob!' she cried.

Drawn by that cry, Fergus came dashing from the kitchen. Raynor was conscious of a hand gripping him savagely by the shoulder, of a voice that bellowed furiously in his face, then his grip was wrenched away from the girl, and a clenched fist smashed him with savage, sickening force, under the chin, sending him staggering wildly back to go down with a crash near the hearth.

The Mind-Reading Pen Moves On

Raynor rose slowly and dazedly to his feet, one hand pressed against his chin. Fergus was standing in the doorway, his arm protectingly around the girl.

'Interfere wi' my lass, would ye?' he said furiously, lapsing into broad vernacular in his anger. 'By gor', but I've a ruddy good mind to give ye some more, ye beggor!'

'Get out!' said Raynor thickly.

'Ay, I'll git oot!' shouted Fergus. 'And I'm taking Diana wi' me! This is nae hoose for her wi' a feller like ye in it!'

'Get out!' said Raynor again.

'Ay, we're gannin', so shut your gob or I'll shut it for ye!' said Fergus roughly. He turned to the girl.

'Ha' way, lass! Git your bag packed and I'll take ye alang to Shawcross Banks,' he went on. 'Mother'll be glad to ha' ye, and we'll send ower for the rest o' your things either th' morn or after the funerol. There'll be things o' your Aunt Hannah's ye'll be wanting as well, I s'pose!'

The girl made no immediate response. She was watching Raynor. He was leaning weakly against the mantelpiece, holding his chin, his sullen gaze on the floor. Then slowly he raised his eyes and looked at her, and she saw the bitter contempt in their depths.

'Come on, Bob!' she said quietly.

The pair of them withdrew, the girl closing the door. Left to himself, Raynor lowered his gaze to the carpet again and remained where he was, leaning against the mantelpiece.

He was feeling sick with pain, anger, and humiliation. To have been knocked down in his own house by a swab like Fergus, and to have been unable to retaliate, he thought bitterly. For retaliation would have been worse than useless — Raynor knew that. When it came to fisticuffs, the heavily-built Fergus would be more than a match for him every time.

When it came to fisticuffs, yes, reflected Raynor, but not when it came to a question of intellect and brain. The lout would be no match for him then, thought Raynor, and, properly directed, brain could beat brawn every time.

Raynor wondered how he could get even with the clod, for, by heavens, he swore viciously, he meant to get even with him somehow or other.

Never in his life before had Clive Raynor hated anybody as he now hated Bob Fergus, for he hated him with a bitter, burning venom which fed on itself until it consumed him like fire, causing him to tremble with rage and bringing again the red mist of fury swimming before his eyes.

By an effort he got a grip on himself and stood there by the mantelpiece plunged in deep and profound thought. Then suddenly he started, his eyes glinting.

It wasn't that he had found the answer he was seeking as to how he could get even with Bob Fergus and make the swab pay one hundredfold for what he had done. No, he hadn't found the answer yet, bu, by heavens, he knew how he *could* find it!

With a vicious, triumphant laugh, Raynor straightened up from the mantelpiece and crossed towards the door. Quitting the room, he went upstairs to the bathroom and bathed his face. Then, going along to his bedroom, he unlocked his dispatch case and took from it the unfinished manuscript of his story.

Descending to the dining-room again, Raynor placed his manuscript on the table in front of him. He sat studying it for a while, then, picking up his pen, he commenced to write at the point where Claude Royston, his hero, had felled his blackmailing hag of a housekeeper to the floor, then pushed her out of a top floor window. That was as far as Raynor had got, and, picking up the thread of the story, he wrote rapidly.

Giving fictitious names to Colonel Blakeney and his daughter, Edith, Raynor described their arrival at the house that morning, and dealt faithfully with everything which had followed.

Faster and faster raced his pen as he drew nearer to the incident which had happened less than an hour ago. He described his visit to the kitchen, the finding of Bob Fergus there, and the ensuing scene in the dining-room.

Without a pause his pen sped on, its swift, faint scratch the only sound which disturbed the hushed stillness of the room. Sheet after sheet he covered with his fine, small writing, and steadily the pile of manuscript by his elbow grew.

He was well ahead of the events of the evening now, and

was writing like a man inspired. For Clive Raynor was inspired, infused again with that sweeping, irresistible flood of inspiration which he had found came to him so strangely in this quiet room.

Ceaselessly, without pause or break, the thread of the story spun swiftly on through his mind, and he transcribed it all to paper with such speed that he scarce knew what he was writing.

Now and again he smiled, a faingt flicker on his lips, as though he found amusement in what he was writing. But he was supremely conscious of it, and his pen raced on until at length it suddenly became borne in upon him that he was not alone in the room.

Startled, he paused in his writing and looked up. Diana was standing near the table, watching him.

'What the devil d'you want?' demanded Raynor harshly.

'What time will you be taking dinner?' inquired the girl. 'I knocked twice, but you did not answer.'

'I never heard you!' snapped Raynor. 'I don't want any dinner — I'm busy. Anyway, what the devil are you doing here? I thought you were off to Shawcross Banks.'

'No; I never intended to go,' said the girl evenly. 'It was Bob's idea, not mine!'

Raynor flung down his pen.

'Wel, it happens to be my idea as well,' he said harshly. 'I don't want you here, so you can get out.'

'Do you mean that?' said the girl.

'Yes, I mean it!' grated Raynor. 'I hope you'll be happy at Shawcross Banks cleaning out byres and playing second fiddle to your clodhopper's mother!'

The girl smiled.

'Poor child,' she said. 'Can't you control your jealousy any better than that?'

With an oath, Raynor thrust back his chair and leapt up.

'What did you say?' he shouted, his face livid with passion. 'How dare you talk to me like that? Get out of here — go on, get out, before I throw you out!'

The girl was already going. Moving from the room, she quietly closed the door behind her. Panting with the violence of his outburst, Raynor stood with fists clenched, glaring at the closed door.

Recovering himself at length, Raynor slumped down on to his chair. It would be hopeless to attempt to write any more just now. He knew that. The thread of the story was broken, and, for the moment, inspiration had fled.

With fingers which trembled with anger, Raynor gathered together the sheets of manuscript he'd just written. Placing them in their right order, he leaned back in his chair and proceeded to read them.

And as he read, the anger died in the face of Clive Raynor, to be replaced by a cruel and cunning smile. For unfolded in the closely written pages before him was the fate which lay in store for Bob Fergus.

A dreadful, horrible fate it was, and one which, in order to be carried through to a triumphant conclusion, meant the involving of another person. The fact that this other person would be an innocent, unsuspecting, and defenceless victim mattered not a whit to Clive Raynor.

Ridden by hate and spite as he was, all that mattered to him was that he knew now how he could deal with Bob Fergus and avenge himself a thousandfold!

The Shape in the Candlelight

Placing his manuscript in a neat pile, Raynor rose. He lit a cigarette, then crossed to the sideboard an splashed himself out a drink from one of the bottles.

So he had added a few more chapters to his story of Claude Royston of Graylings, he mused, as he leaned with his back against the sideboard, his glass in his hand.

It was the story of himself, of course, and of his life at Broom Manor. But it was extraordinary, he reflected, how he could deep the story shooting ahead of present events, and, in its pages, accurately record what would take place in the future.

He had the room to thank for that, of course, this room in which he always found such supernatural and vivid inspiration.

Setting down his glass on the sideboard, he looked at the clock. The time was almost ten-thirty and Raynor was feeling hungry. He wished he'd let that strange and haunting girl get him some dinner before dismissing her so brusquely. He began to listen.

How quiet the house was, he thought, how deathly still! Nothing moved, nothing stirred. There seemed a strange tension about the place, almost, thought Raynor, like that of a crouching beast preparing to spring.

He tried to put the thought from him. It was his house, he told himself, and he was happy here. But, all the same, he wished he wasn't alone.

He started. Alone? Merciful heavens, no, he wasn't alone. There was a body in the house. The body of Hannah Moffat. It was lying upstairs in her room.

Raynor turned out the lamp. Returning to the dining-room, he splashed himself out another drink. He drank it neat and the raw spirit heartened him.

To blazes with Hannah Moffat, he thought. What if she was lying upstairs dead? She couldn't hurt him. She was dead and gone now.

Raynor took another drink. Now was the time, he thought, to make a thorough search for that damning spill. He had the whole house to himself and he could search everywhere, starting with the woman's room.

Reaching the second floor, Raynor hesitated a moment outside the closed door of Hannah Moffat's room. Then, moving on, he turned the handle of Diana's door.

The door was locked. Raising his hand, Raynor knocked sharply on the panels.

'Diana!' he called. 'Are you in there, Diana?'

His voice echoed loudly in the hushed and brooding stillness. But that was all. There was no other response. Again Raynor knocked and again he called.

'Are you in there, Diana?'

Only silence answered him, silence as heavy and oppressive as a pall. No, the girl had gone, and she had locked her door to prevent anyone prying amongst her things before Bob Fergus could send over from Shawcross Banks to collect them.

Moving to the door of Hannah Moffat's room, he turned the handle and slowly entered. In spite of himself his heart was pounding and his fingers, holding the candle, were trembling.

The body of the woman was lying covered with a sheet on the single bed against the wall. His face white, Raynor stood motionless, staring in the feeble illumination of the candle at that still and shrouded form.

Long moments passed as he stood there staring. Then, getting a grip on himself, he moved to the dressing-table on which he placed the candle.

Opening the top drawer, he commenced to rummage quickly through it. But there was nothing there save handkerchiefs, some black woollen stockings, a few pairs of old gloves, and similar articles of personal use and apparel.

Closing the drawer, Raynor opened the next. It contained old-fashioned underclothes, neatly ironed and folded, but that was all. Satisfied that what he sought was not there, Raynor closed the drawer and turned to the next, the bottom one.

Placing the candle on the floor beside him, he squatted down and pulled open the drawer. It contained a number of aprons and old-fashioned blouses, all of them neatly folded away. But beneath them, at the back of the drawer, Raynor found a bundle of old letters and documents tied togehter with a piece of tape.

Untying the tape, Raynor went swiftly through the letters, not troubling to read them, but looking in every envelope in case the woman should have chosen to hide the spill in one of them.

Several of the letters and documents were minus their envelopes and Raynor unfolded each, then quickly refolded it again, in the course of his search.

Suddenly he stiffened, his eyes narrowing. He had unfolded an official-looking document filled in in ink. It was a birth certificate and the name Diana caught his eye.

Squatting by the candle, Raynor examined the document. It *was* Diana's birth certificate, and as he read the other names it bore he caught his breath.

Diana was the daughter of Major Burton, who had died so tragically in the house twenty years ago! And Hannah Moffat was not her aunt, but her mother.

Raynor could scarcely believe his eyes. But there it was in black and white in front of him, with the registrar's signature and everything.

In blank astonishment, Raynor studied the document again. This, then, accounted for the undoubted breeding of the girl and for other things about her which had often puzzled him, reflected Raynor.

He wondered if she knew the truth of her birth. She couldn't possibly know it, he thought, else she wouldn't have called Hannah Moffat her aunt.

He felt a new interest in Diana. If he could see her again he might question her. He wondered how much she really knew.

Crouching there by the candle on the floor, Raynor was so engrossed in his find that he failed entirely to hear a slight movement behind him. Then suddenly he froze, the blood congealing in his veins with fear and horror — *for a hand had been laid on his shoulder from behind.*

For a long moment Raynor did not move. He could not. Then, with eyes dilating, he slowly turned his head. Next instant a dreadful scream of stark terror burst from his lips and he recoiled so violently that he overbalanced, falling on the candle and plunging the room into Stygian darkness.

For what Clive Raynor had seen, standing towering behind him, was a tall, white figure which his quilty heart told him could have come only from the death-bed of Hannah Moffat.

Nothing but Evil

Moaning with terror, half-fainting, Raynor lay where he had fallen. He could not have moved had he attempted to, for so great had been the shock that his limbs seemed paralysed.

He was dimly aware of a quick scraping sound, then a match flared into life. He stared up with horror-stricken eyes. The white figure was still there, standing beside him. It was holding the match. It spoke.

'What on earth are you doing?' it said, and the voice was the voice of Diana.

Raynor stared up at her. He could see her lovely face quite plainly now in the light of the match. She was wearing a white silk nightdress.

The match went out and the girl struck another.

Clive Raynor's guilty heart froze.

'Do get up,' she said impatiently. 'You don't know how stupid you look lying there. Where's your candle?'

Stooping, she retrieved it from where it was lying beside Raynor. Lighting it, she placed it on the dressing-table. Deathly sick and trembling, Raynor got unsteadily to his feet.

'My heavens, but you gave me a shock!' he said hoarsely, supporting himself against the dressing-table.

'I should think so, as well,' said the girl sharply. 'What are you doing in here?'

Raynor made no answer. The girl looked down at the scattered letters and documents lying on the floor. Prominently on top of them lay the birth certificate where it had fallen from Raynor's hand.

'I see,' said the girl coldly. 'You were going through Aunt's things. Why? Never mind, we can't talk here. Go downstairs and I'll put these things away, then I'll cone down and talk to you. Go on!'

Raynor went. He was incapable of refusing. He was still sick with shock and was trembling violently. Never in his life, never in his wildest imaginings, had he thought possible such a moment of unutterable horror as that which he had just experienced.

He went downstairs, feeling his way by the wall, his eyes fixed and staring in the darkness. Reaching the dining-room, he poured himself out a drink with hands which shook so badly that he spilled a lot of the spirit on the sideboard. The glass rattled against his teeth as he raised it to his lips.

He drank off a half tumbler of neat brandy, then crossed to the fire. He felt cold, deathly cold, so cold that it seemed to him as though he would never get warm again. He spread his trembling hands to the embers reddening in the grate.

'My heavens!' he whispered. 'Oh, my heavens!'

He turned his head with another terrified start as the girl

came into the room. Her bare feet were encased in slippers, and she was wearing a light wrap over her nightdress.

'Now what were you doing in Aunt Hannah's bedroom?' she demanded.

'I — I was looking for something,' said Raynor.

'What were you looking for?'

'I can't tell you,' said Raynor; then he reiterated desperately: 'I can't!'

'Is that what you were looking for?'

Like a man hypnotised, Raynor stared at the half-burned spill suddenly disclosed in the palm of the girl's hand. Coolly and unhurriedly the girl unfolded the spill and showed it to him again. It was the spill he had been searching for, the half-burnt bill-heading from James Lewis.

'Then you — then you know?' he gasped, his voice little more than a whisper.

'Know what?' asked the girl evenly.

'That your aunt was blackmailing me?'

'Yes, I knew that,' said the girl.

Raynor stared at her. His face was ghastly in its pallor. If she knew that much, what else did she know, he asked himself in mounting terror. What did she suspect abou Hannah Moffat's death?

With a quick movement the girl flung the spill into the fire. It was consumed in the flames.

'There, probably you'll feel happier now,' she said.

Raynor did not feel happier. He felt terrified. His mind was in a whirl. If only he could think coherently, he told himself desperately. If only he could think!

'Why have you burned it?' he asked hoarsely.

'Because it's of no use to me,' replied the girl. 'I don't intend to blackmail you.'

'But you didn't mind your aunt doing it!' burst out Raynor. Then he added wildly: 'But she's not your aunt — she's not your aunt at all, she's your . . . your mother!'

'I knew that also,' put in the girl coolly.

'You knew it?' exclaimed Raynor. 'But you haven't acted as though you knew it. You haven't shown much grief about — about her death to-day!'

'I didn't love her,' replied the girl. She was leaning slightly forward, her dark, unfathomable eyes fixed intently on Raynor's face. 'Haven't you learned yet that there can be no love in this house,' she asked, '*that love cannot exist here?*'

'I — I don't know what you mean,' stammered Raynor.

'You don't?' said the girl. 'Then think. Since coming here, have you known one thought which, judged by the standards of the world, is decent, clean, and pure?'

'I don't know,' faltered Raynor. 'I cannot say. But, yes, of course; I'm sure I have; I must have known some decent thoughts —'

'Listen to me,' murmured the girl. 'There is nothing here save what the world calls Evil. But you belong here as I belong here, and you will become as I have become. You will not shrink from Evil as you have done in the past. You will breathe it as I breathe it, embrace it as I embrace it, and become its faithful servant even as I have become.'

'You must have been surprised to find me in the house to-night,' she went on conversationally. 'I suppose you thought I'd gone to Shawcross Banks; I hadn't. I was lying in bed reading when I heard you coming up to the top floor. I wondered what you wanted, so I put my light out and locked my door. I heard you try the door, then I heard you in the next bedroom. I went in to see what you were doing. I'm sorry I startled you.'

Raynor paid little heed to what she was saying. His mind, bemused and dazed, was groping desperately back over the past half-hour.

'Diana, what were you saying to me just now?' he burst

out hoarsely again. 'About the house being evil and — and you being evil, and about me being evil.'

The girl laughed.

'You've got nothing to worry about now,' she went on soothingly. 'Go to bed. Remember, the inquest's tomorrow.'

Sudden terror gripped Raynor again.

'The inquest,' he gasped. 'What are you going to say? You knew she was blackmailing me!' His voice rose, shrill with terror. 'I had nothing to do with her death. I never touched her — I swear it!'

'There's no need for you to swear it,' put in the girl calmly. 'No one except yourself is suggesting you had anything to do with her death. She fell out of the window. That's obvious.' Then she added, with slow deliberation: 'Even if she did take up the wrong bucket for the first time in twenty years.'

Raynor groaned aloud and buried his face in his trembling hands. Pitiful heavens, he asked himself with a sob, why did this girl torment him so by her hellish innuendos and her half-concealed revelations of what she knew?

'Well, now I'm going to bed,' she said, 'and you'd better go yourself. Good-night!'

She moved silently away. Raynor sat a few moments, his face buried in his hands. Then slowly he raised his head. As he did so, his eyes dilated. For the girl had not left the room. She had halted by the table and was looking down at the manuscript of his story, reading it as it lay there.

With a hoarse cry, Raynor blundered to his feet. Rushing forward, he swept her aside.

'You mustn't read that!' he cried furiously. 'It's mine!'

With an hysterical, childish movement, he snatched up the manuscript and hugged it to him. The girl stood rubbing her arm where he had handled her. Her eyes had momentarily blazed, but now they were steady again.

'You've hurt me,' she said. 'If you don't want me to read

what you've been writing, you shouldn't leave it lying about.'

'I didn't mean to leave it lying about,' said Raynor hoarsely. 'I didn't think there was anybody in the house but myself when I left it there. I'm sorry if I've hurt you.'

'You have hurt me,' said the girl, still rubbing her arm. Then she asked curiously: 'Is it your new novel?'

'No, it's no,' lied Raynor.

'Then why have you called it "The Whispering House"?' demanded the girl. 'That sounds like the title of a story. It would even fit a story about this house. Is that what it is?' she went on quickly. 'A story about this house?'

'No, it isn't!' shouted Raynor violently. 'Why should I want to write a story about this house?'

'Because there is a story in this house,' returned the girl. 'But it would take a pen dipped in the red brew of hell to write it. Good-night!'

With that she was gone.

Left to himself, Raynor stood a few momenst staring dumbly at the door. Then with trembling hands he replaced his manuscript on the table and sank heavily down into his chair by the fire.

Merciful heavens! What a night he'd had, he told himself quaveringly. What a nightmare of horror it had been!

And he was in the girl's power. He could see that only too well. She knew about the blackmail, and she suspected there was something wrong about the death of her mother, Hannah Moffat. Her references to the wrong bucket proved that.

She had only to get up at the inquest and tell all she knew, and if he, Clive Raynor, wasn't promptly arrested then he'd be a darned lucky man.

But she had as good as promised she wouldn't tell. She had said she was glad her mother was dead. Heavens above, thought Raynor helplessly, what sort of a girl was she?

He stirred at length. Rising, he picked up his precious

manuscript and turned out the lamp. Then, taking the manuscript up to his bedroom, he locked it away in his dispatch-case and went to bed. A few minutes later he had drifted off into a slumber of sheer mental exhaustion.

He awoke when Diana brought him his morning tea.

The inquest was to be held that morning. Raynor felt strained and nervous, and knew that he would feel so until the grim proceedings were safely over. He wondered what the girl would say when the actual moment came. He wondered, also, if she would divulge the truth of the relationship between herself and Hannah Moffat.

The inquest opened at eleven o'clock. Raynor was the first witness called. He gave his evidence to the effect that about nine-thirty on the morning of the tragedy he had asked the deceased to clean the windows. He had then returned to the dining-room, he said, and had sat there writing until he had received an unexpected visit from Colonel Blakeney and his daughter. He was talking to the colonel and Miss Blakeney in the dining-room, he said, when he heard the errand-boy rush into the house crying that Hannah Moffat was lying dead in the courtyard. He had run out with Colonel Blakeney, and had found the woman lying beneath a bedroom window which was open on the top floor.

Diana was the next witness to be called, and Raynor's heart beat sickeningly as he watched her step forward. What would she say, he asked himself in gnawing fear and dread.

'You were not present in the house at the time of the tragedy, I understand?' said the coroner to Diana.

'No; I had gone over to Firfield on an errand,' she replied. Then she added: 'When I left the house Aunt was getting the water ready to wash the windows. She said she would start on the top floor.'

Raynor stared at the girl, sudden exultation in his heart. No matter what she might suspect about the death of Hannah

Moffat, she was on his side and was protecting him. Why else should she have uttered this deliberate lie about Hannah Moffat making preparations to clean the windows? For Raynor knew it was a deliberate lie.

'There is only one other question I wish to ask you,' said the coroner to Diana. 'Have you any reason to think that this sad affair might have been anything else but a complete accident? Have you at any time heard your aunt speak of suicide or do you know of any cause which might have led her to contemplate taking her own life?'

'No,' returned the girl emphatically. 'Aunt would be the last woman in the world to take her life. Recently, however, she has complained several times of bouts of giddiness, and that is what I think must have happened when she fell. I think she must have had one of her attacks and slipped and fallen.'

'Did she consult a doctor about these bouts of giddiness?' asked the coroner.

'No, she said they were nothing,' replied the girl. 'She wasn't the sort of woman who would go to a doctor unless she could really help it.'

The coroner consulted his notes for a moment. Then he said:

'Thank you, that is all!'

The girl stepped down. Deliberately she avoided Raynor's eyes. Even in a small matter like that she showed her complet self-possession and common sense, thought Raynor.

What a grand girl she was, he thought. He was absolutely jubilant. In view of the evidence there could be but one possible verdict. Raynor was confident of that.

His confidence proved justified. After hearing the evidence of the other witnesses, the coroner summed up very briefly, and a verdict was returned to the effect that Hannah Moffat had accidentaly met her death by falling from a window whilst carrying out her household duties. A few formal words of sympathy from the coroner to Diana concluded the proceedings.

Colonel Blakeney had been driven over from Hollerton Hall for the inquest by his daughter Edith. The girl had not attended the inquest, but had gone back with the car, having arranged to call for the colonel later.

'I would like a word with you, colonel,' said Raynor, when the proceedings were over and the coroner, the police, and Dr MacTavish had departed.

'Yes, certainly, Raynor,' replied the little colonel readily.

'It's about Fergus,' said Raynor. 'You know, Bob Fergus, who farms Shawcross Banks. He's a tenant of yours, I believe.'

'Yes, that's right,' assented the colonel. 'What about him?'

'He struck me last night,' said Raynor quietly. 'He knocked me down, in my own house!'

The little colonel stared at him in astonishment.

'Knocked you down?' he exclaimed. 'Good gad, what for?'

'Because I ordered him out of the place,' replied Raynor.

In spite of the gravity of his manner he was enjoying himself immensely. Now that the inquest was safely over, he was feeling a new man. All his doubts, cares, and fears had vanished, and with inward zest he was now embarking on his plan of vengeance on Bob Fergus.

What was more, he was doing it all according to the chapters he had added to his story the previous night. He was acting in exactly the same manner as the hero of the story, Claude Royston, of Graylings, had acted.

'You say Fergus knocked you down because you ordered him out of the house?' exclaimed the colonel, in angry astonishment. 'Good Godfrey, I've never heard of such a thing, dashed if I have. I can hardly believe it. Was he drunk?'

'No, he wasn't drunk,' said Raynor. 'He was perfectly sober. At least, I think so. Perhaps I'd better explain. Apparently he's courting Diana. 'I've no objection to that, of course; but I do object to the fellow knocking about my house as though he owns the place. From what I can gather, he seems to have had the run of the house until I came here. I expect Hannah Moffat encouraged him. He'd be a good match, I suppose. Anyway, he's been here practically every night since I arrived. Had he confined himself to the kitchen during his visits, I mightn't have said anything; but when I found the fellow using my bathroom, I thought, rightly or wrongly, that it was time to protest.'

'Good gad, yes, I should think so,' ejaculated Colonel Blakeney. 'D'you mean to say you found him doing that?'

'Yes, I did, last night,' replied Raynor. 'I found him coming downstairs, so I asked him where he'd been. He said he'd been to the bathroom for a wash. I told him I considered he'd taken a most impertinent liberty. I'd have let it go at that, but he turned round and told me I was a stuffy snob. A stuck-up toff was the expression he used. I thereupon ordered him out of the house and told him never to come back. He asked me what chance I thought he'd have of seeing Diana if he didn't come back. I told him that had nothing to do with me. He then had the colossal impudence to suggest that I had designs on the girl myself, and, for that reason, was forbidding him the house. I'm afraid I lost my temper rather, and I told him if he didn't get out of the house at once, I'd throw him out. That was when he struck me. He knocked me into the hearth.'

'The scoundrel!' exclaimed the colonel wrathfully. 'I know he's got a temper when he's roused, and I know he likes a drink occasionally; but I've never heard of anything like this before. Are you sure he wasn't drunk?'

Rayston hesitated.

'Well, he certainly didn't appear to me to be drunk,' he said. 'He seemed to be more jealous than drunk, though why the devil he should be jealous of me, I can't think. The girl's a servant of mine, that's all.'

'Quite, quite!' agreed the colonel. 'But jealousy's a deuced queer thing sometimes — worse than drink — particularly with a fellow of Fergus' type. Not much sense there really, y'know — no gentlemanly restraint — bull at a fence sort of methods every time, don't you know? Anyway, what're you going to do about it? Take out a summons for assault?'

'Good heavens, no!' disclaimed Raynor hastily. 'I wouldn't dream of it. The reason I've mentioned it to you is that you're his landlord, I understand, and I thought a word from you to the fellow, advising him to keep away from here, might save any further unpleasantness.'

'Yes, certainly; only too pleased!' agreed the little colonel readily.

'I'd also like an apology from him,' said Raynor.

'You'll have that as well,' promised the colonel.

Raynor heard a car draw up outside, and he guessed it would be Edith Blakeney arriving for her father. In order to forward what was in his mind, he had to feel his way very carefully now.

'I don't require a written apology from Fergus,' he said. 'A verbal one will do quite as well. But I don't want him coming to my house. Perhaps it would be better if we both saw him together,' he suggested. 'You couldn't run me out to Shawcross Banks now, I suppose?'

'Yes, certainly, I can!' assented the little colonel, with alacrity. 'That'll be best, as well — much the best. Nothing like striking while the iron's hot!' He glanced at the clock. 'We'll catch him at his dinner,' he announced.

He turned to his daughter.

'Edith, m'dear,' he went on, 'I want you to run Mr Raynor and me out to Shawcross Banks. We've got a little private business to discuss with Fergus.'

'Yes, certainly,' replied the girl, with a smile for Raynor.

As he looked at her in her well-cut tweeds, Raynor thought again what a fine-looking girl she was.

'Well, suppose we get along?' he suggested.

The Guile of Raynor

Edith's car quickly bore Raynor and her father to Shawcross Banks, a fair-sized farmstead some two and a half miles from the manor.

'We won't be long, m'dear,' said the colonel as the car pulled up in front of the farmhouse. 'You wait here!'

Descending from the car he strode to the front door, followed by Raynor, who was taking covert but careful stock of the outside of the house. In response to the colonel's ring, a young girl of about fourteen years of age came to the door and looked shyly at the two visitors.

'Hallo, Annie!' said the colonel gruffly. 'Is your brother in?'

'Yes, sir, he's having his dinner,' replied the girl.

'You might tell him I want to see him, will you?'

The blushing Annie withdrew and a few moments later Fergus came along the passageway towards the door. He was wearing an old sports jacket, breeches, leggings, and mud-stained boots. At sight of Raynor his plump face darkened and he scowled. His expression was not lost on Colonel Blakeney, who said curtly:

'I want to speak to you, Fergus!'

'Yes?' growled Fergus, without the customary 'sir' which he invariably used towards the colonel.

'Indoors, not here!' snapped the latter gentleman. 'I don't intend to discuss what I've come to see you about standing here on the doorstep, Fergus!'

Fergus hesitated a moment, then sullenly led the way into a large, comfortably furnished living-room, the windows of which looked out on the front of the house.

As he followed Fergus and the colone into the room, Raynor glanced swiftly about him. There was no doubt that the room was used a lot, probably in the evenings when the day's work was over, reflected Raynor.

A fire was laid in the grate, ready for lighting, a few magazines and one or two newspapers lay where they had been carelessly thrown on to an old-fashioned horse-hair sofa, and a wireless set stood against one wall.

But what drew Raynor's covert gaze was a fishing-rod, a pair of waders, and a double-barrelled sporting gun standing in a corner of the room beneath a small shelf on which were a few books and a square, cardboard box. Raynor took careful note of these.

'Now, look here, Fergus,' began Colonel Blakeney without preamble, 'I understand that you so far forgot yourself last night as to knock Mr Raynor down!'

'Ay, I knocked him down all right,' admitted Fergus grimly. 'But I didn't forget myself. He asked for what he got!'

'That'll do!' snapped the colonel. 'Don't you talk to me like that. Mr Raynor is a friend of mine, a newcomer to the neighbourhood, and I'm not going to have him knocked about by a fellow like you or by anybody else. You ought to think yourself dashed lucky that he hasn't taken out a summons for assault against you. Anyway, I'm here to warn you to keep away from the manor in future and to demand that you apologise to Mr Raynor in a proper manner!'

'What, apologise to him?' sneered Fergus, red with anger. 'I would be soft! Has he told ye what I knocked him doon for?'

'Yes, he has,' rapped the colonel. 'And I quite agree with him. It's a confounded impertinence your using his house as though it belongs to you! Mr Raynor was quite right to tell you to go!'

'And he was quite reet, I suppose, to be hitlin' and skahin' my lass, was he?' shouted Fergus, lapsing into broad vernacular as his anger burst its bounds, and her struggling wi' him and yelling for help? By gor', he roared, his fists clenching, his eyes blazing, 'what d'ye think I was to do? Stand theer and let him git on wi' it? No, by gor,' I gie'd him what he was asking for and I'll gie him some more if he interferes wi' th' lass again!'

'There seems little point in prolonging this interview,' Raynor said, with a shrug of his shoulders. 'As I have said before, I believe he's mad. You'd better warn him, however,' he went on sternly, 'that if he persists in repeating these ridiculous accusations against me, he will leave me no other option than to consult my lawyers with a view to proceeding against him for malicious and criminal libel. I will see you outside!'

Had anything been required to convince the little colonel of Raynor's complete innocence of the charge levelled against him by Fergus, Raynor's words and attitude would more than have sufficed.

'By gad, Fergus, I don't know what you expect to gain by this!' he burst out furiously. 'I can only agree with Mr Raynor that you must be mad —'

'I'm not mad!' roared Fergus. 'It's the truth I'm telling ye.'

He bounded forward, gripping Raynor by the arm as the latter moved towards the door.

'Tell the truth, ye beggor!' he roared, swinging Raynor savagely round. 'Tell the truth, or, by gor', I'll break your dirty neck for ye!'

'That's enough!' burst out the colonel, his ruddy complexion purple with anger. 'Take your hands off Mr Raynor at once. You can take your notice to quit, and you'll get out of here just as quick as you like!'

Fergus glared at him, but he took his hands off Raynor.

'Ay, I'll gan!' he shouted. 'I wouldn't stop here noo, not if ye asked me to. There's a pair o' ye, I can see that. But never mind. One day ye'll be sorry for this, so I'm telling ye. Noo git oot o' here — gan on, git oot!'

With a snort of disgust and anger, the colonel got out, stalking furiously from the room; Raynor had already gone, and was walking towards the car.

'Confounded boor, that fellow!' exploded the colonel, overtaking him.

'I don't think he's right in the head,' remarked Raynor evenly.

As they reached the car, Edith said:

'What on earth's been going on in there? It sounded like a riot. Was that Fergus who was shouting?'

'Yes!' snapped the colonel, climbing in beside her. 'I've just been giving the fellow his notice to quit, and he didn't like it. Now, drive to the Hall! Mr Raynor'll have lunch with us!'

'It's very kind of you, but I don't think I'll stay for lunch, if you'll excuse me,' said Raynor, as the car slid forward. 'I want to go into Newcastle this afternoon to do some shopping.'

'That's all right, then,' said the colonel to Raynor. 'You come and have lunch, then Edith will drive you into Newcastle this afternoon.'

Thus it was arranged, and, with an inward smile, Raynor leaned back in his seat. Everything was going according to plan, he reflected, just as he had written it in his story.

He had got Bob Fergus kicked out of his farm. That was the first step in his scheme for vengeance on the lout. The second step would be taken that afternoon, when he, Raynor, went into Newcastle; and the third and final step would be taken that same night.

Could He Go On?

As the car purred up the tree-lined drive of Hollerton Hall and swung into the broad sweep of gravel in front of the house, Raynor studied the place with interest, for this was the first time he had seen it. Hollerton Hall, Colonel Blakeney's home, was a fine old house, of mellow red brick, covered with creeper. There was an air of warmth and friendliness about the old place, so different from the grey and forbidding stonework of Broom Manor.

Nor, as Raynor discovered, did the inside of the house belie the promise of its exterior, for there was a homeliness and comfort which told its own tale of happiness and security.

By an adroit remark or two, Raynor quickly inveigled the colonel into showing him over the house, a tour upon which that unsuspecting little gentleman was only too ready to embark, for he loved the old place, which had been in his family since it was built more than a hundred years ago.

It was not through idle curiosity that Raynor wished to see over the house, nor was it because of any desire to please his host. The truth was, that in order to further his scheme of vengeance on Bob Fergus, it was essential that Raynor learn the layout of the interior of Hollerton Hall.

There was only he, Edith, and the colonel at lunch, for the latter was a widower, and Edith was his only child. Ecxellent though the meal was, however, and pleasant though the company, Raynor did not enjoy it, for now that the excitement at the farm was over he was beginning to feel again the fears and self-loathing which he had experienced whilst taking his solitary tramp across the lonely moors.

It was strange, he reflected, that he never felt this way at the manor. It was only when he was away from the manor that he found himself beset by fear, dread and remorse for the evil things which he had done.

Once again, he reflected how that evil and forbidding house seemed to work on his mind in some ghastly and mysterious way. Resolutely he fought to stifle his fears, however. He was a brilliant conversationalist when he wished, and he now exerted himself to such good effect that not for an instant did either the colonel or Edith suspect the turmoil in his heart.

It was the same when Edith drove him into Newcastle after lunch. To all outward appearances he was his normal self, but only he knew the effort it cost him.

If this girl knew the truth about him, he thought bitterly, if she knew him for the murderous monster he really was, how she would shrink from him with fear and loathing instead of chatting gaily to him like she did as the car purred smoothly on along the Great North Road to Newcastle.

Reaching that grey city of Tyneside, Raynor parted temporarily from Edith on the pretext that he wished to visit his late Aunt Bertha's lawyers, Grimmett, Grimes & Grimmett. He arranged to meet the girl an hour later in Stanwick's Tea Rooms in Northumberland Street.

But Raynor paid no visit to the offices of Grimmett, Grimes & Grimmett. Instead, he went in search of a gentleman's outfitters, and, finding a large, plate-glass emporium in Grainger Street, he went in and made a number of purchases which took him upwards of an hour.

Edith had parked the car in Eldon Square, and, having deposited his parcels in the car, Raynor made his way towards Stanwick's Tea Rooms.

His black and bitter mood of haunting fear and remorse was still heavy upon him, and as he walked along the crowded pavements, he felt himself to be a man apart — a man who, by his own hand, had made himself an outcast and a pariah, who had no part amongst this hurrying throng.

It was only by an effort, and by telling himself that he

need not really use them, that he had forced himself to go and make his purchases at the outfitters, for the things he had bought had an important part to play in his plan of vengeance on Bob Fergus.

Over tea, in the large and crowded tearooms, where an orchestra was playing softly above the babel of conversation, he was quiet and depressed in spite of his utmost efforts to conquer the blackness of his mood. However, he managed to grope his way through the afternoon, and in less than two hours, Edith's car turned in at the gates of Broom Manor and purred along the fir-lined drive to the house. Alighting, Raynor collected his parcels from the back of the car.

'Well, thank you very much indeed,' he said to Edith. 'I've enjoyed this afternoon immensely. Now that I know where Hollerton Hall is, I'll come over and see you again, if I may.'

'Yes, certainly; any time you like,' replied the girl, with a friendly smile. 'We'll always be pleased to see you.'

As she drove back down the drive, Raynor stood motionless, watching until the red tail-lights of the car had vanished from view round a bend.

Yes, he was going to visit Hollerton Hall again, he reflected, but much sooner than either Edith Blakeney or her father dreamt, for he was going to visit it that very night.

But was he, he thought wretchedly, as he stood there alone in the darkness. Merciful heavens, hadn't he sufficient black and dastardly crimes on his account already without adding another to the list—another which would be far more frightful and more horrible than any which had gone before?

Why not abandon this vile and awful thing which he was contemplating, he asked himself with a shudder. A sudden wave of terror and self-loathing surged up in him. He must abandon it, he cried wildly in his heart—he must. He couldn't go on with it any longer.

He became conscious that the front door of the house had opened. Yellow illumination from the lamp in the hallway was streaming out into the darkness. Raynor turned. Diana was standing in the doorway, her slim figure silhouetted against the lamp-light.

'I heard a car,' she said. 'I thought it might be you.'

Without a word, Raynor entered the house and the door closed on him.

A Thief in the Night

Raynor took his purchases straight up to his bedroom. Locking them away in his wardrobe, he pocketed the key, had a wash, then descended to the dining-room, where he splashed himself out a drink.

Drinking was becoming almost a habit with him these days, he reflected, as he crossed with his glass to the fire. But if ever a man had reason to drink, he had, he told himself.

The almost overmastering terror which had seized him out there in the darkness had left him by now, and he was no longer conscious of the gnawing fear and remorse which had been with him since lunch.

But it was always the same, he reflected. When he was outside, away from the house, he became a prey to fear and dread; but when he returned and rested in this quiet room, his fears vanished as though smoothed away by some protective and invisible hand.

It was the room, of course, which had this soothing effect on him, he told himself; this dear old room, in the warm and intimate atmosphere of which he became himself—a man dominant, supreme, and unafraid.

He was a fool to go out, even for a walk, he reflected. Why should he go out when he felt so restful here, so content with his thoughts? He had a sudden, queer impression that the room resented his going out as might some lovely, jealous woman resent the absence of her man.

The thought brought a smile to his lips. It was a strange and whimsical fancy, he reflected, but he liked it, and felt that it held in it something akin to truth. Anyway, reflected Raynor savagely, Bob Fergus was doomed and before many hours had passed he would find himself in the grip of relentless and inexorable forces which would not release their hold on him until they had marched him remorselessly to the grave.

A few minutes later Diana came in.

'The funeral's at eleven o'clock in the morning,' she said. 'Will you be coming?'

Raynor hesitated. He hadn't the slightest desire to attend Hannah Moffat's funeral; but he knew convention demanded that he should. Not that he cared a tinker's curse for convention now, he told himself angrily; but there were gossiping tongues to be considered. His absence from the funeral would certainly arouse comment.

'Yes, I'll come,' he said.

'We'll be the only two mourners', said the girl.

'Mother wasn't popular in the village. She never associated with anyone there.' Then she added cynically: 'There'll be plenty of sightseers, of course.'

She withdrew. Raynor sat on, plunged in thought. Staring with unseeing eyes into the heart of the glowing coals, he turned over in his mind every step in the grim night's work which lay before him.

It was close on midnight before he stirred. Diana would be in bed by this time, he reflected. She had not looked in to say good-night to him, but she never did.

Rising, Raynor poured himself out a drink at the sideboard and drank it down neat. He needed a bracer for what lay ahead of him, he told himself.

Turning out the lamp, he went through into the kitchen. The place was in darkness, and the rear door was locked, the key being on the inside.

Satisfied that Diana had gone up to bed, Raynor went up to his own room. Locking the door behind him, he lighted the lamp. Then, opening his wardrobe, he took from it the parcels which he had brought with him from Newcastle.

Unwrapping the parcels, he spread the contents out on the bed. There was an electric torch, a pair of leggings, a pair of breeches, a cap, a mackintosh, and a couple of sports jackets, one of which was much roomier than the other.

Divesting himself of the suit he was wearing, Raynor dressed himself in the clothes spread out on the bed. He put on both sports jackets, donned the mackintosh, then pulled the cap well down over his eyes.

Picking up the lamp, he surveyed himself carefully in the wardrobe mirror. The two sports jackets and the mackintosh gave him the appearance of being much broader across the shoulders than he really was, and, satisfied, he replaced the lamp.

Thrusting the torch, a handkerchief, a pair of gloves, his keys, and his knife into his pockets, he turned out the lamp and stealthily unlocked his bedroom door. Stepping softly out on to the landing, he listened intently. But nothing moved, nothing stirred to break the deathly, brooding stillness which enfolded the house like a black, oppressive pall.

Quietly locking his bedroom door on the outside, Raynor slipped the key into his pocket and crept silently downstairs. Letting himself out into the night through the rear door of the kitchen, he locked the door behind him and put the key in his pocket. Then taking Diana's bicycle from the outhouse he wheeled it round to the front of the house and down the drive.

Pausing at the drive gates to turn on the bicycle lamp, he

mounted the saddle and rode boldly through the darkness in the direction of Shawcross Banks.

Save possibly for some poacher or tramp, or, maybe, Constable Podger from the village out on his beat, Raynor knew it was extremely unlikely that there would be anybody about on the lonely country roads at that late hour.

But he didn't care if there was. In fact, he'd welcome it. He had chosen his leggings, breeches, mackintosh, and cap with the greatest care, and if, in the darkness, he didn't look exactly like Bob Fergus, he was satisfied that at least he looked sufficiently like him as to pass for him.

He didn't intend to stop for anybody. If anyone spoke to him he would give them a grunted 'good-night' and ride on without dismounting. Nor did the fact that he was riding a lady's bicycle matter, either. In fact, it was all to the good, for everybody in the district knew that Bob Fergus was courting Diana, and there would be nothing strange in Fergus—or someone who looked extraordinarily like Fergus—being seen riding from the direction of the manor late at night on the girl's bicycle.

Raynor hoped he was seen by someone. That was one of the reasons why he had lighted the bicycle lamp. For although his scheme was absolutely water-tight, it would help a lot if somebody was able to come forward later and say they had seen Bob Fergus abroad late on this particular night, mounted on a bicycle.

He rode along the by-road until he was within a quarter of a mile of Fergus's farmhouse. Then, dismounting, he turned out the lamp and stood a few momenst looking about him in the darkness. He knew he had to hurry, for, once away from the house of evil, it didn't take long for him to change back into a normal, decent person—so different from the cold-hearted animal which Broom Manor had made him.

Not a sound disturbed the intense stillness of the sleeping

countryside, and, satisfied that there was no one in his immediate vicinity, Raynor wheeled the bike quietly on along the road towards the farmhouse.

Leaving the bike in the hedge beside the entrance gate, he drew on his gloves, then cautiously approached the house. He trod with the utmost stealth, fearful lest his footsteps might be heard by some farm dog which would raise the alarm.

Reaching the windows of the room in which he and Colonel Blakeney had interviewed Fergus that morning, Raynor tried them cautiously with his gloved hands, hopeful that one of them, at least, might have been left off the latch. He was careful to make no sound.

He found all the windows fastened, but he had come prepared for that. Taking his knife from his pocket, he opened it and inserted the blade between the sashes. Next instant there came a faint click as he thrust back the catch.

Returning the knife to his pocket, he stood a few moments peering about him in the darkness. Then, turning his attention to the window again, he stealthily raised it and clambered through into the room.

Straightening up, he stood rigid and motionless, listening with bated breath and straining ears. But nothing broke the hushed stillness of the sleeping household save the ticking of a clock on the mantelpiece and what sounded like a faint, muffled snoring from somewhere overhead.

Drawing his electric torch from his pocket, Raynor pressed the switch. The golden beam swept the room, giving him his bearings, then, switching off the torch, he moved silently and carefully towards the corner of the room where stood the fishing-rod, waders, and double-barrelled sporting-gun which he had seen that morning.

Reaching the corner, he raised his hand and groped cautiously along the small shelf above. His fingers closed on the square, cardboard box he had seen that morning, and he lifted it down.

A swift flash of his torch showed him that the box contained cartridges for the gun, as he had anticipated it would. Thrusting four of the cartridges into his pocket in the darkness, he carefully returned the box to the shelf. Then, groping cautiously for the gun, he picked it up and stealthily retraced his steps towards the window.

It had been a bit of splendid luck seeing the gun there that morning, he reflected jubilantly. But it wouldn't have mattered if he hadn't seen it. The poker from the fireplace, or some such weapon as that, would have suited him equally well for the grim porpose he had in mind—provided, of course, that it came from the Fergus household.

But the gun was first-class—the very thing. It would make a quicker, better job than would a poker, and there'd be less chance of bungling.

Thus thinking, Clive Raynor climbed cautiously out of the window, closed it gently behind him, then, carrying the gun, trod stealthily through the darkness towards the bicycle.

The Third Victim

Mouting the bicycle and carrying his gun as best he could, Raynor pedalled away into the darkness, taking the road which led to Hollerton Hall.

He had not relighted the bicycle lamp, but he was still uncaring as to whether or not he was seen in the darkness, for he didn't intend to stop for anybody.

Save for himself, however, the lonely road was deserted at that late hour, and it was without meeting anyone that eventually he reached the drive gates of Hollerton Hall.

Dismounting from the bicycle, he left it in the black shadow of a clump of bushes just inside the gates. Then, cyrrying the gun and treading on the grass verge which fringed the gravel, he set off on foot up the drive.

Reaching the top of the drive where it opened on to the broad sweep of gravel which fronted the hall, he halted and stood motionless, staring intently at the black bulk of the house which loomed up in front of him through the darkness.

Not a light showed in any of the windows at the front of the house, and, satisfied that the household was safely abed, Raynor moved stealthily round to the rear.

When Colonel Blakeney had shown him over the house that morning, Raynor had taken particular notice of the windows of the ground-floor rooms at the rear of the house, and he had noted with inward satisfaction that they were fitted with old-fashioned fasteners, as were the windows at Shawcross Banks.

With the gun in his hand, however, he prowled about for a while in the hope of discovering some window which had been left unfastened. His search proving unsuccessful, he paused at length in front of the kitchen window and took his knife from his pocket.

He was still wearing his gloves in order to avoid leaving any incriminating fingerprints, and inserting the blade of the knife between the window-sashes, he forced back the catch. Then, returning the knife to his pocket, he gently raised the window and clambered through into the kitchen.

Straightening up in the darkness, he stood listening with straining ears. But not a sound broke the intense stillness, and, satisfied that no one was stirring, Raynor stealthily lowered the window, taking the precaution of leaving it open about an inch from the bottom.

Taking his torch from his pocket, he switched it on and flashed the beam swiftly about the kitchen. Having got his bearings, he laid the lighted torch on the floor, so that the beam would not be visible to anyone outside the window.

Then, kneeling down, he slipped a couple of cartridges into the gun.

With the gun loaded in both barrels, Raynor straightened up, and propped it against the table. Then, taking his handkerchief from his pocket, he tied it carefully round the lower part of his face, leaving only his eyes showing. Pulling his cap well down over his eyes, he picked up the gun, and retrieving his torch, switched it off.

Feeling his way cautiously from the kitchen, he emerged into the inky black darkness of the passageway which led to the main entrance-hall. A swift flash of his torch showed him the baize-covered connecting door immediately in front of him. Switching off the torch, he passed silently through the swing door and gained the main entrance-hall, where again he stood rigid and motionless, listening intently.

The main staircase was only a few paces from him in the darkness, and from the landing above came the slow, ponderous tick-tock, tick-tock of a grandfather clock, clear and distinct in the stillness.

No other sound broke the tense, hushed silence, and satisfied that so far his entry had gone unheard, Raynor felt his way silently to the stairs and commenced a cautious ascent.

Gaining the landing, he stood motionless, listening with straining ears. But apart from the slow and heavy tick-tock, tick-tock of the grandfather clock somewhere near him in the darkness, not a sound disturbed the hushed and brooding stillness.

Tense and rigid, taut in every nerve and muscle, Raynor pressed the switch of his torch. The golden beam split the darkness, showing a wide, carpeted corridor leading from the landing. The first door along the corridor was that of Edith Blakeney's bedroom. The second door was that of the colonel's bedroom. Raynor had learned all this during his tour of the house with the unsuspecting colonel.

Switching off his torch, he slipped it into his mackintosh pocket and moved cautiously forward. Pausing outside the door of Edith Blakeney's room, he pressed his ear to the panels.

Not a sound came from the room, and satisfied that the girl was asleep, Raynor moved silently on to the door of the colonel's room.

In the darkness his groping fingers closed silently on the handle of the colonel's door. With the utmost stealth, a fraction of an inch at a time, he turned the handle. As he pushed the door softly open there came to his ears a sound of snoring.

Slipping silently into the room, Raynor softly closed the door behind him. Raynor's gently groping fingers found the light switch just inside the door of the room. As he pressed the switch there came a faint click, and the room was flooded with warmly shaded light.

Tense and motionless, his gun held menacingly at the ready, Raynor stood staring towards the bed. Colonel Blakeney was sound asleep, his grey-haired head resting on the pillow.

Raynor took a slow, menacing step forward, and then another, his tread deadened on the soft carpet. Then suddenly he froze, rigid and motionless, as, roused by the light, the colonel stirred restlessly, his eyes blinking sleepily open.

For a few moments the colonel lay where he was.

Then, as though realising that the light had been switched on, he gave a grunt and raised himself inquiringly on his elbow.

As he did so he started violently, his eyes dilating as they took in the masked and mackintoshed figure standing within a few paces of the bed, gun raised menacingly.

The Ring at the Bell

What thoughts flashed through the colonel's mind in that dreadful moment will never be known. The cap, mackintosh, and leggings were as worn by Fergus, of Shawcross Banks, and the gun was the same type as used by Fergus. It may be that Colonel Blakeney realised this; but before he could move or utter one single startled word the inhuman devil that Raynor had become sent the gun roaring into life.

The charge struck the colonel full on, and he collapsed heavily on to the pillow.

Following hard on the roar of the gun, Raynor fancied he had heard a cry from the next room. Whirling now on his heel, he bounded for the door and wrenched it open. As he did so he came face to face with Edith Blakeney.

At sight of the masked man suddenly confronting her, the girl uttered a cry of terror. Next instant a savage sweep from Raynor's arm sent her staggering wildly aside, then Raynor was gone, rushing along the landing in the darkness and bounding downstairs.

As though in his haste he dropped his gun; but actually he dropped it deliberately, and it came clattering down the stairs behind him as he bounded down to the hallway below.

Above, Edith Blakeney was screaming at the top of her voice, and from the direction of the servants' quarters, higher still in the house, came cries of questioning and alarm.

Blundering along the darkened hallway and through the swinging baize door, Raynor gained the kitchen. Thrusting up the window which he'd left open at the bottom, he swung himself out into the night.

Next instant he was running madly round the house and racing down the darkened drive towards where he had left his bicycle. Hollerton Hall was on the telephone, and Raynor knew that before many minutes had passed the alarm would be put through to Firfield police station. Before that happened it was essential that he was well away from the place.

Whipping his handkerchief from about his face, he thrust it into his pocket. Then, seizing the bicycle, he ran it out through the drive gates, leapt into the saddle, and pedalled swiftly off into the darkness, heading for Broom Manor.

Raynor rode without a light, and more than once, in his haste, he was almost into the hedge which bordered the narrow road. He avoided any serious spill, however, and meeting no one on the lonely road at that late hour, it was without any untoward incident that eventually he turned in at the drive gates of Broom Manor.

He was safe enough now, he reckoned, so, dismounting, he wheeled the bike along the fir-lined drive until he came to the house, which was in as complete darkness as it had been when he had set out on his murderous, nocturnal mission two hours or more ago.

Returning the bicycle to the small outbuilding where Diana always kept it at the rear of the house, Raynor let himself into the darkened kitchen. Locking the door behind him, he crept softly upstairs to his bedroom, where he lighted the lamp and quickly divested himself of the clothes he was wearing.

No pangs of conscience or remorse for his latest fiendish crime kept Clive Raynor awake that night. He lay awhile in the darkness, speculating upon what would be happening at the manor, then gradually he drifted off into slumber.

How long he slept he did not know, but suddenly he awoke with a start. Was it imagination, he asked himself, or had he heard a peal on the front-door bell?

Next moment his guilty heart missed a beat, and he started up on his elbow, for, from downstairs, came the jangling, raucous peal of the old-fashioned, front-door bell.

Who could be ringing at this hour of the morning? Raynor asked himself in fear. Had it anything to do with the murder of Colonel Blakeney?

The grey light of early morning was filtering through the curtains drawn across the windows. Raynor peered at his bedside clock. The time was close on seven-thirty.

Propped on his elbow, Raynor listened intently. The ring had not been repeated. He wondered if Diana had heard it and gone down to answer it. That was more than likely, he thought, for by this time the girl should be up and about her daily duties.

Listening with straining ears, Raynor heard a light step outside his bedroom door. It was followed an instant later by a knock, then the door opened and Diana came into the room. In the greying light which filtered through the curtains, she saw Raynor propped on his elbow.

'You're wanted downstairs,' she said quietly.

'Who is it?' demanded Raynor hoarsely.

'Superintendent Clayton and Sergeant Anstruther, from Firfield,' answered the girl.

The Investigation

The chill fingers of deathly fear clutched for an instant at the guilty heart of Clive Raynor. Had anything gone wrong? he asked himself desperately. Had he slipped up anywhere? Were the two police officers here to arrest him?

No, that couldn't be, he assured himself. If they were here to arrest him, they wouldn't have sent upstairs for him. They'd have come up themselves and arrested him in the bedroom.

The girl was still standing by the door, watching him curiously. With an effort, Raynor got a grip on himself.

'What on earth do they want at this hour of the morning?' he demanded, striving desperately to keep his voice steady.

'I don't know,' replied the girl. 'They merely asked to see you.'

'Where are they?'

'I showed them into the dining-room.'

'All right; I'll get up,' said Raynor unsteadily. 'Tell them

I'll be down in a minute. I won't keep them waiting long.'

'Very well,' said the girl.

She withdrew, closing the door behind her. Waiting a few moments to try to get a better grip on himself and make himself more composed, Raynor pushed back the bedclothes and rose.

As he thrust his feet into his slippers and pulled on his dressing-gown, he wondered if he should take his loaded revolver down with him, hidden in his dressing-gown pocket.

There wasn't the slightest doubt that this visit by the police had something to do with the murder of Colonel Blakeney. It might even have something to do with the deaths of his Aunt Bertha or Hannah Moffat, thought Raynor suddenly.

He felt suddenly sick again with deathly fear. Merciful heavens, what was he to do, he asked himself wildly. Take the revolver with him and shoot them down if they tried to arrest him?

Again, Sergeant Anstruther was no fool, reflected Raynor. The sergeant had struck Raynor as being a singularly efficient type of officer when Raynor had met him on the day of Hannah Moffat's death. Those keen eyes of Anstruther's were almost certain to spot the ominous bulge of a revolver in a dressing-gown pocket, thought Raynor, and if he and Superintendent Clayton were here on a peaceful mission, Anstruther would wonder at once why Raynor had come downstairs to meet them armed with a revolver.

No, best leave the gun where it was, thought Raynor desperately. Best leave it where it was. He could keep on the alert, and if he foresaw the slightest risk of arrest, he could make a dash for the stairs, rush up to his room, and grab the gun. Even if they happened to be armed they wouldn't fire on him unless they were certain he was armed, and they wouldn't think he was armed if he was running away.

With trembling fingers, Raynor picked up a comb and

passed it through his hair. Then, bracing himself for whatever the next few moments might bring, he went slowly downstairs and entered the dining-room, which was chill and cheerless at that early hour.

The two police officers were standing by the table. Superintendent Clayton was a grey-haired, well-built man, with a neatly clipped military moustache.

'Good-morning!' said Raynor inquiringly, pausing just inside the open doorway.

'Good-morning, sir,' said the superintendent. 'I'm sorry to disturb you so early, but I'm afraid I have bad news. Colonel Blakeney, of Hollerton Hall, has been murdered during the night!'

'What?' exclaimed Raynor, with every appearance of being horrified and aghast.

'Colonel Blakeney was shot dead as he lay in bed,' went on Superintendent Clayton. 'From evidence in our possession, we have detained Robert Fergus, of Shawcross Banks, on suspicion of having committed the murder, and have conveyed him to Firfield Police Station.'

'Fergus?' ejaculated Raynor, in well-simulated astonishment and dismay. 'D'you mean to say he broke into the Hall and shot Colonel Blakeney?'

'He denies it emphatically,' replied the superintendent. 'He admits, however, that there was trouble between himself and Colonel Blakeney—trouble in which, according to his statement, you were concerned. Is there any truth in that allegation, sir?'

'Yes, I'm sorry to say there is,' replied Raynor quietly.

Inwardly, he was conscious of a relief so vast that it was akin to jubilation. The superintendent and the sergeant weren't here to arrest him. They'd already roped Fergus in, and were here merely to take a statement from him, Raynor. Well, thought Raynor sardonically, he'd be only too happy to help.

'Would you care to give us your version of this trouble, sir?' asked the superintendent.

'Yes, certainly,' replied Raynor readily. 'I'll tell you all I can.'

He waited obligingly whilst Sergeant Anstruther produced notebook and pencil.

'The trouble really started the evening before last,' he commenced, when the sergeant was ready. 'Apparently Fergus is courting Diana Moffat, my late housekeeper's niece whom I have kept on here in my employment. From what I can gather, Fergus seems more or less to have had the run of this house until I came to take up residence here. Two evenings ago I found him using my bathroom. I considered this a liberty, and I told him so, whereupon he was sufficiently impertinent to me for me to order him out of the house and to forbid him to visit here again. He then asked me what opportunities I thought he'd have of seeing his girl if he couldn't visit her here. I told him that that had nothing whatsoever to do with me, and that I wasn't interested in the matter. He thereupon accused me of having designs on the girl myself. My reply to that was to tell him to get out of the house at once, or I would do my best to throw him out. He lost his temper completely and struck me, knocking me into the fireplace there. By the time I had recovered, he had left the house.'

'Did the girl see this happen, sir?' put in the superintendent.

Raynor thought swiftly. A statement was almost certain to be taken from the girl. He had to be careful not to contradict what she might say.

'She may have seen a little of it,' he said. 'I cannot really say. The incident took place in here, the door was open, and I'm afraid our voices were raised, particularly that of Fergus. I didn't see the girl myself, but she may have been standing somewhere out there in the hall, attracted by the row.'

'Then you didn't discuss it with her afterwards?' asked the superintendent.

'No, I didn't,' said Raynor, a trifle stiffly. 'I saw no necessity to discuss it with her. Beyond telling her that I had forbidden Fergus the house, and that he had had the unmitigated impudence to strike me, I said nothing. I was not a matter I cared to discuss with a domestic, however interested in the fellow she might be.'

'No, quite,' agreed the superintendent. But didn't she want to know why you had forbidden him to visit the house?'

Raynor moved restlessly. Where the devil were these questions leading to, he thought impatiently.

'I told her that I resented Fergus using my house as though he owned the place,' he said. 'She appeared to understand what I meant.'

'I see,' said the superintendent. 'Well, what happened between you and Fergus after that, Mr Raynor?'

'The day following the incident—which was yesterday—was the day of the inquest on Hannah Moffat,' continued Raynor. 'Colonel Blakeney was one of the witnesses. After the inquest I consulted him as to what I should do about this trouble with Fergus. He suggested I might issue a summons for assault. I hesitated to do that, for apart from a natural reluctance to have the affair ventilated in the columns of the local press, I had no wish to be vindictive towards Fergus. All I wanted was an apology from the fellow, and some sort of assurance that he would keep away from here in future. Colonel Blakeney told me he was Fergus' landlord. He was exceedingly angry at what had happened, and he went so far as to say that unless Fergus furnished me with a fitting apology and promised to keep away from here he, Colonel Blakeney, would no longer have him as a tenant. He insisted upon our seeing Fergus without delay and having the matter out with the fellow. He seemed quite wrought up.'

'Why was he in such a hurry to see Fergus?' put in the superintendent.

'Because, as I've told you, he was exceedingly angry,' replied Raynor. Then he added stiffly, 'I would like you to understand that Colonel Blakeney had been good enough to give me his friendship, and I think I can safely say that he resented almost as deeply as I did the treatment I had received from Fergus.'

'I see,' said the superintendent. 'So you and Colonel Blakeney went out to see Fergus?'

'Yes. Miss Blakeney motored us out to Shawcross Banks,' continued Raynor. 'We saw Fergus. He firmly refused to apologise and to give an assurance to keep away from here in future. He then accused me of having struck the girl. This so angered the colonel that he lost his temper completely and gave Fergus his notice to quit.'

'How did Fergus take it?' asked the superintendent.

Raynor hesitated.

'Well, personally,' he said, 'he seemed to me to be completely mad. He was shouting at the top of his voice, saying that he wouldn't stay at Shawcross Banks not even if the colonel asked him to, but that one day the colonel would be sorry. He said he'd get the pair of us, even if he had to swing for it. When Colonel Blakeney told him to calm himself, he made a rush at him and tried to strike him. I got between them, and he turned on me. He was acting like a maniac. There were plenty of witnesses. His mother, his kid sister, and a boy and two or three farm labourers saw him and heard him. They were standing looking into the room.'

'What happened then?' asked the superintendent.

'Nothing,' replied Raynor. 'Colonel Blakeney and I simply came away, leaving Fergus' mother hanging on to him trying to quieten him. Both the colonel and I realised that we were doing more harm than good by remaining. When we reached the car where Miss Blakeney was waiting, she asked us what the shouting had been about. Even she, sitting out in the car, had heard the row Fergus was making.'

'Did Colonel Blakeney tell her why Fergus had been shouting?' asked the superintendent.

'No, not at the time,' replied Raynor. 'He confined himself to saying that he had given Fergus his notice to quit, and that the fellow hadn't liked it. He may have told her all about it afterwards, of course. I cannot say.'

Superintendent Clayton was silent a moment. Then he said:

'I have just one other question to put to you, Mr Raynor, and, in putting it, I trust you will understand that I am merely doing my duty as the police officer in charge of this case. Had Robert Fergus the slightest grounds whatsoever for making this accusation against you of interfering with the girl Diana Moffat?'

'No, none at all!' answered Raynor firmly. Then, in a voice which appeared to be trembling with suppressed anger, he added: 'I understand, of course, that in fairness to Fergus, you must ask the question. That it why I am endeavouring not to resent it!'

'Thank you!' said the superintendent quietly.

'Are there any questions you would like to put to Mr Raynor?' he asked the sergeant.

'Yes, there is one, sir,' said the sergeant briskly, looking up from his notebook. 'According to what Mr Raynor has told us, the trouble between Robert Fergus and Colonel Blakeney seems to have been a direct result of the quarrel which took place here between Mr Raynor and Fergus two evenings ago. Is that not so, sir?' he asked, turning to Raynor.

'Well, no, I wouldn't say it is!' lied Raynor, speaking slowly and carefully. 'From what I could gather when we were out at the farmhouse, Fergus seemed to have one or two pretty deep-rooted grudges against Colonel Blakeney. He seemed to think that the colonel, as landlord, should have expended more money on the farm, and he was shouting something about some repairs to the farm buildings not having been attended to. I know he called the colonel some pretty choice names. I'll repeat them to you, if you like.'

'Yes, we'd better hear them,' said the superintendent.

Raynor gave them—and foul and unpleasant names they were. The fact that they existed only in his own imagination worried Clive Raynor not a whit. For his own sake, he told himself, he must paint as black a case as possible against Bob Fergus.

'What exactly was the question you wished to put to Mr Raynor?' asked Superintendent Clayton, turning again to the sergeant.

'What Mr Raynor has just told us rather alters the position, sir,' replied Sergeant Anstruther thoughtfully. 'But the question I was going to ask him was this.' He turned to Raynor. 'Assuming, sir, that you were the cause of the trouble between Colonel Blakeney and Robert Fergus—the quite innocent cause, of course—Fergus would probably feel as bitter against you as he did against Colonel Blakeney. In fact, you say that he threatened both of you. That being the case, it is quite possible that he meant to get both of you last night. Did you hear anyone prowling about or hear any suspicious sounds last night, sir?'

'It's peculiar thing you should ask that,' answered Raynor slowly. 'At a matter of fact, I thought I did hear someone outside the windows there last night. It was close on midnight and I was sitting here writing when I fancied I heard a step outside on the gravel. I listened, but the noise was not repeated, so I came to the conclusion I must have imagined it.'

'Would the house be locked up then, sir?' asked the sergeant.

'Oh, yes, the girl always locks up for the night before she

goes up to bed,' answered Raynor with great conviction.

Sergeant Anstruther glanced at his superior officer.

'If it was Fergus out there, sir,' he commented, he would see the light through the curtains and would know that Mr Raynor was sitting up. He might have thought it better to clear off and come back later when Mr Raynor had retired for the night. There would be more chance of his taking Mr Raynor unawares then.'

'This is all supposition of course, Anstruther,' said the superintendent, 'but I see your point. You are trying to establish why Fergus, if he is the guilty man, should have made Colonel Blakeney his first victim when he had reason perhaps for feeling more bitter against Mr Raynor. If your assumption is correct, Mr Raynor has certainly had an extremely lucky escape.'

'By Jove, yes!' put in Raynor feelingly. 'I never dreamt—never suspected—such a dreadful thing for a moment.'

The superintendent turned to him.

'Well, thank you very much for your information, Mr Raynor,' he said. 'We would now like to speak to Diana Moffat. If you will be good enough to ring for her, we will trespass no further on your time.'

The Burial

Raynor cursed inwardly. This suggestion that he should ring for Diana instead of being permitted to go in search of her, effectively baulked any chance he might have had of having a word with her in private.

He knew, however, that he dared betray to these two police officers nothing of what he was feeling, so, crossing to the fireplace, he rang the bell. A few moments elapsed, then, in response to the ring, there came a knock at the door and Diana entered the room. She inquired what he had rung for.

'Superintendent Clayton wishes to speak to you,' said Raynor curtly.

The girl looked inquiringly at the superintendent. Raynor, in an agony of doubt and fear as to what she would say, would dearly have liked to remain. But he knew he dared show no undue anxiety to be present at the interview, so he walked from the room, closing the door behind him.

Out in the hallway he stood irresolute, a prey to fear and indecision. But he knew the stupidity of remaining there. He could hear nothing, and if Sergeant Anstruther or the superintendent suddenly opened the door of the dining-room and found him lurking in the hallway, they'd wonder what the devil he was doing there. They might even suspect him of eavesdropping—probably would suspect him of it—and their suspicions would be aroused at once that there was something wrong somewhere in thsi particular household.

Turning away, Raynor mounted the stairs and went into his own bedroom. Diana had evidently been up there in his absence, for the curtains were drawn back from the windows.

Crossing to the windows Raynor stood with his hands plunged in his dressing-gown pockets, staring out with unseeing eyes at the dismal autumn landscape.

Supposing the girl told the police officers the truth, what exactly would the position be, he asked himself. Supposing she told them just what had happened between himself, her and Fergus, what bearing would that have on the murder of Colonel Blakeney?

None at all, except to indicate to the police officers that he, Raynor, had lied, Raynor assured himself. And even then it didn't prove he had lied. It would merely be his word against the girl's. No, that was hardly it, he recollected: it would be his word against the girl's word and Fergus'.

Well, supposing the police did accept the girl's and Fergus' version of the incident which had led to the quarrel, reflected Raynor, what then? They would look upon him, Raynor, as a liar and would discredit the rest of the information he had given them; but that didn't alter the fact that there had been a row between Fergus and Colonel Blakeney, and that it was Fergus' gun which had been found at the scene of the murder.

That, however, was taking the worst possible view, reflected Raynor. There was no earthly reason why the police should accept the word of Fergus and the girl instead of his. After all, Raynor reminded himself, his name did stand for something, and so far as the world knew his reputation was above reproach. Why should the police accept the word of a lout like Fergus and the servant-girl he was courting, against the word of Clive Raynor, popular novelist and decent, respected citizen?

No, the whole thing was absurd, Raynor assured himself. He had nothing to fear, nothing at all. There wasn't the slightest dobt that he would have to appear as a witness for the prosecution against Fergus, but the very worst that could happen to him would be that he might become the target for the malicious tongues of idle and bad-minded gossips.

He wondered what Diana would think of this arrest of Fergus. The news must come as a decided shock to her, he reflected. But she couldn't suspect him, Raynor, of having a hand in it. No, by heavens, he'd covered his tracks much too well for that, and, clever though she undoubtedly was, he'd proved himself the cleverer thi time.

The sudden whirr of a car engine starting up below the windows caused him to look down. Superintendent Clayton and Sergeant Anstruther were leaving in the police car which had brought them out from Firfield.

Raynor stood watching until the receding car had vanished round a bend in the drive, then, turning quickly from the window, he quitted the bedroom and went swiftly downstairs in order to look for Diana.

He found the girl in the kitchen preparing breakfast. If the news that Fergus had been detained on suspicion of murder had upset her she showed no signs of it, thought Raynor, but looked, as usual, calm and self-possessed.

'Well, what d'you think of the news?' demanded Raynor. 'What d'you think of your precious Fergus now?'

'He's evidently got more nerve than I gave him credit for,' replied the girl evenly.

Raynor stared at her. Of all the answers he had expected, this was tle last. Confound the girl and this devilish self-possession of hers, he thought angrily.

'Then you think Fergus is guilty?' he rasped.

'I don't know,' replied the girl. 'I haven't learned the details. The police weren't very communicative.'

'What did they ask you?' demanded Raynor.

'They wanted to know if I'd ever heard Bob speak threateningly about Colonel Blakeney,' answered the girl, 'and they asked me if he had any grounds at all for quarrelling with you about me.'

'I don't know what the devil they want to keep dragging me into it for,' said Raynor savagely. 'What did you tell the superintendent?'

The girl ingnored the question.

'I don't see why you should be surprised at being dragged into it,' she said. 'After all, if it hadn't been for you, Colonel Blakeney wouldn't have given Bob his notice to quit Shawcross Banks, and the pair of them wouldn't have quarrelled.'

'Never mind about that!' grated Raynor. 'What did you tell the police?'

'I told them I'd never heard Bob speak threateningly about Colonel Blakeney,' replied the girl. 'I also told them that he hadn't the slightest ground for being jealous of you, so far as I was concerned, or for quarrelling with you about me. I told them,' she added, with the slightest hint of mockery in her voice, 'that you had always behaved towards me as a perfect gentleman.'

Very audible was the sigh of relief which Raynor gave. His tautened nerves relaxed, and he laughed weakly.

'You told them that, did you?' he asked shakily. 'Honestly?'

'Yes, honestly,' replied the girl.

She turned to face him, her eyes steady and direct.

'I have told you before that you have nothing to fear from me,' she said. 'Now go and get your bath, and I'll have the fire lighted in the dining-room and your breakfast ready for you by the time you come down.'

'Yes, but wait a minute, Diana,' begged Raynor. 'Hasn't this business upset you? Aren't you worried about Fergus?'

'He's not hanged yet,' said the girl.

'No, but, damn it, he might be!' burst out Raynor.

'Well, worrying about him won't save him,' she answered. Raynor stared at her.

'No, but it might help to save him,' he said unsteadily. 'You could have made things pretty unpleasant for me if you'd told the police the truth about the row between me and Fergus. Defending counsel would make the most of it, you bet. He'd do his best to prove that if Fergus did commit the murder, he committed it whilst burning with justifiable rage and resentment!'

'The row with Colonel Blakeney took place yesterday midday,' said the girl, 'and the murder appears to have been committed some time in the early hours of this morning. That gave Bob more than twelve hours to cool down. I don't think burning rage and resentment would be much of a defence. If that's the best defending counsel can do for him, then there's not much hope for Bob.'

'Good heavens, girl, how can you talk about it so calmly?' burst out Raynor. 'The fellow's been courting you for months, hasn't he? Haven't you any affection for him at all?'

'I've told you before, I don't wear my heart on my sleeve,' replied the girl. 'Perhaps the affection was all on Bob's side.' Then, with an abrupt change of subject: 'Are you coming to the funeral?'

'Yes, of course,' said Raynor readily, for in his overwhelming relief at the girl's attitude he would have done anything to please her, and he felt it was as little he could do to be with her at the funeral.

'Then go and have your bath,' she said. 'Time's getting on if we're to be ready by eleven o'clock.'

Raynor departed upstairs, and at eleven o'clock that morning he and Diana, in a car sent from Firfield, rode slowly behind the hearse which bore the body of Hannah Moffat to the grave. As they were driven down to the village, a large black car swept by them at terrific speed, causing the driver to swerve violently.

'Talk about a road-hog,' exclaimed Raynor angrily.

'If you ask me, that was a police car,' said the girl coolly. Raynor frowned. What could a police car be doing rushing around the country at that speed?

He and Diana were the only two mourners—if mourners they could indeed be called, thought Raynor sardonically. Personally, he was fiercely glad the blackmailing hag was dead, and as for Diana—well, he had learned from the girl's own lips that she had had no love for her hard-faced mother.

As he sat beside her in the slowly-moving car his hand crept along the seat and closed on hers, slim and black-gloved. She softly returned the pressure of his fingers, and looked at him and smiled.

To Raynor, it was a smile of friendship and understanding. No matter what she knew of him, no matter what she suspected, this bewitchingly lovely girl would never betray him. Raynor was as certain of that as he was that by no wilful word or act would he ever betray himself.

The girl and he belonged to the manor, that dear old house which held such an extraordinary and untold fascination for him that he knew he could never bear to leave it. She loved the house as he loved it, she belonged there as he belonged there, and beacuse of that, surely he and she belonged to each other—a duet of utter, ghostly and ghastly evil?

The girl spoke to him.

'I told you there'd be plenty of spectators,' she said.

The hearse and car had turned in at the gates of the little cemetery. A group of villagers consisting mainly of women in sombre black was waiting there.

'Damned vultures!' said Raynor.

The girl laughed amusedly, then composed her face as the hearse drew up in front of the door of the little chapel in which the funeral service was to be held.

The simple service was soon over, and the interment followed. As he stood bareheaded beside the graveside with Diana, Raynor felt not the slightest twinge of remorse as the coffin of his victim was lowered into the grave.

The Man from Scotland Yard

Meanwhile the police car which had flashed past Diana and Raynor had pulled up outside Firfield police station. From it descended a fat, untidily dressed man wearing an old mackintosh and an old felt hat. As he lounged into the police station, the officer on duty, sitting writing at his desk, looked at him inquiringly:

'I want to see the officer in charge here,' grunted the fat man. 'Superintendent Clayton or whatever his name is.'

'What's your name and what d'you want?' demanded the other.

'My name's Detective-Inspector Bullock, of Scotland Yard,'

replied the fat man, 'and what I want is a nice hot cup of tea, with plenty of sugar in it—four pieces. I've got a sweet tooth!'

The officer on duty moved—quickly.

Sprawled in a chair with his feet stretched out to the fire in Superintendent Clayton's office, Detective-Inspector Bullock set down his empty cup and said:

'Well, come on, give me the dope. Let's have the whole thing from beginning to end.'

Superintendent Clayton wasted no words, but gave him a breif yet comprehensive résumé of the murder of Colonel Blakeney, and the arrest of Fergus.

'Well, it seems a clear enough case,' grunted Bullock, feeling in the pocket of his roomy, ill-fitting jacket, and producing a boiled sweet wrapped in paper. 'You've got the motive, you've got the gun, the fellow was recognised by the colonel's daughter, so what else d'you want? What have I been called in for?'

'Because, in spite of the evidence, Sergeant Anstruther here isn't satisfied that we've got the right man,' replied the superintendent. 'He's persuaded Captain Norman, the Chief Constable of the county, that there's doubt in the case, and that's why Captain Norman has called in Scotland Yard.'

'Ah!' said Detective-Inspector Bullock, popping the sweet into his mouth and staring hard at Sergeant Anstruther, although he continued to address his remarks to the superintendent. 'And has Sergeant Anstruther persuaded you that there's a doubt in the case?'

'No, he hasn't, although he's tried hard enough,' replied the superintendent. 'I agree that he's hit on a very good point; but I think we've got the right man in Fergus.'

'Well, what is this very good point?' demanded Bullock. 'You tell me yourself, Anstruther.'

'It's this, sir,' said the sergeant quickly. 'When we went to the farm to get Fergus, he swore that he'd gone to bed shortly after ten o'clock that night, and hadn't stirred from it until roused by us. When we showed him the gun with which the murder was apparently committed and asked him if he could identify it, he admitted at once that it was his; but he swore that he'd never been near the Hall that night, and that the last he'd seen of his gun was downstairs in the living-room of the farm, when he'd turned out the lamp to go to bed. He kept the gun in a corner of the room, he said, with his fishing-rod and waders. If this story of his was true, therefore, someone must have broken into the farm that night and taken his gun. I thought I'd check up on it. I examined the area around the window of the living-room, and I found a faint, freshly-made scratch on the catch of the window. A similar faint scratch was on the catch of the window through which entry had been gained into the Hall.'

'Uh-huh, a good point!' grunted Bullock. 'But hasn't it occurred to you that this fellow Fergus might have been clever enough to make that scratch on his own window-catch to support the yarn he meant to pitch in case anything went wrong?'

'Yes, sir, it has,' replied the sergeant; 'but I'm certain Fergus hasn't the brains to think of a thing like that. He's rather a stupid, dull-witted sort of chap. Again, the man who committed the murder was not only seen by Miss Blakeney, but he also left the gun behind. Now if that man was Fergus, would he have gone straight back home to bed? Surely, in spite of the handkerchief he'd got tied round his face when he encountered Miss Blakeney, he must have known that the game was up, and that the only thing to do was to make a bolt for it.'

'No; not if he was relying on this yarn of his about having his gun stolen,' replied Bullock. 'Bluff it out, that was the game—bluff it out!'

He lounged lazily to his feet and took a turn up and down the room.

'Anyway, let's have a look at him,' he said, turning to Superintendent Clayton. 'Have him brought in here.'

Whilst Fergus was being brought from his cell Bullock turned to Sergeant Anstruther.

'You're smart!' he said bluntly, groping in his pocket for another sweet. 'I like the way you've raised these points.' Then, as the sergeant flushed with pleasure at this praise from the man from Scotland Yard, the latter added: 'Not that I expect they'll lead anywhere.'

He popped the sweet into his mouth, sucked noisily for a moment, then went on:

'But all the same, supposing this murder has been framed-up on Fergus, it must have been done by somebody who had a grudge against either him or Colonel Blakeney, or against both of'em. D'you suspect abybody?'

'No, sir,' admitted the sergeant helplessly. 'That's just where my case falls down. I don't know of anyone who would shoot Colonel Blakeney so cold-bloodedly and deliberately. He was one of the most popular men in the district. He was liked by everybody.'

'What about Fergus?' demanded the detective. 'Is he liked by everybody?'

'No, there's a few who don't like him,' answered the sergeant, 'but not badly enough to want to stop him like this. Anyway, they wouldn't have the guts—the nerve, I mean, to carry a job like this through.'

'I don't know,' grunted Bullock. 'I've come up against nerve when I've least expected it. You can't always judge!'

He broke off as Superintendent Clayton entered the room, followed by Fergus and a gaoler. Fergus was hand-cuffed, his weak, blue eyes were red-rimmed as though he'd been crying and his plump, ruddy-complexioned face was pale.

'This is Detective-Inspector Bullock, of Scotland Yard, Fergus,' said the superintendent quietly. 'He wishes to speak to you.'

Bullock was staring hard at the prisoner with his heavily lidded, baggy little eyes. Then he spoke to Fergus in a kind and understanding tone.

'So it wasn't you who shot Colonel Blakeney?' he said.

Wild hope flared in Fergus' eyes, and he tried to take an eager, impulsive step forward, but was restrained by the gaoler.

'No!' he cried hoarsely. 'I swear to Heaven it wasn't me. I was never oot o' my bed. Ha' ye got him—ha' yet got the beggor what did it?'

'No,' said Bullock. 'Who d'you think did it?'

'I divvent kna'!' cried Fergus desperately. 'I kna' nowt aboot it. I was in me bed all neet. Oh, sor, sor, do believe me. I wouldn't dee a thing like that—not to me worst enemy, I wouldn't—'

His voice broke in a sob.

'All right, pull yourself together!' said Bullock gruffly. 'Crying won't make things any better. According to your statement, you say your gun must have been stolen from your living-room. Did anybody know you kept the gun there?'

'Ay, plenty!' said Fergus hoarsely. 'Most everybody knew I kept it theer.'

'Then that doesn't help us much,' commented Bullock.

He took a slow, lounging turn up the floor, then turned to Fergus again.

'Just what was this trouble between you and Colonel Blakeney?' he asked. 'Come on, let's have the truth!'

'I've telled the truth!' cried Fergus. 'I've telled Superintendent Clayton the truth. I swear by gor' I have!'

'All right, come on, tell me!' invited Bullock.

'It was all through that theer Raynor o' Broom Manor!'

he burst out passionately. 'If it hadn't been for him and his dirty ways I wouldn't ha' got me notice to quit, and there'd ha' been no trouble at all between the colonel and me. He telled the colonel a lot o' dirty lees aboot me using the hoose—his hoose.'

'Ay, my lass!' went on Fergus fiercely. 'She's a servant at the manor—there's just Raynor and her theer alone—and I catched him havin' a fight wi' her and I nigh knocked his head off, and the next day he comes along to th' farm wi' Colonel Blakeney and denies to me that he ever touched the lass, the dirty liar. He wanted an apology, and I wouldn't gie him one and, man, it maddened me, him standing theer saying I was daft and didn't kna' what I was talking aboot so I lost me temper and tried to set aboot him again, but the colonel stopped me and gie'd me notice to quit!'

Bullock's heavily lidded eyes switched to Superintendent Clayton.

'You've interviewed the girl?' he asked.

'Yes, and she denies this story of Fergus' emphatically,' replied the superintendent. 'She says there is not a word of truth in his statement. She says that Mr Raynor has always behaved towards her as a gentleman.'

'She denies it?' cried Fergus hoarsely, his face ghastly white. 'She denies it, d'ye say—Oh gor'!'

His knees sagged and he would have collapsed completely had he not been supported by the gaoler and by Sergeant Anstruther, who stepped swiftly to the gaoler's assistence.

'Get him a drink!' grunted Bullock.

A glass of water was quickly procured and held to the prisoner's lips.

'It seems to have knocked you, your lass denying your story,' commented Bullock, eyeing Fergus intently.

'She canna ha' denied it!' croaked Fergus desperately. 'It divvent believe it—she canna ha' denied it—she knows it's true, and she wouldna' deny the truth!'

'She has denied it,' put in the superintendent firmly.

Fergus groaned aloud, his head lolled on his chest, and his body shook with sobs which came right from his heart.

'Then I'm beat,' he moaned. 'She's turned ag'in me—him and her—they're both in it—'

'In what?' demanded Bullock sharply.

Fergus made no reply. Supported by the gaoler and Sergeant Anstruther, he was sobbing in great retching gulps. Bullock strode to him and gripped him by the shoulder.

'Pull yourself together, man!' he rapped, shaking him. 'You say Raynor and the girl are both in it. In what?'

'In calling me a lee'or!' sobbed Fergus. 'In saying he—he wasn't havin' a struggle with her when he was—'

Releasing his grip on Fergus' shoulder, Bullock stepped back.

'Take him away!' he said.

On the Trail

Waiting until the door had closed on Fergus and the gaoler, Detective-Inspector Bullock lounged by the fire. Watched expectantly by Superintendent Clayton and Sergeant Anstruther, he turned his back to the fire and straddléd out hi fat legs.

'Have you got a fish-and-chips shop in Firfield?' he demanded.

'Yes,' said the superintendent in surprise. 'Why?'

'Because I want some supper,' replied Bullock. 'I've had nothing to eat since we passed through Weatherby. You might send out for some fish-and-chips, will you. And don't bother about a plate or anything. I'll have 'em in the paper!'

'But we can provide a better supper than fish-and-chips,

right here at the station,' protested the superintendent.

'You can't!' said Bullock bluntly. 'I like 'em!'

Sergeant Anstruther grinned. This was the first time he'd met Detective-Inspector Bullock, but he'd heard a lot about him, and he knew that this man from Scotland Yard coupled a brilliant record with a reputation for most peculiar and unorthodox behaviour.

'Are you sure you won't have a plate?' asked the superintendent when the fish-and-chips, wrapped in a newspaper, had been brought.

'No, don't want one!' grunted Bullock. 'Now then,' he went on, standing in front of the fire and using his podgy fingers as a fork. 'New then, about this identification of Fergus by Miss Blakeney. She's prepared to swear it was him coming out of her father's bedroom, is she?'

'Yes, quite prepared to swear it,' assented the superintendent.

'What sort of a girl is she?' demanded Bullock. 'Easily frightened?'

'No, I wouldn't say that,' replied the superintendent. 'She's a strong, healthy girl with plenty of common-sense.'

'Well, how did she happen to identify Fergus when he had a handkerchief tied round his face?' asked Bullock.

'She recognised his cap, mackintosh, and leggings,' explained the superintendent. 'He was dressed as he's always dressed.'

'Always?' grunted Bullock.

'Well, nine days out of ten,' said the superintendent.

Detective-Inspector Bullock took a large fish-bone from his mouth, licked it, then threw it into the fire behind him.

'So the chap is daft!' he commented. 'He breaks into the Hall wearing a cap, mackintosh, and leggings which are about as well-know as his face. But so's he won't be recognised, he ties a handkerchief over his face. Why the heck didn't he bring a sheet to cover the rest of himself with?'

Superintendent Clayton stared at him in silence, but an eager, expectant look was dawning in the eyes of Sergeant Anstruther. Taking a long, nicely browned chip from the greasy newspaper, Bullock levelled it at the sergeant.

'I'm beginning to believe you're right, Anstruther,' he said. 'A chap who would act as daft as this chap Fergus seems to have acted at the Hall wouldn't have the brains to fake just a little scratch on the catch of his living-room window. If he'd wanted to fake a break-in there he'd have made a proper bull-in-a-china-shop sort of job of it. That little scratch showed finesse—a French word meaning ingenuity, artfulness, slyness!'

He looked at the superintendent as though supplying the translation for his benefit.

'I am aware of the meaning of the word,' said the superintendent stiffly.

'Yes, well, now if this chap Fergus was artful enough to fake that scratch on the window-catch of his living-room,' went on Bullock, 'why wasn't he artful enough to go to the Hall in some other clobber than the cap, mackintosh, and leggings which he usually wore? The two things don't seem to make sense, do they? Sort of contradict each other, eh?'

He crammed the remainder of his chips into his mouth, wiped his hands on the newspaper, then crumpled it into a ball and flung it into the fire.

'Anyway, what sort of a chap is this Raynor?' he demanded.

'Quite a nice fellow,' replied the superintendent. 'Steady and reliable, I'd say.'

'Well, either he or Fergus is lying,' said Bullock. 'Which of' em d'you think it is?'

'Oh, Fergus!' said the superintendent without hesitation.

Bullock switched his baggy little eyes inquiringly to the sergeant.

'I don't think Mr Raynor was lying, sir,' admitted the sergeant. 'I don't think he appears to be the sort of man to intefere with his domestics and to knock them about.'

'Well, what about the girl?' demanded Bullock, turning again to Superintendent Clayton. 'What's she like?'

The superintendent hesitated.

'Well, I don't want to say anything against her', he said slowly, 'but she's always been a bit of a mystery. She's lived at the manor all her life, with her aunt, who was housekeeper there; but she's never associated with any of the villagers. She's always kept herself to herself.'

'What d'you think, Anstruther?' demanded Bullock, turning to the sergeant.

'It's difficult to say, sir,' sait the sergeant. 'She's the sort of girl who you can't get next to. She's deep, if you know what I mean, sir. My own impression is that she was telling us the truth when she said Mr Raynor had never molested her.'

Bullock turned again to the superintendent.

'You say her aunt was housekeeper at the manor,' he went on. 'Isn't she housekeeper there now?'

'No; she was killed by a fall from a window on Thursday of this week,' replied the superintendent. 'She was buried this morning.'

'What caused her to fall?' demanded Bullock.

'According to the evidence at the inquest she slipped and fell whilst cleaning a top storey window of the house,' replied the superintendent. 'Apparently she was subject to bouts of giddiness. Unfortunately, that is not the only tragedy which has happened at the manor this week. Last Sunday night Mr Raynor's aunt was burned to death there in her bedroom.'

Bullock stared at him.

'Good lor'!' he ejaculated. 'He's had some bad luck, that fellow, hasn't he? How did this particular tragedy occur?'

'According to the evidence at the inquest, the old lady's nightdress caught on fire whilst she was sitting in front of the bedroom fire,' replied the superintendent. 'It is thought she must have fallen asleep. A verdict of death by misadventure was returned at the inquest.'

Bullock was silent a moment.

'Did she leave any money?' he jerked out.

'A considerable amount, I believe,' replied the superintendent.

'Who did she leave it to?' demanded Bullock.

'I understand that Mr Raynor was the sole heir; but I am only speaking of what I have heard,' replied the superintendent. Then, noting Bullock's stare, he went on sharply: 'There was not the slightest suspicion of foul play, I can assure you. It was as clear a case as possible of accidental death.'

'Well, that's your bussines, of course, and I'm not doubting it,' grunted Bullock. 'What's the time? Half-past ten!'

He lounged across to the desk and picked up his old felt hat.

'You might see if my car's waiting out there,' he said. 'I'm going to see Miss Blakeney.'

Your Word May Mean — The Scaffold

Edith Blakeney was on the point of retiring for the night when a maid entered her bedroom to say that Detective-Inspector Bullock of Scotland Yard wanted to see her.

'He insisted upon seeing you, Miss Edith,' said the girl, 'so I've shown him into the drawing-room.'

'Yes, all right, Ellen,' said Edith. 'I'll go down at once.'

Putting on a warm dressing-gown over her pyjamas, she went down to the drawing-room where the man from Scotland Yard was standing warming himself with his back to the dying embers of the fire.

'Mis Blakeney?' he said inquiringly. 'I am Detective-Inspector Bullock of Scotland Yard. I would like a talk with you. Will you sit down? I am sorry to disturb you so late.'

Obediently the girl seated herself.

'Now, Miss Blakeney,' went on Bullock without any further preamble, 'I understand that you met Robert Fergus last night coming out of your father's bedroom. Is that correct?'

'Yes,' assented the girl.

'But you did not see his face because he had a handkerchief tied over it?' went on Bullock.

'No, I did not see his face,' assented the girl.

'Then how did you recognise him?' demanded Bullock.

'By his cap, mackintosh, and leggings,' replied the girl. 'I would know them anywhere.'

Bullock was silent, then abruptly he jerked out:

'What colour are Fergus' eyes?'

The girl hesitated, taken aback by the suddenness with which the question had been shot at her.

'Why, I—I don't know,' she faltered. 'They're—they're blue, I think. Yes, Fergus is fair. He has blue eyes!'

'You don't seem quite sure,' said Bullock.

'I am sure,' replied the girl. 'I just couldn't think for a moment. Fergus has blue eyes.'

'Did you see those blue eyes of his last night when you met him face to face?' demanded Bullock. 'The handkerchief wasn't over his eyes, I take it. You must have seen his eyes!'

'I—I didn't ,' said Edith unsteadily. 'It all happened so quickly. I didn't have time to see his eyes.'

'But you must have looked into his face,' pressed Bullock.

'Yes, but I didn't notice his eyes,' admitted the girl falteringly. 'I—I was so shocked and startled at seeing him.'

'Mis Blakeney,' said Bullock earnestly, 'I want you to realise that a man's life is at stake and it may be on your word alone that he is sent to the scaffold. Bearing that in mind, are you still prepared to swear that the man you saw was Robert Fergus?'

The girl was silent a moment. Then, in a voice which was little more than a whisper, she said:

'Yes—yes; it was Fergus I saw last night! I am prepared to swear it.'

'Only because you recognised his cap, mackintosh, and leggings?' pressed the man from Scotland Yard.

The girl was silent, and Bullock repeated his question:

'You are prepared to swear the man you saw was Fergus simply because you recognised his cap, mackintosh, and leggings? There is nothing else about him that you recognised. Is that correct?'

'Yes, that is correct,' admitted the girl, in a low voice.

Bullock waited a few moments to enable her to compose herself. Then he said:

'Now listen very carefully, Mis Blakeney. Suppose I suggest to you that the man you saw wasn't Robert Fergus. Suppose I suggest to you that the man you saw was someone of Fergus' build, and dressed exactly like Fergus—in Fergus' cap, mackintosh, and leggings, even. Woul you swear on oath that such a suggestion in an absolute impossibility—on oath, I said.'

'No, I couldn't swear it was impossible,' faltered the girl.

'Then the man you saw might have been someone dressed as Fergus?' pressed Bullock.

'Yes, he—he might have been,' admitted the girl. 'But I'm certain it was Fergus I saw.'

'Well, we'll forget that for the moment,' said Bullock. 'Now, tell me this—you knew, I suppose, that there was trouble between your father and Fergus, and that Fergus had threatened him? Did your father take those threats seriously?'

'I cannot say,' replied the girl. 'Daddy didn't discuss it with me.'

'But you knew about the trouble, of course?'

'Yes, I knew about that.'

'How did you know about it if your father didn't discuss it with you?'

'Mr Raynor told me about it.'

'When?'

'Yesterday evening, when we were coming back from Newcastle,' said the girl.

'When *who* were coming back from Newcastle?' demanded Bullock. 'You and Mr Raynor?'

'Yes; we'd been into Newcastle to do some shopping,' said the girl.

Bullock's heavily lidded eyes took on a peculiar glint.

'This shopping expedition into Newcastle would be after the row at Shawcross Banks between Fergus and your father and Mr Raynor?' he suggested.

'Yes, it was yesterday afternoon,' replied the girl. 'Daddy invited Mr Raynor here for lunch, but Mr Raynor said he was going to catch the bus from Firfield into Newcastle to do some shopping. Daddy suggested I should drive Mr Raynor into Newcastle after lunch, and I agreed bacause I wanted to do some shopping myslf.'

'And you and Mr Raynor were together the whole time you were in Newcastle, I suppose?' suggested Bullock.

The girl rose swiftly to her feet.

'Mr Bullock,' she cried, her voice quivering, 'I do not understand the nature of these questions.'

'Never mind—answer them!' retorted Bullock harshly. 'Were you and Mr Raynor together the whole time you were in Newcastle?'

The girl's face was white.

'No; we parted for about an hour,' she said unsteadily. 'Mr Raynor wanted to see his lawyers.'

'And you did your shopping then?'

'Yes.'

'When did Mr Raynor do his?'

'After he left his lawyers.'

'Were you with him when he did this shopping of his?'

'No; he did it before we met for tea. He got away from the lawyers earlier than he expected.'

'But you saw this shopping of his, I suppose?' demanded Bullock. 'You saw what he'd bought?'

'I only saw the parcels,' quavered the girl. 'They were in the back of the car.'

'What sort of parcels were they?' demanded Bullock.

The girl was silent, her face deathly.

'What sort of parcels were they?' repeated Bullock harshly. 'Describe them!'

'There was one rather large parcel,' faltered the girl, 'and a smaller, circular one.'

'How big was the circular one?' demanded Bullock. 'About this size?'

He held his podgy hands about a foot apart.

'Yes, about that,' admitted the girl.

'And about half as thick, eh?' demanded Bullock.

The girl nodded dumbly.

'I see,' said Bullock. 'Well, that's all, Mis Blakeney. You go to bed now—I can let myself out.'

Outside on the step he stood a few moments, deep in thought. Then he moved to the police car which was waiting for him.

'Broom Manor,' he ordered. 'But don't go right up to the house. Pull up at the bottom of the drive, if there is a drive!'

Clive Raynor Sees the Reckoning

The hour was past midnight. Seated in his dining-room, Clive Raynor was writing busily. The fire had been built up, and he was immersed in his task of bringing up to present events the incredible story he was in the process of writing.

It was, as he well knew, his own strange and evil history since he had come to live at the manor.

Suddenly he started, the point of his nib digging itself into the paper, for the hushed stillness of the lonely house had been broken by a raucous, jangling peal on the front door bell.

As he listened, tense and motionless in his chair, the quilty heart of Clive Raynor missed a beat. Who could be ringing at this hour, he wondered, the chill fingers of vague and nameless dread clutching at his heart.

As he sat there the ring was repeated, more prolonged and insistent this time. He would have to answer it himself. Raynor knew that, for Diana had gone to bed.

Pushing back his chair, he rose. His face strained and set, he quitted the room and went along the darkened hallway. Unlocking the front door, he pulled it open. Standing in the darkness was a fat man in a battered old felt hat and an old mackintosh.

'What the devil d'you want?' demanded Raynor harshly.

Detective-Inspector Bullock touched the brim of his shabby hat.

'Sorry to trouble you, guv'nor,' he said in a hoarse, beery voice, 'but I'd like to 'ave a word with you.'

'What about?' demanded Raynor. 'Who the dickens are you, anyway?'

'Name o' Simpson, guv'nor,' replied his visitor hoarsely. Turning his head, he peered about him in the darkness, with elaborate care, then looked at Raynor again. 'I've got to speak to you in private, guv'nor,' he said, in a husky whisper.

'Look here, what the devil are you getting at?' grated Raynor. 'State your business and clear off!'

'It's about some things what you bought in our shop in Newcastle yesterday afternoon, guv'nor,' said the other, in a guarded voice. 'The manager's sent me to see you,'

Raynor tensed, the blood draining from his face. Merciful heavens, what was this, he asked himself in fear. What had happened?

'Come in!' he said jerkily.

Detective-Inspector Bullock stepped briskly across the threshold, waited until Raynor had closed the door, then followed him into the dining-room.

'Now what's the trouble?' demanded Raynor harshly, turning to face him.

'We've 'ad the coppers around, guv'nor,' replied his visitor, his podgy hands fumbling with his hat. 'They wanted to know if Mr Clive Raynor, of Broom Manor, 'ad an account with us.'

Raynor said nothing. He could not. He was shocked into speechlessness. Stark terror held him dumb.

'The coppers described you, guv'nor,' went on his visitor. 'That's 'ow we knew it was you. They said you was a tall, dark, 'andsome man, and they wanted to know if you'd bought a mackintosh, a cap, and some leggings at our shop yesterday afternoon. The salesman remembered you, sir, because you took a long time to choose the mackintosh, the cap, and the leggings he said.'

'Did he tell the policeman that?' burst out Raynor, then cursed himself for a fool. But he had to know—he had to know!

'Well, 'e did, and 'e didn't, sir, if you see what I mean,' replied his visitor. ''E said 'e remembered a gent buying the things described, but 'e said 'e didn't know the gentleman's name, and wouldn't know if 'e'd know the gent again if 'e saw 'im, if you see what I mean.'

Raynor didn't see what he meant. He was incapable of taking in this garrulous rigmarole. All he did know was that the police were making inquiries about the purchases he had made the previous afternoon and the terrifying revelation froze his heart with fear.

'What's brought you here at this time of night to tell me this?' he demanded hoarsely, fighting desperately to get a grip on himself and to think coherently.

'I know I'm late, sir,' admitted his visitor, 'but the shop didn't shut till eight, then I 'ad to 'ave a bite of supper and catch a bus to Firfield. I've walked out 'ere. The manager sent me.'

'But why?' demanded Raynor hoarsely. 'Why should the manager send you?'

'Well, you see, I'm the 'ead tally-man outside the shop,' explained the other. 'I've been with the firm ever since I was a lad, and the manager trusts me, like. So 'e says to me this evening: "Joe," 'e says, "there's some mistake 'ere. A gent answering the description of Mr Raynor did buy one or more of them articles 'ere yesterday afternoon," says the manager to me, "but so did other gents, and we don't want to to offend any customer or get in wrong with the police, because we've always 'ad a good name, so I think you ought to go and see this Mr Raynor, of Broom Manor, and get this mistake cleared up, because," says the manager, "it is a mistake, there's no shadder of dout about that." So 'ere I am, sir, and that's why I'm 'ere, if you see what I mean.'

He wetted his lips and stared anxiously at Raynor.

'The whole thing's a lot of absolute nonsense!' burst out Raynor agitatedly. 'Your manager's put you and himself to a lot of stupid, unnecessary trouble. I had the parcels stolen from my car, and I reported the matter to the police, describing the articles, and saying where I'd bought them. The police were probably checking up on my story when they visited your shop, but why the devil they couldn't take my word for it instead of troubling you, I don't know.'

'Ah, they're queer, the coppers,' said his visitor darkly.

'Suspicious like. I know 'em. Howsumever, sir, I see 'ow it is. The things what you bought were stolen from your car, and you told the police. That's what brought 'em to our shop. A pity they 'aven't something better to do. Well, sir, I'm glad we've got the matter cleared up, and we'll always be glad of your custom. I'll be getting along now, sir.'

He stared pointedly at the decanter on the sideboard as he took a backward step towards the door.

'I've got a long walk back to Firfield, and it's chilly out,' he said huskily. 'You couldn't spare a nip, could you, guv'nor?'

'Yes, all right,' said Raynor impatiently.

With trembling fingers he poured his visitor out a drink.

'Well, 'ere's your good 'ealth, guv'nor!' said the latter, raising his glass, then draining it at a gulp. 'And now I'll be going. Good-night, sir!'

A few moments later he had gone, and, locking the front door on him, Raynor turned to retrace his steps to the dining-room. As he did so, he halted with a quick intake of breath, for Diana was coming silently downstairs, the pale oval of her face illumined in the yellow flame of the candle she was carrying.

The Devil Claims His Own

Without a word, Raynor strode on into the dining-room. The girl followed him in. Her dainty, bare feet were encased in crimson slippers, and she was wearing a crimson silk wrap over black silk pyjamas.

Blowing out the candle, she set it down on the table and looked curiously at Raynor's face, deathly in its pallor.

'Who was that?' she asked quietly.

Raynor did not speak—his brain could not find an answer. The police were on his track. That was all he could think of.

The police were on his track. Somewhere, somehow, his devilishly cunning scheme had slipped up, and the knowledge paralysed him with terror.

The girl crossed to where he was standing by the fire. Laying her slim fingers gently on his arm, she looked up into his tortured face.

'Who was it?' she asked quietly.

Raynor moved away from her and commenced to pace the room.

'I can't tell you!' he burst out hoarsely. 'I can't tell you!'

Heavens above, how could he tell her, he asked himself desperately, without admitting everything?

With a groan he flung himself into the chair by the fire and buried hi face in his hands. The police were after him. The net was closing in about him. Heavens! What was he to do? Make a bolt for it while he had the chance?

Yes, that was it, he told himself wildly. That was what he must do. But how far would he get? Not far. Even now he was probably being watched.

He became conscious that the girl was kneeling beside him.

'What is the matter?' she asked gently. 'You know you can trust me. I have not failed you yet.'

No, that was true, thought Raynor, clutching desperately at the straw of comfort proffered in the thought of being able to confide in someone.

But how could he confide in her, he asked himslelf despairingly. How could he tell her that it was he who had murdered Colonel Blakeney, and that the police were at his heels?

'Who was that man who come here?' she insisted gently. 'If you tell me perhaps I can help you.'

Help him—help him—thought Raynor wildly. Merciful heavens! That's what he wanted beyond all things—help!

He stared into her eyes so dark and warm with sympathy. Her nearness to him was in itself a thing of comfort. She was his friend—his one and only true friend!

With a groan which was almost a sob, he dropped his face to his hands again. Then before he knew it, scarce realising even what he was saying, he was pouring out to her the whole wretched story.

'I did it because I hated Fergus,' he concluded desperately. 'I did it because he knocked me down and would have taken you from me. And now they're after me—the police are after me—the police are after me—'

He broke off with a shuddering groan. The moments passed, then slowly he raised his drawn and haggard face and looked at the girl. She was still kneeling beside him, still smiling.

'You have nothing to fear,' she said gently.

'Nothing to fear!' burst out Raynor hoarsely. 'What d'you mean—nothing to fear?'

'I knew all that you have told me,' whispered the girl. 'I know all that you have done.'

'Knew it?' gasped Raynor. 'How did you know it?'

'I read your story,' said the girl softly. 'I was curious to read it, for I knew that here, in this house, you would write only of things that were evil. I took your keys and dispatch-case up to my room whilst you were asleep the night of the say you killed my mother!'

With an oath of fear and rage Raynor leapt to his feet. The girl had risen as swiftly.

'Listen to me!' she said tersely, gripping him by the arms and looking into his face. 'This had to come sooner or later. You belong here, and I belong here. We belong to each other, and we belong to the house. We are three in one. A trinity of evil. You do not understand yet; but one day you will. There can be no going back for you now to the world you knew. But you are safe here. You have nothing to fear!'

'What d'you mean, I have nothing to fear?' cried Raynor

hoarsely, seizing on these latter words of hers.

The girl's lovely fave had relaxed. She was smiling again, and now her voice was soft as she whispered:

'I can save you. You never left the house the night Colonel Blakeney was murdered. I can swear to that on oath.'

Raynor stared into her lovely face, wild hope surging in his heart.

'Diana, would you swear that for me?' he cried. 'That I never left the house that night?'

'I would swear that,' she whispered.

Unresistingly she led him from his chair to the chair at the table. He moved like a man in a daze. The events of the past hour had stunned him. He felt lost, frightened, helpless, content to leave everything to the girl.

She drew a sheet of paper towards him and handed him his pen.

'Now write!' she said softly.

Raynor wrote as her gentle, murmuring voice dictated. No thought of refusal was in his mind for he was completely dominated by her. His trust in her was blind and unquestioning, for had she not proved herself his loyal and kindly friend not once, but many times?

He finished what he was writing and he signed it. Then something stirred in his mind, and with a tremendous laugh, he added a postscript.

The girl was leaning over his shoulder.

Raynor's eyes dilated. There was something black and gleaming in her hand. He glimpsed it and in that same instant the world of Clive Raynor dissolved in a shattering roar and flash of flame.

Before the last echo of that roar had died away the door of the room crashed violently open. The girl whirled, the smoking revolver still in her hand. She had a vision of a fat man in a shabby old hat and mackintosh plunging towards her. She screamed and fired, but he was already diving across the table towards her.

The lamp fell with a crash to the floor, shattered into fragments, rivulets of burning oil spreading over the carpet. Borne back by the hurtling dive of the fat man, the girl crashed to the floor with him on top of her. She fought like a wild cat in the eerie illumination of the burning oil which was seizing on the carpet. From her scarlet lips came a screaming torrent of foul and vile invective. Then her wrists were jerked together, and the cold steel of handcuffs locked shut on them.

The End of the House

Dawn found Detective-Inspector Bullock sprawled in a chair in Superintendent Clayton's room at Firfield Police Station. With him were the superintendent and Sergeant Anstruther.

'I had nothing to go on against Raynor except suspicion,' said Bullock. 'I suspected him of lying after I'd seen Fergus, because I reckoned Fergus wasn't lying, so Raynor must have been. I was favourably impressed with Fergus, that's straight. So after I'd seen Edith Blakeney I went and saw Raynor, and I took a chance — what they call a bow at a venture. It went home, by Jove. I shot the fear of death into him. Then I left the house and nipped into it again through the kitchen window. I wanted to see what he was up to after I left him. I can move as silently as a shadow, mind you, although I'm running to weight a bit, and he'd never have known I was in the house. I heard the girl and him talking in the dinign-room. I listened at the door, but I couldn't hear what they were saying. Then she shot him — shot him right through the mouth. I heard that all right!'

'But why did she shoot him?' demanded Superintendent

Clayton unsteadily, for all this had been a shock to him. 'What did she stand to gain by his death?'

'She shot him after he'd made a will in her favour,' replied Bullock. 'It's lying on your desk there along with the story he was writing. He'd left her every ha'penny he'd got. She was to spend it on the upkeep of the manor. Spend it on the manor, my foot — she'd have spent it on herself.'

'But how, if she shot him?' demanded the superintendent. 'That was murder, and she'd have hanged!'

Bullock laughed shortly.

'It was suicide!' he retorted. 'At least, that's what she meant it to look like. The police were after him. She knew that — must have known it. And there was his confession all neatly written, lying on the table in front of him.'

'His confession?' repeated the superintendent in bewilderment.

'Yes, his story, if you like,' replied Bullock, lounging towards the door. 'I've been looking through it. It is a confession. What's more, it'll make your hair stand on end. He killed the lot of 'em — his Aunt Bertha, Hannah Moffat, and Colonel Blakeney. You'll find all the details in his story. It fits him like a glove.'

'There's more to the story, as well,' he added.

'Hannah Moffat was in service in the manor, and she was going to have a baby — this girl Diana,' replied Bullock, pausing in the doorway. 'Major Burton was the father, but he ordered her out of the place. So she killed the lot of them — left no witnesses, see? Then she went off to Hockley, where Diana was born. She applied to the trustees of the estate to be kept on as housekeeper at the manor. Not suspecting anything of what had happened, the trustees gave her the job, seeing she'd been in service there. So she turned up at the manor again, passing Diana off as her niece. Oh, you have some nice goings-on in these country places, I must say. Well, I'm going to get some kip. I'll see you in the morning, before I leave for London. Good-night!'

The door closed on his retreating form. Superintendent Clayton looked at Sergeant Anstruther.

'The manor's been burned to the ground,' he said unsteadily. 'The overturned lamp in the dining-room did it. The place went up like a bonfire, I understand. The fire brigades couldn't get there in time to save it. If you ask me, it was a thundering good job they couldn't. That house was a menace. It brought only blood, horror, and misery upon everyone who lived there.'

Six months later Jacob Markham, publisher, was sitting with a friend of his in his club.

'Yes,' he said quietly, 'I will always remember Raynor's last words to me before he left London. "My next book," he said, "will make your fortune!"'

'And I'll bet it has done,' said his friend enviously. 'It's simply swept the country. It's the most sensational autobiography of a criminal ever published. But how the devil did you ever get the publishing rights of such a manuscript?'

'Raynor left them to me in a postscript of his will,' replied Jacob Markham, 'and the Home Office gave me pemission to use 'em. The original manuscript, of course, is in the Black Museum, at Scotland Yard.'

He sighed.

'Poor Raynor!' he said. 'I can never think badly of him. I wish he'd never gone up to that beastly house in Northumberland. The place was like a man-eating tiger, except it didn't *eat* its victims—it made them evil!'

The Ancestor Who Returned

by JAMES GARNETT

It was dead of night in the old manor of Shrewford. A thin mist, creeping up from the silent river, had cloaked the house in a grey mantle that shrouded the lower floors from sight; but in the clearer air above were tall chimneys and turrets, sharply outlined in the bright light of the moon.

Inside the manor all was still. A brooding silence hung on the oppressive air in the spacious rooms, with their heavy antique furniture and oil portraits of long-dead knights and ladies, past owners of that ancient house.

One such painting had but recently been hung up, and as the eddying mist outside the tall windows swirled, straggling beams of moonlight came and went across the newly gilded frame and the sardonic face of the man within.

He was a tall man, with a thin face and a peaked beard. His dark hair was brushed back from his high, narrow forehead, and his jet-black eyes seemed to glow with life. And just as vital were the eyes of a raven that perched upon his shoulder, its coal-black plumage matching the cloak he wore, its whole expression as queerly life-like as his own. In fact, of the two, man and raven, it was the bird that many people thought to be the artist's finest work.

The man himself was the late owner of the manor, and upon a metal plaque beneath the painting his name was etched — Sir Richard Grey. He had been dead a year, and upstairs, in the vast old bed-chamber he no longer needed, slept his heir and nephew, Sir Francis Grey, now owner of the manor and a man of wealth and standing.

So deep was the silence of the old house that Sir Francis was aware of it even in his slumber, and presently he awoke from his dreams, a sudden look of fear in his drowsy eyes, and a muttered word of alarm upon his lips. He sat up in bed and listened intently, his head to one side. After a while he thrust one leg out of bed, and cautiously threw aside the clothes. Then, step by step, listening as he went, he walked to the end of the bed and put on a heavy dressing-gown.

Crossing to the door, he opened it wider and looked out. In front of him was a wide corridor leading to a landing that overlooked the hall below, and leaning over the stair rail was a man, his whole attitude one of strained attention to something that was happening beneath.

He made not the slightest sound or movement until Sir Francis drew near, and then he turned round, his finger to his lips.

He was an old man, with silvery hair and an honest, kindly face. He was Giles, butler to Sir Francis, just as he had been butler to Sir Richard and to Sir Richard's father before that.

'Listen, Sir Francis!' he commanded in a whisper; and then he leaned over the stair rail again, this time with his master beside him.

He gripped his master by the arm and spoke again in lowered and impressive accents.

'It is the tapping,' he murmured; 'the tapping that we hear at dead of night.'

Sir Francis gave a little shudder and drew his arm free, bidding Giles be silent whilst he listened.

Oddly loud against the brooding silence of the manor was an endless tapping, a hollow sound that struck a chill upon his mind, so full of purpose did it seem. Listening to it, he felt his breath come quicker and his mouth go dry with fear.

'It is a mouse gnawing at a loose plank that taps against the wainscoting,' he muttered uneasily.

Giles shook his head doubtfully, and his whisper came faintly to his master's ear.

'No mouse ever made such a noise as the one we hear,' he said.

With this he fell silent, and the two men leaned over the stair rail, their minds intent upon the faffing problem of the mysterious tapping that echoed upon the air.

It had awakened them nightly since Sir Richard's death, at first at fairly infrequent intervals, but now night after night, as though whoever it was that tapped was getting impatient as the weeks slipped by. Many times the two men had crept cautiously down the stairs to trace the tapping to its source, but a year had now passed, and they were no wiser as to its cause, except that they knew it came from Sir Richard's library, the room where his portrait hung.

Thinking of all this, Sir Francis stood erect, and his voice rang out in querulous anger.

'I cannot sleep,' he cried fretfully. 'What is this tapping? What does it mean? And who makes it?'

At the sound of his voice the tapping ceased abruptly, as though the hidden tapper had taken alarm, and the two men stared at each other in utter silence.

Presently Sir Francis spoke abruptly, trying to cover his fear by a show of anger.

'Get back to your bed, Giles,' he commanded. 'I'll not worry myself about this tapping any more.'

Turning on his heel, he went back to the bedroom, and the door slammed shut behind him. But the old butler still stayed on alone, motionless, sunk in thought.

He was thinking that Sir Francis had no right to own the manor or enjoy the ample income that the estate provided.

So abandoned had been his ways that Sir Richard had rightly considered him unfit to take possession of the manor and uphold the family name, and in a will made shortly before his death, Sir Richard had therefore left the manor to his niece, Frances Grey, cousin to Sir Francis himself.

But upon Sir Richard's death this will had not been found. Instead, Sir Francis had produced an earlier will that the old knight had carelessly failed to destroy. This early will gave Sir Francis possession of the manor.

He treated his cousin with intentional harshness, refusing to allow her the smallest income from the estate, and sending her away to earn her living as best she could. Then he devoted himself to a life of pleasure, his sole worry being the eerie tapping that nightly broke his slumbers, mocking him by reason of his inability to find out what it was that caused it.

Such were the thoughts that the old butler was thinking as he stood alone after Sir Francis had left him and the tapping had ceased, and because he bitterly resented the wrong that had been done to Frances Grey, he made a resolve that he would try to trace the tapping to its source, unknown to Sir Francis.

He remained silent a little longer, working out a plan, and then, half-hopeful, half-doubting, he slipped away into the shadows, away to his bed to finish his sleep.

But to Sir Francis sleep would not come. Fretful and angry, he moved continually about in his bed, fearing that the tapping, however it was caused, boded him no good. His ancestors had all been men and women of high honour and unsullied name, and it was said that the ghosts of those long dead knights and ladies still walked at night through the manor they had loved so well.

It might be, thought Sir Francis, that they were responsible for the tap-tap-tap, that it was a prelude to some kind of punishment they would mete out to him for sullying the family name and robbing his cousin, Frances, of the manor and money that were rightly hers.

Next day neither Giles nor Sir Francis referred to the events of the night before. Sir Francis had resolved to make a determined effort to ignore the tapping, and Giles was full of his plan to discover what it was that caused it.

Night fell too early for Sir Francis, who feared what the darkness might bring; but the old butler was eager to put his plan into operation, and no sooner had his master retired for the night than Giles lit an old-fashioned oil-lamp and made his way to the library in which hung the picture of Sir Richard.

Holding up the lamp, the butler studied the portrait carefully for several minutes, fascinated for the hundredth time by the eerie vitality of the coal-black raven that was perched on the old knight's shoulder.

The bird had been Sir Richard's pet, taking titbits from his fingers when he dined and perching motionless upon his arm whilst he read in his library or walked about the manor grounds. At his death the raven had vanished, and no one had set eyes on it since.

This thought made Giles shake his head disconsolately, for he would have loved to tend the bird of which his old master had been so fond. Then, setting down the lamp on the table, he began to prepare the room for the long vigil he proposed to make. He pulled out a high-backed settee from the wall just enouth for him to squeeze in behind, and then drew up a chair so that when he was in the hiding-place he would be entirely hidden from anyone in the room.

His next step was to go round the library with the lamp, to make sure that no one was hidden in any of the nooks and alcoves, and finally he closed the door and window. He was alone, with only the portrait of his old master to keep him company in the deserted room.

For some time he stood, sunk in thought, wondering whether he dare go on with his scheme. He knew by heart all the many legends of the manor, and when he recalled some o them he felt a qualm at acting as he was doing.

Eventually he summoned up his courage and extinguished the oil-lamp, thus plunging the library into darkness. Feeling his way cautiously through the gloom, he secreted himself in the hiding-place he had made between the settee and the wall.

When the tapping began, as he was sure it would do, he proposed to peer suddenly over the settee. It would then be after moonrise, and the library light enough for him to discern what it was that caused the tapping.

But what that thing might be Giles did not try to imagine, est his courage fail him. Therefore, during his long vigil, he tried to keep his mind upon things of the everyday world and upon the girl who had been robbed of her rights, and for whose sake he was undertaking his vigil.

Hour after hour he sat behind the settee, as motionless as he could manage, and presently the rising moon shone in through the window, dispelling some of the gloom.

And now he heard a faint noise, vague and indefinable, something like the rustling of a silken dress or the sighing of the wind in the trees. It seemed to come from all parts of the library at once and, secreted behind the settee, he found it impossible to decide where the source of it was located.

He was sure, however, that neither door nor window had opened, for both were long past the stage of quiet opening, and the tiniest noise of a squeaky hinge or rattling pane would have been clearly audible in the silence.

Where then had the intruder come from? This was the thought that was in the old butler's mind when the first tap rang out, surprising him so much by its suddenness that he almost cried aloud.

Immediately there was another tap, and then a third —

hollow, echoing taps that came so swift after one another that he marvelled at the persistence of the unseen tapper.

So far, he had not dared carry out his plan and peer over the settee into the moonlit room, for an inexplicable fear held him motionless. He remained on hands and knees, ready to rise, yet dreading what he might see.

At last he summoned up his courage, and, rising inch by inch, with bated breath and fast-beating heart, he stood erect and looked out into the library.

It was filled with a luminous blue haze as the moonlight streamed in through the windows. It fell full upon the portrait of Sir Richard, but all around were impenetrable shadows, and it was from the shadows that the tapping came.

So much Giles realised in one embracing glance, and then he tried to see into the shadows. For a time he saw nothing, but then he slowly made out a dim outline that caused him to grip the edge of the settee in stark amazement.

Perched upon the back of a chair was a raven, and the sound of its beak as it pecked at the wall was the tapping that had bewildered him and Sir Francis for so many months.

And yet it was hard to see the raven, for its plumage merged imperceptibly into the dark shadows, and Giles, looking at the portrait of Sir Richard with the raven on his shoulder, wondered for a moment whether it was not some kind of optical effect, an after-image or something of the sort, that caused him to see a similar bird in the shadows whence the tapping sounded.

Then, cautiously, he began to climb over the settee, hoping to approach and set his doubts at rest, when, suddenly, without the slightest warning, the door opened and Sir Francis sprang into the room. He had been awakened by the tapping, and had come down once again to try to find out what it was.

At the sight of Giles he recoiled in terror, but when the

old butler quickly struck a match and lit the lamp Sir Francis recovered himself with an effort.

Giles gave one fleeting glance at Sir Francis, and then he looked towards the chair on which he had seen the raven.

But there was nothing there. The bird, if indeed there had been one, was gone, and with a curiously awed feeling Giles realised that there was nowhere it could have gone in those few swift seconds of alarm.

'What is this? What do you want here?'

Raising his hand, Giles pointed to the chair upon which he had seen the raven.

'The tapping!' he cried in excited tones. 'I've found out what it is!'

Then he paused to collect his thoughts, for he was beginning to doubt whether he *had* found out. Then in slow and impressive accents he told Sir Francis everything.

The latter considered things in silence for a while, and at length his glance strayed to the picture of the raven that was perched on Sir Richard's shoulder.

'It must have been an illusion, Giles,' he suggested. 'You had been looking at the picture, and the image remained in your eyes for a time.'

Then Giles, too, studied the picture. Sir Richard's eyes gleamed in the lamplight as though he were a living man, and to the old butler's excited nerves it seemed almost as though Sir Richard knew the meaning that lay behind all these queer happenings, and that he was, in some uncanny way, responsible for the tapping and the illusion of the raven that had pecked at the panel of the wall.

A cry from his master interrupted his train of thought. Sir Francis had drawn near to the panel, and was scrutinising it closely; but now he had drawn back, and was pointing at it with a trembling finger.

'It is pitted with tiny dents!' he cried.

Then he lowered his voice and spoke in confidential tones, drawing near to Giles and gripping him by the arm.

'That was a real raven you saw, Giles,' he said. 'See, here are the marks of its beak.'

Giles shook his head doubtfully, but Sir Francis impatiently ordered him to fetch some tools so that they might break the panel open.

'The tapping was to guide me to something that is secreted in the wall,' he said. 'Perhaps it may be the gold and jewels that were hidden away during the Civil War, and were never found because the man who hid them was killed that same day in battle.'

Giles nodded his head, infected by his master's inthusiasm.

'Stranger things than this have happened in this old manor,' he agreed.

Then he fetched tools, and the two men removed the panel. It was fastened by a catch that they might have undone had they known its secret, and inside was an oblong cavity, in which, covered with dust and cobwebs, lay an envelope. Giles picked it up to wipe it clean before Sir Francis handled it, and as he did so he read aloud the words that were written on it.

'*The last will and testament of Sir Richard Grey, Baronet.*'

Almost before the last word had left his mouth the envelope was snatched from his grasp by Sir Francis, and as the old butler drew back in alarm from the fury in his eyes he realised that it was the missing will — the will that would give back to Frances Grey the possessions that were rightly hers.

For several moments the two men stared at each other in silence, and then Sir Francis mastered his rage with an effort.

'I'll take charge of this will,' he said.

A mocking light burned momentarily in his beady eyes; and then, leaving Giles to put the library straight, he passed out of the room, taking the precious document with him.

Next evening found Sir Francis alone in the library where the will had been so strangely found. It lay on the table before him — a single sheet of parchment, upon which, in plain terms, Sir Richard bequeathed the manor to Frances Grey.

All day long Sir Francis had been racking his brains for a means to retain the manor. He dared not destroy the will, for Giles had seen the inscription on the envelope, and the best that Sir Francis had been able to do was to tell the old butler that he had sent the will to the solicitors to be dealt with. This had given him a short respite.

'There is no chance of my persuading Frances to marry me after the way I have treated her,' he muttered, as he paced up and down the floor. 'Of course, she'd allow me a small income from the estate, but that's no use to me. I want the manor and the money — and I'll have it!'

His voice rang out, charged with menace against the girl he meant to rob; but scarcely had the sound died away than there came an answering echo, hoarse, unnatural — a sound that caused the colour to ebb from his cheeks, leaving him pale and agitated.

It was like the croak of a raven, and instinctively he stared over his shoulder at the picture on the wall. But the raven depicted in it could not have made the sound; the idea was so ludicrous that he wondered how he could ever have entertained it. Yet he had done so in that brief moment of terror.

Uttering a snarl of contempt at his own stupidity, he continued to pace up and down the floor, evolving and rejecting a hundred schemes, until at last he found one that seemed to meet his needs. It was to write to Frances Grey and invite her to the manor, and then to make her a cunning offer that he was sure she would accept; and, once she had accepted it, he would be able to produce the will and flaunt it in her face, and she would have no means of taking from him the manor and the fortune that were rightly hers.

Sir Francis went carefully over his scheme and found it flawless, and then he set to work — first to write to his cousin, and then to prepare a document that she was to sign.

Two days later he drove over to the local station to meet her, for it was essential that she should not have any communication with Giles and hear of the discovery of the will.

A gleam of delight burned in his eyes when he noted the lines of worry on her face and the poor quality of the clothes she wore. His assurance increased as he drove her back to the manor, for a few shrewd questions told him that she was finding it hard to earn her living in a sphere to which she was a virtual stranger.

When they sat in the library, facing one another across a table upon which a document was laid face downwards, Sir Francis dwelt upon her obvious poverty. He pointed out that she was not trained to earn her own living, and that she would never achieve by her own efforts the life of ease and security to which she had once been accustomed. This, he continued, had preyed on his mind, and he had bitterly repented of his harshness in turning her adrift without a penny at their uncle's death.

Finally, he leaned across the table and looked her straight in the eyes.

'And, therefore, Frances,' he said impressively, 'I am going to settle upon you an income of thirty pounds a week for life.'

For a moment she sat silent, stunned by the unexpectedness of his offer. The realisation of what such an income would mean to her momentarily deprived her of speech; but then she flushed with gratitude, and a flood of words poured from her lips.

Sir Francis interrupted her expressions of thanks with

a wave of his hand, and then he spoke again.

'Before I grant you such an income you must sign this document,' he said.

At these words a change came over the girl's face, for she knew her cousin's treacherous ways.

'It is a statement,' he continued, 'which binds you upon your solemn oath never to lay claim to the manor of Shrewford in the unlikely event of a will turning up in your favour.'

He paused and eyed her shrewdly, noting her hollow cheeks and the tiredness of her eyes, expecting her to jump at his offer, but she asked a question.

'The reason?' he echoed. 'Well — I am tired of living in suspense. At any moment a will may be found depriving me of the manor, and it is worth thirty pounds a week to me to know that should such a will turn up you will never claim your rights. Not that I expect such a will to be found, for the manor was well searched after our uncle died, but — one never knows.'

Frances Grey thought this plausible reason over. She had given up all hopes of regaining the manor, and thirty pounds a week would be a fortune to her in her present reduced circumstances.

'Give me the paper,' she said suddenly. 'I'm tired of being poor. I'll sign it, but —'

She paused, and her eyes grew cold and an unusual sternness crept into her voice.

'But both you and I know,' she continued, 'that the manor is rightly mine, no matter what the lawyers say. You had your money whilst our uncle lived, and I — I have had nothing.'

So saying, she took up the pen that Francis gave her and set its nib upon the paper. Then she paused.

Suppose she signed it and next day the missing will turned up? This was the question she asked herself, but quickly came another question. Suppose she refused to sign and the will never turned up? That would be to lose a certain thirty pounds a week.

At this thought she tensed her finger round the pen, but even as it began to move across the paper there came a sound that stopped her hand, whilst Sir Francis recoiled from the table, his face white with terror.

It was a raven's croak, harsh and sinister, and again Sir Francis turned to stare at the picture on the wall. His action and his look of horror did not pass unnoticed by his cousin, and she turned to look at the portrait of her dead uncle, too.

To Sir Francis the old knight's eyes seemed filled with icy contempt, but to Frances Grey they looked quite different. Slowly she drew herself erect, reminding herself that she was of the same family as that stern old man, a family to whom courage and honesty were virtues desirable above all others.

Then, turning swiftly to the table, she seized the document she had nearly signed, and as Sir Francis turned in amazement she tore it into tiny pieces and cast them fluttering to the ground.

'I'll not give up my rights because I fear hard work and poverty!' she cried. 'I would despise myself for doing so. I am a niece of that stern old man whose portrait hangs behind us, and he would hold me in contempt were I to be so weak.'

She paused, noting the evil rage that flamed in her cousin's eyes, and then, avoiding the arm he put out to seize her, she walked from the room.

Uttering a growl of rage, Sir Francis sank into a chair.

'But for that sudden noise, that raven's croak, she would have signed the paper I had drawn up,' he snarled. 'Who — or what — made that noise? Or was it only my imagination?'

He stared wildly around the room, but nothing living met

his eye, and, shaking with anger, he spoke again.

'And now she'll speak with Giles on her way out, and he'll tell her that the will's been found.'

His fury was amazing to see. His eyes blazed and his face worked as he pulled the will from his pocket and slammed it down on the table before him, but then his rage died down, for he has seen something that brought a cunning smile to his thin lips.

The will left the manor to 'Frances Grey'. Surely, he thought, it would be easy to alter this name, wherever it occurred, to his own name, 'Francis Grey'. It was only a matter of turning a letter 'e' into a letter 'i', and with an expression of impatience he hurried away to find a pen and ink to alter the will before his cousin returned and demanded to see it.

Frances came back to the library sooner than her cousin had expected, for Giles had told her of the discovery of the will directly he had greeted her.

She came in at the door with the old butler hard at her heels, and Sir Francis, pen in hand, raised his head and darted at her a look that was so venomous that she came to a halt, appalled at what she saw in his eyes.

Then she plucked up courage and approached the table, and a single glance told her that the parchment sheet upon which her cousin had been writing was the will that had never been found at Sir Richard's death.

For a moment she stood motionless, transfixed with shame and horror at her cousin's wicked duplicity and the heartless way he had tried to trick her such a little while before.

Then she leaned across the table to take the will, but she was too slow. Her cousin had seized it and had sprung back out of his chair. He took the will between his fingers and stared menacingly at her and at the old butler who stood by her side.

'Give me that will,' she said sternly.

Sir Francis recoiled in horror from the figure before him

She stretched out her hand, but he drew back still farther, and gave a mocking smile.

He paused a moment.

Then he gripped the will between his fingers, preparing to tear it into fragments. But as the strong parchment buckled in his grip the raven's croak rang out again, harsh and sinister, causing him to drop the will from his shaking fingers.

It fluttered to the floor, and Frances darted forward to pick it up. Uttering a cry of rage Sir Francis moved to snatch it from her, but in the very act of moving he recoiled, his face blanching to an ashen whiteness, his eyes dilated with terror.

Between him and the girl he meant to rob was a shadowy figure, vague and formless in the gathering gloom, but its face was plainly that of Sir Richard Grey, and upon its shoulder perched a coal-black raven, just as in the picture behind him on the wall. Sir Richard's eyes blazed with stern contempt, and his uplifted hand was thrown forward, forbidding Sir Francis to approach the girl he meant to rob.

Both she and the butler had not seen the phantom, for they were bent to the ground, and Sir Francis, cowering back in mortal fear, saw them take up the will, and without a backward glance, fled from the room.

Then the figure of Sir Richard began to fade until at length it was gone, and Sir Francis, was able to collapse into a chair. It was the end of all his wicked plans, and he knew that he would be lucky to escape imprisonment, since his incomplete attempts at forgery would be plain to see.

Actually, he was treated with great generosity by Frances Grey. She allowed him a generous income from the estate.

He is now abroad, and though he often racks his brains to account for the inexplicable events that accompanied the finding of Sir Richard's will, he is still as far as ever from any ordinary, everyday explanation.

The Golden Amulet

by SYDNEY PHILIPS

It had been a strange, unusual, disquieting week, thought Evan Knock to himself as he sat in a tiny back garden in south-east London one Sunday afternoon. Of his extraordinary experiences nobody had been able to offer the remotest idea of an explanation. Yet it had all happened so clearly, in such a matter-of-fact manner. The most amazing thing was that it seemed as though history, in some inexplicable fashion, had repeated itself after four hundred years.

Yesterday, Mr and Mrs Tomlinson, Julian's parents, had been to tea, and talked the whole matter over with Evan's father and mother. They had all agreed it was one of those things which defied description. After a while, Mr Tomlinson and Evan's father had gone round to the local, 'The Brown Cow', and consulted the regulars there. At first they had been laughed at, and then the talk had grown more serious, but nobody had been able to throw any light on the affair.

Still in a state of shock, Evan had only been able to remember bits in flashback, odd disjointed things, but as he sat quietly in the garden with all the usual Sunday afternoon noises, planes overhead, a lawnmower clanking away in the distance, he began to piece out the week's happenings in an orderly sequence. His mind jerked back to last Monday morning. He could remember parting the boughs in front of him, and pushing the leaves away from him . . .

Evan turned his head, calling to his two companions.

'John! Julian!' he cried. 'Over here, come and look.' A crashing of heavy feet breaking twigs underfoot, and muttered curses, meant that John Blair was on his way in response to Evan's summons. John was heavy and well-built for his sixteen years and his method of moving about rather reminded everyone of a well-meaning elephant. But for all his size and strength, John would not have harmed a fly. Evan knew that he wouldn't be able to hear Julian, because although he was the same age as John, he was slim, wiry and very light on his feet, the best half-miler the school had ever had.

'It's a good job we're collecting botanical specimens, and not trying to observe the animal wild-life,' said Evan with a laugh as John came pounding into view. 'You'd frighten everything off within miles.'

John snorted. 'Didn't you know,' he said, 'I'm understudy to Mr Universe!'

Julian Tomlinson came padding along, his black face wreathed in smiles as he caught the end of John's last remark.

'Behold!' he said, 'the human hippo! Guaranteed to make a trail a mile wide!' Then he ducked to avoid John's playful swipe, laughing uproariously.

Julian's parents had come over from the West Indies during the war, and Julian and his sisters and brother had been born in England. All three boys went to the same comprehensive school in south-east London and were filling in time between finishing their exams and the end of the summer term.

The form had been divided up into groups and given projects to fulfil. The projects had been designed to test 'initiative, resourcefulness and application'. Evan gave a small groan to himself when he heard this. The three boys had been friends since primary school days, and always went round together. They were known as 'the three musketeers'. When their turn had come, the master's eyes twinkled as he said:

'Now you three, here's botanical specimen tin each. I want you all to go to Crown Woods up by Shooter's Hill, and bring back speeimens of every tree, bush, grass and flower you can find. Between the three of you, you must be able to present a complete botanical picture of Crown Woods to the form on Thursday week.'

'Cor, what a drag,' Evan commented as he slung the specimen tin over his shoulder. 'Sounds deadly dull to me.'

'Might have been a lot worse,' grunted Julian. 'At least we'll be in the open air, enjoying the sun; thar's something we can never get enough of in England, at least so Mum and Dad say.'

'We'll need something to eat on this expedition. I'm starving already,' John grumbled.

'Sandwiches, that's the answer,' said Evan, 'but we don't want to waste time going home today — we'll have to live off the country.'

'Live off the country? You sound as though we're going to take a pot at a rabbit or snare an unwary squirrel or something.'

'Living off the country means you take advantage of what the locality has to offer,' Evan explained. 'Now there's a shop not a thousand paces from here, which sells excellent pork pies.'

'Oh, I see!' John slowly realised that Evan was pulling his leg yet again. He wondered privately if he'd ever get used to it. The other two had a quick-fire line in repartee, and were always playing jokes on him. His patient, thorough mind was no match for the satirical humour of his two friends.

They pooled their financial resources and bought pork pies, a bottle of lemonade and three slabs of thick, rich, fruit cake. Then they set off.

Because it was a weekday, Crown Woods were absolutely still and quiet. Not a sound except bird song broke the silence.

The hot sun beat down on the boys so they were soon carrying their blazers, taking off their ties and loosening their collars.

'Tomorrow we must be properly equipped,' said Julian. 'Jeans and tee shirts to start with.'

'Yep,' broke in John, 'I'll bring my father's old army haversack and we can carry the gear in that.' He looked in his pocket. 'I'll have to eat my pie by licking it up; it's almost in crumbs,' he said.

The approach to the woods was up a twisty path amongst low lying bramble bushes. They decided to collect specimens of trees first. As they went farther, the bushes gave way to slight, delicately-leaved slender trees, silver birch and larch, then to thickets of hawthorn and wild roses. The larger older trees towered above. They plucked two or three leaves from each tree, writing an identifying label and sticking it to the leaf stems with a sliver of sticky tape. Each tree was drawn to show its shape, and a quick sketch made showing the placing of the leaf on the bough.

'All my trees look like cauliflowers,' complained John, whose drawing was not his strong point.

By twelve o'clock they were hungry, and it was at this point that Evan pushed the twisted boughs in front of him, and parted the branches away from his face. Through the pattern of leaves, he could see a long glade of oak trees, sunlight filtering down through the leafy ceiling making a mottled, uneven pattern on the ground. Insects danced in the shafts of light shining downwards.

'Just the place for lunch,' Julian said as he brought up the rear. The boys pushed through and made a beeline for a grassy bank beneath a massive oak.

Evan carefully laid his specimen tin down, slipped his Biro to his notebook and placed them all in a neat pile. Julian looked around and hung his specimen tin from a convenient branch. John threw his tin down, tossed the notebook after, opened his bag of provisions, and started to wolf down the pork pie.

'I could eat this three times over,' he grumbled. 'Aren't you going to eat yours?' He looked at Evan outstretched on the bank, hands clasped below his head, staring up into the mighty branches of the oak tree.

'Look,' Evan said quietly, nodding upwards. A squirrel chattered angrily at being disturbed, then whisked his tail and disappeared with a scurry.

Julian laughed. 'Wonder if he'd like a piece of my pie?'

'What?' John was horrified. 'While I'm still hungry? Not on your life!'

When the squirrel had scuttled away, Evan still looked up into the tree branches.

'Y'know,' he said to his two friends, 'this oak must be terrifically old, like all the others in this glade. Oaks take ages to mature — look at the thickness of the trunk, and the spread of the branches. The roots run underground to the same extent as the branches, to balance the weight of the tree.'

'I see what you mean,' said Julian. 'If the roots were tiny, the tree would topple over.'

For a while there was no sound except the chomping of three pairs of jaws.

'Why are they called Crown Woods?' asked Julian.

'Because they're the property of the Crown, I suppose,' Evan explained. But he made a mental note to find out more.

'I think we've got a book at home about this area. I'll look up the details.'

That evening when he had finished writing up the day's botanical findings, Evan hunted through the bookshelves in his room. At last he found what he was looking for — a history of Eltham Palace. He settled down on his bed, the book supported on the pillow, and read steadily until bedtime. His mother stuck her head round the door.

'Aren't you going to watch the programme at ten o'clock?' she asked. But Evan was so deeply absorbed, he didn't even hear; he had no idea that history could be so interesting . . .

On Tuesday the boys were again resting in the same leafy oak tree glade for lunch. John had fallen asleep in a most ungainly attitude, spread-eagled on his back, a rich assortment of grunts and whistles issuing from his wide-open mouth. Evan went over and looked at his friend.

'What awful snores,' he said, 'you can't hear yourself think!' He gently rolled John on to his side. John's mouth closed, he breathed quietly and the snores stopped as if by magic.

'Did you find that book?' asked Julian quietly.

'Yes, and very interesting it was, too,' replied Evan. 'As we guessed yesterday, these woods have their name because they're the property of the Crown, and have been for donkey's years. At one time they stretched right over to Eltham Palace, that's about three or four miles away, and they were the hunting ground of kings. They used to stay at Eltham Palace, and have a good day's sport hunting deer and wild boar.'

'I wouldn't have thought there'd be enough cover for deer,' put in Julian.

'Well, the woods would have been much thicker then, remember; they're thinned out nowadays by the G. L. C. parks department. Look, do you want to hear the rest of the fruits of my painstaking research or not?'

Julian laughed. 'I'm hanging on your every breath. Pray continue.'

'Thank you, kind sir!' Evan gave a mock bow. Well, it seems that these woods were a favourite spot for Henry the Eighth. He used to come here with crowds of courtiers and servants, and hangers-on.'

Julian looked round him; it seemed impossible to believe that these woods, so quiet and peaceful, had once been the scene of the chase so many hundreds of years ago. And yet there was an indefinable sense of mystery about the woods, almost as though they were waiting for something or someone.

'Perhaps some of these great trees were just young saplings then, since they take so long to grow?' Julian asked.

'More than likely,' said Evan. Then he went on:

'Sir Thomas More used to walk here with his daughter, Mary. Remember she married Sir William Roper? He was lord of the manor of Well Hall.'

'I've never seen any manor house in Well Hall,' said Julian, waving away a wasp which was buzzing round his apple core.

'It was pulled down over thirty years ago. My Mum can remember it,' said Evan, taking a swig from the lemonade bottle.

'It was an enormous house with a big garden all round it. Some of the garden walls are still there. If you look closely you can see the ancient bricks. They're smaller than modern bricks, and they've weathered a deeper red in colour.'

'How long ago did you say?' asked Julian.

'About four hundred years.'

Julian whistled.

'How come you know so much about it all anyway?'

'Well,' Evan poked with a stick at the leaf mould beneath his feet, 'as a matter of fact, there have been Knocks living hereabouts for five hundred years. My ancestors were grooms at the Well Hall manor house. We've got records to prove it!'

Julian whistled again.

'Five hundred years ago my ancestors lived in Africa, and we have *no* records to prove it. My great grandfather was a slave, you know,' he said. 'Sometimes I wish I could have know him; by all accounts he was a fine man. *His* father, that's my great, great grandfather, was brought to the West Indies in a slave ship. In Africa he was of a royal house.'

John stirred slightly in his sleep, then settled down again.

'I don't think it really matters what our ancestors did, it's what we are that matters,' said Evan slowly.

'Come on, man,' Julian chipped in, 'you're proud of your ancestors because they were attached to the great manor house, but I'm proud of *my* ancestors because, despite all adversity, they won through and we are free. Perhaps you don't understand that because you've always been free.'

Julian hesitated, and then he pulled out a curiously worked amulet attached to a gold chain from under his shirt, and held it out to Evan.

'What is it?' he asked.

'It's a good luck charm. It's solid gold and those signs mean that the wearer is protected from evil spirits. I mustn't ever take it off because it's handed down from father to son — the eldest son of the family always wears it.'

As Evan held the charm in his hand, the most extraordinary feeling came over him, as though in some inexplicable way this had happened before, at another time but in this very place. He felt as though he'd had an electric shock; his whole arm shook with tremors, the flesh crawled, the skin tingled violently. He grew very thirsty and a strange mixture of awe, fear and apprehension filled his mind.

All at once there was a tumult of shouting, a crashing as though some frightened animal were bounding through the undergrowth running for its life, breathing heavily. It was all over in a split second; when Evan turned to speak to Julian, he realised that Julian had heard it too.

'What happened?' he asked Julian.

'I don't know, but please give me back my charm,' and Julian slipped it inside his shirt once more.

'Well I never', thought Evan to himself as he finished off his lunch, 'all this time I've known Julian and he never mentioned it before.'

Julian's brown eyes grew dark as he gazed into the distance. He shivered slightly.

'I remember my grandmother said the amulet had magical powers, but I've always laughed at the idea before.'

'But how could the magical powers possibly affect *me?*' asked Evan.

'There are lots of things we don't understand,' replied Julian. 'My father says the present and the past are all mixed up, that there's no such thing as time — everything's happening at once, and we can only see part of it because our ability to understand is so limited.'

Evan's brow crinkled — it all sounded double dutch to him, and yet the experience he had just had was so real — as soon as he turned the gold amulet over in his hand it seemed as though the whole glade had come alive with other people, and strange unaccountable noises.

'Let's go, anyway,' said Julian. 'It's time we were moving. We've done a great deal of work today and I must get my specimens sorted out properly this evening.'

Evan stirred the still-sleeping John with his toe. He looked at Julian.

'Let's keep this to ourselves. John would think we'd gone off our nuts.' John woke up, yawning noisily, and the three ambled home. Evan felt shaken and upset.

At tea that evening, Evan was unusually quiet and ate but little. His mother looked at his white face and felt his clammy forehead.

'You're overdoing it on that project of yours,' she said. 'I think you've got a touch of the sun. Upstairs with you now.' Evan's teeth chattered violently. 'Go on, hurry up,' she went on. 'Hop into bed, and I'll fetch you a hot water bottle and some aspirins.'

After his mother had drawn the curtains of Evan's room, she went out closing the door quietly behind her.

Evan ran over the events of the day in his mind. This business of the amulet — he struggled to reduce the inexplicable to terms he could understand. When he'd held it in his hand and turned it over, it had seemed as though a door had opened and he could hear and sense that other beings were in the glade, but he couldn't see them, as if something were occurring behind a thick curtain of gauze. What did it all mean? And how had Julian been affected, too? Was it something to do with the fact that he had never taken the amulet from his neck? Had he and Julian been linked together in some past experience by the amulet? *Had* it been in the past or in the future?

Gradually, Evan's tired mind relaxed and he fell into an uneasy sleep.

He slept for several hours before he dreamed.

Suddenly, he was in a thick wood in broad daylight very early in the morning. The sun streamed down on Evan as he stood deep in the undergrowth. In the distance a cock crowed, and the birds began their chorus. It was strangely quiet. Evan noticed there was no usual hum of aircraft, no sound of traffic on the roads.

'It must be too early,' he thought to himself. 'Nobody's about.' Then he heard the hunting horn. His scalp prickled, and the hair stood up on the back of his neck. He lifted his head and sniffed the air. Fear seized him and he plunged deeper into the undergrowth, scratching his sides. The hunting horn blew again a little nearer; at the same time he heard the noise of hounds baying their full throated howl. Hounds on the chase. Could they be chasing *him?* Surely not, a fifth form boy from the comprehensive school? He shook his head to drive the ridiculous thought away — his head was unaccountably and unusually heavy. It was then that he realised he had horns, a great spread of antlers sprouted from his forehead. He looked down at his legs. They were brown, slim and ended in delicately shaped hooves. He was a stag. A *stag*, and the dogs were after him. Now he could hear shouting and the neigh of horses, getting closer and closer. And all the time the dogs howled and the hunting horn blew thin and clear in its message of pain and death.

Fear gripped Evan, and he began to run. Panic stricken, he broke cover and bounded along in great leaps. Instinct took over and he began to jump sideways to throw the dogs off his scent. As he went out into the open, a hoarse cry from one of the men on horseback showed that he had been seen. With a loud whoop of joy the entire company of huntsmen, about fifty of sixty all told, galloped after him. He looked hastily over his shoulder and saw they wore brightly coloured clothes of a bygone age — not modern huntsmen he thought as he tore along, more like the pictures in his history book of Henry the Eighth. He took a second glance and realised it *was* the king — an enormous figure on a grey horse leaning forward with anicipation, the full mouth open with joy, the face flushed in anticipation.

Then Evan realised that he was a royal stag. Only the king and members of his household were allowed to hunt deer in the forests of the Crown. And these were the Crown Woods where he had been with his three friends since Monday.

Evan splashed noisily through a little stream, crossing diagonally, hoping to douse his scent and throw off the following dogs. But it was no good; he was in plain view. He zigzagged up the slope on the other side of the water, and bounded off through the trees again. Coming to a glade of oak trees he made one last dash for the undergrowth, but the dogs were too near him — he could feel their hot breath on his heels, their jaws snapping against his flanks. He parted the leaves in front of his face and tried to push the boughs away, but at that moment his antlers caught in the bushes. He struggled to get free, his sides heaving as he fought for breath — the dogs were on him. He pulled and twisted to no avail; his horns were caught fast. The huntsmen came up laughing and shouting with pleasure at their morning's sport. Evan felt his strength ebbing, his eyes glazing, and all went black . . .

At that moment he woke up, wrestling with the sheet which was wound round and round his arms. He sat up in bed, shaking, not knowing where he was for the moment. It had all been a dream. Only a dream. He wasn't feeling too fit, he told himself. 'A touch of the sun,' his mother had said. He suddenly realised he was hungry.

He got out of bed and crept downstairs, trying to avoid the squeaky steps, raided the larder for a cheese and pickle sandwich and went back to bed. It was two o'clock, he noticed by the kitchen clock.

As soon as he got into bed again and put his head on the pillow, it was early morning. He was in a cobbled yard putting the finishing touches to grooming and harnessing a horse.

'There you are, my beauty,' he said, giving the horse's back a slap. 'You'll do. You look as splendid as I can make you. Today we shall ride with the King.'

Evan put on his tunic of dove green, and brushed a wisp of hay from his sleeve.

'All ready, Knock?' came a raucous cry from the head groom.

'All ready, sir.' Evan swung up into the saddle and took his place at the end of the small procession of men, as befitted his station in life. At sixteen he was assistant to his father in the stables, and this was the first time he'd been allowed to join a hunting party.

'With any luck I may feast on venison tonight,' he thought, licking his lips.

The men on horseback clattered over the cobbles and out of Well Hall manor by the back gate. The king's party was already making its way up the muddy track which led to the forest, so the Well Hall men joined on the end of the troop.

Ahead, Evan could see a large group of men dressed in gorgeous clothes, colourful and bright against the green leaves of the trees. The king, a large figure on a grey horse, was in the lead, laughing and shouting at the top of his voice. At his side rode a Nubian prince on a visit to the king's court. He was clothed in rich satin sewn with pearls, with many rings on his fingers, flashing in the sun as he moved his hands.

Evan couldn't see the Nubian prince's face, but the set of his shoulders and the way he carried his dark head were familiar. 'Ridiculous,' thought Evan to himself, 'how could I, a mere assistant groom, ever have seen such a great personage before?'

Suddenly, the hunting horn came from the right, the dogs were unleashed and they rushed away, tails up, noses to the ground picking up the scent of the royal deer. The huntsmen followed in hot pursuit, first trotting, then galloping. Evan felt the horse's strong muscles beneath him. The air was like wine; he began to shout with excitement, keeping his eye on tke king and the Nubian prince far ahead.

They had put up a stag. It was bounding through the trees in great zigzags with the dogs close behind. The huntsman blew the horn again; one after another, the hunt went through a little stream, watching the stag at its last gasp, dashing into a glade of trees. Evan, still bringing up the rear, trotted into the glade. He could see the stag caught fast by its antlers with the dogs snapping at its heels.

The crowd of courtiers clustered round the king, congratulating him on a fine chase, jostling and pushing in their attempts to speak with his majesty. It was strange, Evan thought, that the whole morning he hadn't been able to see anyone's face, only their crowding backs.

He bent down to adjust his stirrup, and his eye was caught

by something glistening in the grass. It looked like a jewel. Quickly dismounting, he picked up the strange object. It was gold. There were strange markings on it. A charm perhaps? It must belong to one of the great gentlemen in the king's party. He must try to find the owner. He began threading his way through the crowd, holding his horse by the bridle and holding on tightly to the amulet. Perhaps it belonged to the Nubian prince? He would try him first.

'Evan Knock! Evan!' he heard the head groom shout. Again it came: 'Evan!' He woke up with a jerk to find his father standing at the foot of the bed. It had been another dream . . .

'Wake up, lad, it's late.' The dream had been clear in every detail. So sharp was the recollection in his mind that he looked down at his hand to see if he still held the golden amulet. He dressed slowly, feeling confused.

He ate his breakfast, and, brushing aside his mother's protestations that he still didn't look well, set out for Crown Woods.

Joining John and Julian, he said nothing of his dreams, dismissing them in his own mind as the effects of a "touch of the sun"; slight sunstroke, his father had said.

After a hard morning's work, they found the long glade of oak trees quite easily and sank down to rest. As before, John gobbled up his lunch and then fell backwards, asleep almost as soon as his head touched the ground. Julian laughed.

'What a fellow,' he grinned, 'I don't know how he does it!'

Evan finished his food and folded the sandwich paper neatly in his pocket. He leant backwards to tip some lemonade into his mouth. As he was swallowing the cool liquid he heard the hunting horn, clear and sweet. Glancing at Julian, he realised his friend had heard it too. They both stood up and withdrew hastily to the side of the glade in a kind of frozen fear. The sound of the horn grew nearer, then the

A Medieval hunting party was bursting into the glade!

baying of the hounds, and a little farther off the jingle of harnesses, the neighing of horses and the shouting of men engaged in the chase. Both boys stood speechless.

Suddenly, at the end of the glade, a royal stag came into view, its flanks heaving, tossing its splendid antlers as it moved at speed along the leaf mould. Close behind streaked the dogs, snarling and yapping as they closed in for the kill. Then the full hunt burst into the glade with a burly man in rich clothes at its head. Horses in splendid harness, their sides flecked with foam, galloped at full pelt. They were brought up short when the stag, caught fast by the antlers in some branches, was brought down by the dogs to its death.

The courtiers and gentlemen crowded round the burly man on the grey horse offering their congratulations on a successful kill.

'An excellent day, your majesty,' said one.

The king spoke: 'Cut off the stag's head. It was a royal deer and gave us a right royal morning's sport, and it shall be given to a great princeling.' The king turned, looking for the Nubian prince in the general hubbub and melée.

A little farther back, Evan could see one of the young grooms dismount and pick something up from the ground, then the lad moved forward, obviously searching for someone. Both he and King Henry found the Nubian prince at the same time. The boy went to the prince's stirrup, and it was at that moment that Evan saw his face. Evan's jaw dropped; his eyes bulged with horror. The young groom was himself! Just as it had all been in his dream last night. He looked quickly at the Nubian prince and it was his friend Julian! Evan's mouth went dry with fear. He could hear Julian clearing his throat over and over again.

Together the two boys stood and watched themselves as they had been so long ago in this very glade — the young groom handing back the golden amulet to the African prince visiting King Henry the Eighth's court . . .

Both boys stood stock still, transfixed by the scene in front of them. Julian took the amulet out from under his shirt and, holding it in his hand, turned it over twice.

'Now you turn it over,' he told Evan in ringing tones, with a commanding voice quite unlike his own.

Evan turned the charm over twice, and the whole rich, colourful panorama disappeared from their sight . . .

'Evan! Julian! Oi, you two, what's the matter?' came John's voice as if from a long way off. He drew a little closer — 'I say, what *is* the matter? You both look as if you'd seen ghosts.' John stretched. 'I've had a grand sleep. Come on, it's time we were making tracks.' He picked up his things and sauntered off. Evan and Julian followed him automatically, with faltering footsteps, stumbling in John's wake.

'Good old John, so sensible and practical,' thought Evan, 'I'll never laugh at him again!' It was as though John was their only link with reality . . .

Over Saturday tea, Mr Tomlinson could see both his son and young Evan were frightened and deeply disturbed by their experience.

'It's nothing to be terrified about,' he said in his deep musical voice. 'We can't explain what happened in logical terms. We just don't know enough to explain it. Just accept it . . .'

And with that both boys had to rest content. But to this day, Evan, for one, will never go near Crown Woods again, and neither will Julian.

The Phantom of Cursitor Fields

by HENRY POPE

The Iron Box

The last warm golden rays of sunset slid across the house-tops, and streamed through the window to light the frail figure which lay on the bed.

The sun brought a little colour to the old lady's soft cheeks, and gleamed in her white hair as she moved her head and smiled.

'When the sun goes down, I shall go, too,' she whispered.

Little Bob Bryan tried to speak as he looked into his mother's pale face.

The bedroom was not very large, and into it faintly drifted the roar of London's traffic. The noise of engines seemed far away, as though even the great city knew what was happening, and was moving on tiptoe.

The old lady turned and smiled as she looked at the man who bent over her from the other side of the bed. His dark hair was heavily tinged with grey, and he wore the blue uniform of a policeman.

'You've been a very good husband to me, John,' she said softly. 'We've been very happy together — very happy!'

The last words were a whispered sigh, and John Bryan leaned closer.

'You two will get along without me,' she whispered. 'I've been ill a long time — and there's something that I want you to promise before I go.'

Her voice was very weak, but her lips still held the smile which Bob knew so well.

The thin, pale face turned towards the warm rays of the setting sun and the old lady looked out across the roofs beyond the window.

'All my life I've lived here in Cursitor Fields,' she murmured. 'There were green fields here once, but now it's all buildings.'

'We'll stay on here, Mary,' her husband said. 'Bob and me, we'll always live here.'

'Yes, stay here.' She turned to them. 'But there's something I want to tell you about — the Phantom!'

'The Phantom?' John Bryan repeated.

'Yes. You've heard of it, John?' Her voice grew suddenly stronger. 'The Phantom of Cursitor Fields! It comes in the night, and it's terrible to see. It brings dreadfulness and disaster.

'There are papers about it in the iron box in the attic, John. And if ever the Phantom comes again, go away — and take the boy with you!'

There was an intensity of warning in her voice which made even Bob draw back, while John Bryan stood with wide eyes.

'Don't talk about that kind of thing now,' he breathed. 'You'll only—'

'Never forget my warning,' came the answer, and Bob saw his mother fall back against her pillow.

As the last golden rays of the sun faded from the sky she smiled sweetly just once more.

And that was the end.

* * *

The floor of the narrow attic was littered with all kinds of odds-and-ends — broken chairs, discarded oilcloth, battered boxes, and musty old clothing.

Daylight struggled with difficulty through the slanting window in the roof above, showing Bob, as he squatted on the floor.

It was more than a year since his mother had died, and Bob had come to the attic alone. He had found a square iron box, and he was now using a hammer and an old chisel in an effort to force the lid open.

He could remember what his mother had said about the Phantom, and he recognised this box as the one which contained some papers about the spectre which had once haunted Cursitor Fields.

Sitting there, hammering away, he could hear the traffic of London roaring below him. Cursitor Fields was close against Cheapside, almost within a stone's throw of the Bank of England — the very heart of the mighty metropolis.

Bob and his father lived in rooms at the top of a ramshackle old office building. Cursitor Fields was full of similar old places, which frowned over the narrow ways and streets, and towered above the alleys and passages with which the City district was honeycombed.

Bob was strong, in spite of his few years, and presently the lid gave way. It shot up in a shower of rust, and inside he saw papers yellowed from age.

Some were newspapers, with queer, heavy type. Some were documents covered with awkward handwriting. He picked one of these up and read:

'Notes on the Phantom of Cursitor Fields, wrote by James Robert Bryan.'

'It comes in the night,' Bob read, 'mostly when the thickest of mists drifts over the fields from the River Thames. It is seen as a face which grins horribly, and men do say that the Phantom chatters and jabbers to itself as it floats in the air.

'It shines of its own light, in a blue haze, and leaves behind a smell upon the air like brimstone. It forebodes disaster—'

Bob put the document down, and lifted one of the newspapers. He saw old-fashioned type, set in headlines:

'Phantom at Cursitor Fields. Frightened Householders. People Leaving Their Dwellings!'

A little scared, a little fascinated, Bob looked through the papers in the iron box. Each one of them told of some appearance of the Phantom, and of the trail of disasters which had followed.

And right at the bottom of the box Bob discovered a manuscript which was older than any of them, and done in handwriting so strange that it took him time to puzzle it out.

Slowly, word by word, he read:

'Ye Spectre talks of itself as it floats on ye aire, not touching ye grounde. It shynes in ye dark. Those who witness it should fall straitway on yere knees and enter into ye prayers.'

'Ye Spectre is very able to give terror to beholders, and doth mean much trouble.'

Bob read no more. He bundled the papers back into the iron box and lifted it, running for the stairs.

'Dad!' he called down then. 'I've found the iron box, and it tells you all about the Phantom!'

His father met him at the foot of the stairs.

He took the box away from Bob, and would not let him read more of its contents.

But John Bryan sat up late that night, reading all that other men had had to say of the Phantom of Cursitor Fields.

* * *

Lights were burning in the Cursitor Fields branch of the City Bank. All the clerks had been working late, and darkness had long since fallen.

Bob Bryan jerked his hat off its hook, and clapped it on his head as he waved cheerfully to the head cashier, and made for the great mahogany doors which led to the street.

It was more than ten years since Bob had found the iron box in the attic. He was now well-built, with finely moulded features, and clear, clever eyes.

The big doors closed behind Bob, and he turned to the blue-clad figure hardly visible in a deep doorway near at hand.

'That you, Dad?' he called cheerily.

'Hallo, my boy!' came his father's gruff tones. 'I saw through the window, when I came on duty, that you were working late, so I hung around here just to have a word with you.'

'It's a rotten night for your job, Dad — misty!'

Bob looked up and down the narrow street as he spoke. The street lamps on the corners were shrouded by halos of thin mist drifting steadily in from the river. By midnight they would have banked up into fog.

The air was damp, and it had a touch of biting cold.

With the shrouded street lamps and the sweeping mist the buildings took on an unusual appearance. They seemed to lean over the roadway at queer angles. Some of them were so old that they did indeed lean forward.

'These streets look like bits of the past,' the man in blue said, as they reached a corner. 'I often think o' nights that I'll see a sedan chair come around a turn, with linkmen running over the cobbles in front, their torches all flaring, and then—'

'So long as you don't see the Phantom, you needn't worry.'

Both turned as a voice broke in from behind. A tall, broad-shouldered man stood there, smiling down at them, his eyes shining.

'Why, Mr Jolly!' exclaimed John Bryan. 'What d'you know about the Phantom?'

Joseph Jolly lived in the Fields, and everyone knew him

because he held an ancient and official position. He was know as the Warden of the Fields, and he had an office near at hand. He ranked with the City aldermen, and rode every year in the Lord Mayor's Show.

'Haven't you heard?' Mr Jolly asked. 'There's talk that it was seen last night.'

'What — the Phantom of Cursitor Fields?' Bob asked, and glanced at his father.

From the day when Bob, as a boy, had found the iron box, until this moment, neither had exchanged a word about the Phantom. But neither had ever forgotten it, and what he had read in the old papers was ever fresh in Bob's mind. Besides, he had not forgotten his mother's warning.

'Well, duty's duty — and my job is to arrest all ghosts,' said Bob's dad, laughing.

'Keep your eyes open, you might see it,' the warden answered. 'It won't scare you, though, Bryan, you've got plenty of nerve, I know.'

'You can't be more than a score of years in the Force and not have nerve,' Bob's father answered, and he raised a hand to his helmet as he saluted the warden. 'Good-night, sir!'

'Good-night, Bryan! Good-night, Bob!'

'Good-night!' Bob answered.

He watched the big figure vanish in the darkness and the mist. He knew the Warden of the Fields well, because he was a customer at the bank.

'He's a nice fellow,' his father said. 'Always has a word with me when he sees me on my beat. Well, you'd better get along home to your supper.'

'I will, Dad, and if you're passing the house in about half an hour, I'll bring down a can of hot tea,' Bob said. 'You want something like that to warm — you —' His voice trailed off.

Out of the misty darkness on the other side of the narrow street, something was looming with a pale, bluish glow.

'Dad — look! Over there in Sword Alley!'

He heard his father gasp, then both stood transfixed.

Through the mist they saw a mis-shapen form, and thrust out from it was a grinning face. It was without colour, and yet it seemed to shine with a spectral, blue-tinged glow.

They saw glaring eyes — and they heard a babbling.

It was a weird and eerie sound the like of which had never before come to their ears — a muted jabbering of ghostly words, and while they heard it the face grew clearer in the mist, and Bob remembered what he had read years before:

'It comes in the night, mostly when mist drifts over the Fields from the River Thames.'

'It's the Phantom!' Bob cried.

'You're right, boy!'

While he shouted Policeman Bryan drew his truncheon, and hurled it with all his force across the narrow way. In the instant that the weapon left his hand the spectral form disappeared.

Both heard the truncheon crash against the wall of Sword Alley and drop to the ground.

Sword Alley was empty, save for writhing curtains of thick mist which drifted slowly from the Thames.

'That was the Phantom all right — never a doubt of it!'

The old policeman's voice was quite steady, and he stooped to pick up his truncheon.

'Dad!' Bob gasped. 'Mother warned us about it — and it's come.'

'No ghost can scare me!' His father smiled at him through the gloom.

'But you can't stay on duty alone with — with that!' Bob told him. 'And Mother warned us to go if we saw it. She said it meant black trouble.'

'Ay, she did,' old John Bryan said thoughtfully. 'But I'm not going to let it frighten me away from my duty.'

He looked along the alley, then down the street on either hand.

'I'll be all right, Bob,' he said. 'You get along home to your supper.'

* * *

It was past midnight, and Bob's father stood in the shadow of a door at Four Ways. This was where four streets met in the very centre of Cursitor Fields, and although he did not know it, this was where the tree had stood, from which a highwayman had once dangled in chains for a year and a day.

From where he stood John Bryan could see the retreating back of the sergeant, continuing his rounds. It was his job to meet every policeman on his beat and take his report. He would be around again in two hours' time.

The sergeant disappeared, and the sound of his foot-falls was lost, muffled by the mist, which had now grown heavier. But, thick though it was, John Bryan could see the fronts of the buildings across the road.

He could make out quite clearly the steel grille which guarded the window of Maffins, the jewellers. They were said to be one of the oldest and one of the richest firms in the City, although they still kept to the building they had used for two centuries and more.

The window was set back from the pavement so that, with the doorway, it was flung in shadow. Bob's father always watched this well, because the jewellers' premises were a great temptation to thieves.

He stood there a while, beating his gloved hands against the cold, then slowly moved forward through the silent night.

To-night the mist and fog blanketed out all sound, so that he seemed the only living occupant in a world of his own.

And it was a strange world, this queer corner of London. It held wooden buildings which had escaped the Great Fire of about three centuries earlier, and when all the motors and vans, the clerks and workers of the day had gone, Cursitor Fields seemed to slip back to the past.

Slowly treading with rubber-shod boots, Policeman Bryan went on, scanning the fronts of the buildings, and watching the street ahead. He neared Maffins' window, and he was almost level with it — when he stopped dead.

In the darkness of the doorway he saw a bluish glow, and his heart leaped.

The glow hardened into the outlines of the evil, grimacing face he had seen earlier that night. To his ears came the wild babbling of the spectre — and the shape moved towards him.

It appeared to float on the air. He had but the merest hint of an impalpable wraith-like body supporting it, then he raised his truncheon — and in the instant that he made to strike an icy hand gripped his throat.

He gasped at the touch. The terrible face seemed to swell and fill his whole vision, then he was borne backwards.

Something hit his head with awful force, smashing the stout helmet and knocking it from his head.

He fell, and knew nothing more.

Had there been any to see what followed, the spectacle would have daunted the stoutest heart.

The Phantom bent over the blue-clad form of the policeman, and raised him. Holding the helmet, the terrible figure floated with its burden down passages and alleys until Four Ways was left far behind; then, on a corner, the Phantom stopped and the senseles man was lowered to the ground.

The Phantom's terrible, grimacing face seemed to inspect the battered helmet for a moment, then it dashed the helmet with savage force against the nearby wall, crashing it there again and yet again.

The Phantom then bent above the inert figure once more, and moved away and vanished into the night.

It was almost two hours later when the sergeant patrolling the policemen's beats in Cursitor Fields came upon the still insensible figure of John Bryan.

* * *

It was nine o'clock in the morning, and Bob Bryan stood in the inspector's room at the Cursitor Fields police station.

Bob's face was pale and set, and his eyes were glinting.

At the other side of the table stood the inspector in charge of the station, with a chief inspector and a superintendent Close at hand were three detectives.

'It's no good getting excited, Bob!' Inspector Chart was saying. 'You can't get away from facts!'

'I say that my father was afraid of nothing — and he never ran away!' Bob answered.

'Listen,' The inspector leaned forward and spoke quietly. 'Maffins' place was robbed last night. The premises are on your father's beat. He says that he saw the Phantom there and that it struck him down.'

'If my dad says that, then it is what did happen!' Bob exclaimed.

'And yet we found your father two hundred yards away!' the inspector said. 'He was unconscious when we discovered him, and his helmet was crushed in. On a corner above him were marks, showing that the helmet had been smashed against the wall.'

He paused, and looked at Bob steadily before he went on.

'Your father saw the Phantom, and it frightened him. He ran away. He ran headlong into that brick wall, and that is what knocked him out. The mark you can see on the corner proves it, Bob!'

Bob swallowed hard. His father had been taken to hospital, but he was not seriously injured. Bob had heard his story and knew that what his father had said was true. But the police believed differently.

They were saying that he had run blindly away from the Phantom, and had hurt himself in his terror.

'We saw the Phantom earlier,' Bob said, 'and my dad threw his truncheon at it! We saw it just after he had come on his beat.'

'And you think that the Phantom robbed the jeweller?' asked the superintendent. 'There was no Phantom! That's utter nonsense. Undoubtedly, he found thieves breaking into Maffins, and they threatened him and he ran away! The whole thing is plain neglect of duty by Constable Bryan, and I'll see that he answers for it when he has recovered!'

The inquiry was held in a room at the Cursitor Fields Station, and Bob waited outside. Bob knew how strict was discipline in the Force, and he knew that appearances were against his father.

Inspector Chart would speak for him, but the plain fact remeined that Maffins had been robbed and that it seemed as though John Bryan had run away from the thieves.

Bob needed no one to tell him the result of the inquiry when his father came out.

John Bryan's hair seemed to have turned even more white, and his face was lined. Inspector Chart held him at one side, and the old policeman smiled wryly as he faced his son.

'After more'n twenty years — I'm sacked,' he said, 'in sight of my pension, and they're turning me out for something I never did. They're branding me for a coward — and you know I'm not that, don't you, son?'

'You're a better man than ever I'll be, Dad! I'll find the

Phantom!' Bob told him. 'You stood by me when I was a kid, and I promised Mother that I'd fight anybody who did anything to hurt you, and I'll fight for you now!'

He looked from his father to the inspector and drew himself up.

'Inspector Chart, I'll throw up my job in the bank, and I'll join the Force. I'll get myself posted to your station, if you'll give me my dad's old beat to cover. And if the Phantom's there I'll catch it and I'll prove my dad's no coward!'

The two men looked at him speechlessly.

They watched him turn on his heel and hurry away.

Five minutes later Bob had resigned his job in the City bank, and the next month he joined the Force.

The Phantom's Message

Old Sammy Todd sat by the Four Ways crossing in the heart of Cursitor Fields. He was seated close against the wall, on an old wooden box, and over his knees was a wad of half a dozen placards, which were warm as a blanket against the chill of the night air.

Under one arm he clutched half a dozen evening newspapers, the last of his stock, and he was just thinking about packing up and going home.

Old Sammy had been born in the Fields, and he knew all there was to know about them. He knew that, in the middle of the crossing, and not six yards from where he sat, there had once stood a gallows tree. Highwaymen and footpads, robbers and thieves and sheep-stealers had once swung there in chains.

He knew all about the Phantom that was said to haunt Cursitor Fields, too. But he was afraid of no Phantom! He could remember the stories his old grandfather had told him of it when Sammy himself was but a little boy — tales which had sent shudders fluttering up his spine.

But he had sat for twenty years on that same old wooden box and he had never seen the Phantom. The talk that was going around about it was just a scare!

Very slowly his thoughts trailed away.

Where it came from old Sammy did not know, but he suddenly saw a figure in Bankside, and it was moving towards him, just as the moon slid behind a cloud, suddenly flinging cold blackness over Four Ways and the buildings about it.

The form was that of a man, and yet not a man, it seemed to old Sammy, the newspaper seller. It appeared to glide over the flagstones on bent and crooked legs which were half hidden by a black cloak that appeared to merge with the night.

He saw a grimacing head which glowed blue against the humped shoulders behind it. He saw glinting eyes that glared and were ringed about with a dreadful blue fire, and as the figure came swiftly towards him — it babbled!

He heard it muttering while it dragged itself along. It spoke sounds that were not words, but seemed to be the ghosts of words. It appeared to be on the ground, and yet not to touch the ground, and all the while its awful eyes were on him!

'The Phantom!'

Old Sammy framed the name with his lips, but he had no voice with which to speak. His heart seemed to be still and cold in his chest, his limbs were numbed, and he could not move.

The thing came on. He saw it reach the pavement and the very roadway before him. Its gabbling chatter rang in his ears. He saw a thin, white hand come out of the blackness of its garments — a spectral, bony hand which reached slowly and menacingly out towards him.

He shrank back, and with that movement life came again to his limbs. He half fell from his box and dropped his papers. He paused as the Phantom came on, then he backed away.

He went back — back — back on legs trembling so much that they could barely support him, then he turned and ran! He ran blindly, wildly, with his breath sobbing in his throat. He burst around the first corner to which he came — and ran full tilt into two big forms, which yielded before him a moment and then jerked him to a stop.

'It's the Phantom — it came to me! It tried to get me!' old Sammy gasped. 'It's there — round the corner!'

'What are you talking about, Sammy?'

The voice that spoke was gruff, and the old newspaperman saw triple silver stripes against a blue sleeve. He looked up and recognised the startled features of Sergeant Cobb.

With him was Bob Bryan.

'I tell you it's there!' old Sammy gasped.

'Where?' Bob gripped his arm.

'It came down Bankside!' the newspaperman answered. Bob jumped forward, his right hand dropping towards the thong of his truncheon. He was going to the station for night duty, like the sergeant, and Four Ways was on his beat.

The sergeant followed Bob as he leaped around the corner, and old Sammy came fearfully after them.

Bob saw the overturned box and the scattered newspapers. Of the Phantom there was no sign.

'It's gone!' old Sammy breathed.

'It was never here,' the burly sergeant growled. 'You fell asleep, Sammy. You must have been dreaming.'

'I tell you I saw it!' the grey-haired man protested.

'All this talk about the Phantom's playing on your mind,' the sergeant said. 'There's no such thing!'

'I've seen it too, sergeant,' Bob said quietly, as they

moved towards old Sammy's stand. 'It's through the Phantom that my father lost his job.'

'I did see it!' old Sammy said shakily.

'You dreamed it!' the sergeant said. 'You've been —'

'D'you think he dreamed *this?*' Bob broke in, and pointed with a quivering finger.

On the upturned box lay a slip of paper, and it glowed blue in the gloom.

The sergeant exclaimed suddenly, and bent over it with Bob. Both saw that it was a torn piece of parchment, and on it was strange, scrawled writing, full of elaborate capital letters, and it was this which shone.

'That's the colour o' the Phantom's face — blue, like!' old Sammy said.

'Let's have a look at it.'

The sergeant snatched up the parchment as he spoke, and it crackled in his fingers; then all three read the peculiar words written in fiery script:

'Again I will come at Eleven of ye
Clock in Ye Kynges Banquet Room.'

'What the dickens does this mean?'

The sergeant glared at the parchment while he spoke.

'Again I will come at eleven o'clock in the Kynges — that means King's — Banquet Room,' Bob read. 'Where's that?'

'I don't know,' the sergeant answered. 'But I do know that ghosts don't leave messages. Somebody's playing a joke on you, Sammy!'

'It was no joke,' the old man answered. 'I tell you I saw it and I heard it! It was talking to itself!'

'Sammy, did you smell anything?' Bob asked. 'Did it come near you?'

'Ay!' The old man turned to him, his voice still shaky. 'It nigh touched me, and there was a strange smell.'

'Yes, brimstone,' Bob said quietly. 'Sergeant, it was the Phantom, all right. I've seen it, and I know!'

'Well, come along to the station, Sammy, and tell us all about it,' the sergeant suggested.

The three moved off together, with the newspaper seller telling them again how the Phantom had come and what it had looked like.

Ahead showed the blue lamp and the bright lights of the police station, and they all mounted the steps and entered the old charge-room.

'We'll have a word with the inspector,' the sergeant said, and knocked at the door of the inspector's room. When he entered the others followed him in.

Sergeant Cobb reported briefly what had happened.

'I don't doubt that old Sammy did see something,' he ended. 'But I say it's some fool playing a trick on the old chap. Because ghosts don't leave messages like this, sir!'

With these words he slapped the yellow parchment down on the inspector's desk. The inspector picked it up and turned it over in his hands.

'What message?' he asked.

The parchment was blank!

It was yellow and torn and old, but there was now no writing on it at all!

The sergeant snatched it back and examined it, his gaze startled, while old Sammy stood with his eyes almost bulging from his head in dread.

''Twas ghost-writing!' he gasped.

The inspector's eyes had narrowed now, and he looked quickly at old Sam.

'What was the message?' he asked.

'I remember it,' Bob told him. 'It was, "Again I will come at eleven o'clock in the King's Banquet Room." We were wondering what that meant.'

'King's Banquet Room!' repeated the inspector. 'Why, that's the room in Sir Benjamin Lee's house, and the chie superintendent's there to-night. It's Sir Benjamin's birthday, and he's giving a little party for some old friends.'

'Then this Phantom's going to give them a visit, from the look of it!' the sergeant chuckled.

'Heaven help them if it does!' old Sammy breathed.

'Cobb, take young Bob Bryan with you. Go to Sir Benjamin's house, see the chief, and report to him. Go at once!' said the inspector.

'Very good, sir.' The sergeant saluted.

'Inspector, I'm due on my beat at ten o'clock,' Bob said.

'All right, my lad. If you're not back, I'll put a reserve man on,' the inspector answered. 'Get along now! And you, Sammy, stay here, and we'll give you a cup of tea. After that I'll send a man to take you home. You look all shaken up.'

* * *

Bob Bryan stood with his back to a small locked door in the King's Banquet Room in the house of Sir Benjamin Lee, Alderman in the City of London.

Opposite Bob was a leaded window, and three picked policemen stood with their backs to it, facing into the room. On Bob's right there was another locked door. This was broad and heavy, and formed a main entrance. Here stood Sergeant Cobb with two more policemen.

The door which Bob guarded merely led to a cupboard which he had inspected and found empty.

In the centre of the floor was a table spread for supper, and the meal was almost concluded. At one end sat Sir Benjamin, and at the other was his wife. She was very beautiful, for all the fact that her hair was silver.

She had wonderful rings on her fingers in which diamonds flashed with pointed spears of fire, and around her neck were beautiful pearls. Bob had heard that those pearls were worth more than a thousand pounds.

Bob and the others stood stiffly at attention, but Bob's gaze was constantly roving around the room, taking in every detail. Between the other two groups of police was a corner in which stood a small cabinet, and Mr Jolly was reflected in the glass here.

Bob could see the back of his shoulders heaving every time that he laughed or made a joke.

'Five minutes to eleven,' the alderman's daughter commented, as she looked at the clock above the big fireplace. 'How thrilling if the Phantom really does come!'

'If you see him — duck!' Mr Jolly exclaimed, 'because the police will throw their truncheons at him.'

'I hope they're good shots,' the alderman commented.

'I shan't spare your champagne. I'll heave a bottle if the Phantom shows up,' the chied superintendent chuckled.

'He won't come,' Mr Jolly assured them. 'I think that it must have been students from the hospital playing a prank.'

'If I catch them it'll be the last practical joke they'll make for some time!' the chief said grimly.

There was silence for a space. Bob could feel the tension that was creeping over the room as the minute hand of the clock crept nearer the hour.

'Two minutes to eleven!' Marion called cheerily. 'Well, if anything does get into this room it will certainly be a real ghost!'

'It can't come through the doors or window,' commented Mr Jolly. 'And it can't come down the chimney, because there is a roaring fire there!'

'I made that up myself,' said Sir Benjamin. 'I think we're getting excited over nothing.'

'One minute now!' his daughter called.

Silence fell. Bob saw the other police reaching foı their truncheons, and he drew his own. The polished lengths of hardwood gleamed coldly in the lights from overhead.

'If anybody throws those, aim straight!' Mr. Jolly chuckled, as he saw them. 'I've got no hair to protect my head!'

The others laughed nervously.

Bob saw the hands of the clock just touch the eleventh hour, then he heard a faint whirring of the mechanism as the clock started to strike.

It chimed eleven times, and as the last sound quivered away, Mr Jolly spoke.

'There you are, eleven o'clock,' he said, 'and nothing has—'

His voice snapped off.

Every light in the room went out!

For one moment there was absolute and complete silence. Then suddenly it was split by a terrified scream from Lady Lee.

'Oh-h! Something touched me!'

'Are you all right?' Her husband's voice came out of the blackness. 'Strike a match, someone!'

'Oh-h!' she screamed again.

It was then that Bob Bryan saw by the cabinet a blue haze. It materialised swiftly into the terrible features of the Phantom.

They all was it, grinning and grimacing. And through the room came the heart-shaking sound of its wordless mumbling.

It showed clear, with a blueness that was unearthly. The Phantom's eyes glared as it floated into the room. Then came a terrific smash as a truncheon crashed into the glass front of the cabinet.

With that the Phantom vanished.

Bob heard Lady Lee scream again. He heard the chief superintendent shout, then Mr Jolly's voice calling for someone to make a light. And even as he shouted the lights came on in the room again.

Mr Jolly stood clinging to the back of his chair, staring with dilated eyes at where the Phantom had been seen. All the others were on their feet, except the alderman's wife.

Lady Lee had fallen forward, so that she rested on the table. She had fainted.

'Mother!' Marion ran to her side. 'Mother, you — Oh, look!'

She pointed to the silken gown that her mother wore.

Clear against it, near the neck, there was a mark which glowed faintly blue and seemed to smoke.

'The mark of the Phantom!' Marion screamed.

'It was the Phantom!' Sergeant Cobb leaped forward. 'I flung my truncheon at it, and it went clean through the thing. Smashed the cabinet!'

'I saw it myslef!' Mr Jolly panted.

It was then that Marion screamed again.

'Daddy, look! Mother's pearls! They're gone!'

* * *

Sergeant Cobb stood with Bob and the rest in the centre of the King's Banquet Room.

Every inch of it had been examined, and the smashed cabinet had been drawn away from the wall. They had searched for secret panels or hidden doors by which the Phantom might have got in. But there were none. The very structure of the old house wiped out the possibility of any concealed entrances.

'It's a mystery' the chief superintendent said. 'Well, it's nearly midnight, and there's nothing more that we can do here. Cobb, you'd better take your men back to the station and make out your report. Each man will also give a report of what he saw, and I'll consider them in the morning.'

'Very good, sir!'

Bob marched grimly along with the others. He knew now, beyond all doubt, that the Phantom did indeed exist. It had robbed his father of his honour, and Bob was determined to solve the mystery of it — if such a mystery could indeed be solved.

As the moving file of men in blue tramped steadily down the cobbled street, something flashed through the air from above, falling to the narrow pavement at Bob's side.

All the others saw it, and they halted.

'What's that?' the sergeant exclaimed, as Bob stooped over the object.

It was a square packet, and he picked it up.

He felt a thrill when he found that it was parchment, which crackled against his fingers.

'Open it,' the sergeant said.

Bob opened it. As he did so something fell to his hand — something that shimmered and gleamed in the moonlight.

'Lady Lee's pearl necklace!' he breathed. And while he spoke he saw the strange ghost writing on the parchment which had been wrapped round the pearls:

'Y take and Y gyve.'

'I take and I give,' Bob read. 'What's that mean?'

'Where did they come from? Who threw them?' the sergeant panted. 'What's the meaning of it all?'

The group of police looked up and down the street. There was nothing that moved in sight.

Bob looked at the strange writing on the parchment, and he saw that it was already fading into nothingness.

'Someone threw it down from one of the roofs,' the sergeant exclaimed.

Bob looked up. He saw nothing save the roof-tops, showing black against the sky.

And while they all stared there came through the air the jeering, quivering, uncanny laugh which Bob had heard before.

It was the laughter of the Phantom.

It sounded faint and far away, and it shuddered into silence with a last evil chuckle.

The Silent City

Here and there about Cheapside a blue-clad guardian of the law stood, half invisible, in some dark doorway, and of pedestrians there was none at this hour of night, save two men who walked resolutely through St Paul's Churchyard.

The mighty mass of the cathedral flung everything into gloom, and from this the two emerged. They strode with quiet resolution across Cheapside, and almost immediately plunged into a narrow thoroughfare which took them direct to Four Ways, in the heart of Cursitor Fields.

The two men slowed as they crossed Four Ways.

'Where d'you think we'll find Bob Bryan?' one man asked.

'Somewhere around here,' came the reply. 'This is his beat. He knows more about the Phantom than anyone else.'

Suddenly, turning a corner, the men sighted a figure in police uniform. Two steady eyes surveyed the pair from under the brim of a helmet. The men saw a set of very firm and resolute features.

'Excuse me, are you Bob Bryan?' one of the men asked the young policeman.

'Yes,' came the answer.

'Well, my name is Kimber,' the man went on. 'And this is my friend, Cranford. We're both newspaper reporters, and we've come along to-night to try to get a glimpse of the Phantom of Cursitor Fields.'

Bob Bryan looked at them again. Kimber was a thick-set man, with ruddy features and a square chin. Cranford was slender and his face was pale.

'I don't believe that the Phantom exists,' Kimber said, after a space. 'But the editor of our paper has offered twenty-five pounds to the first reporter who can say that he's actually seen the ghost. That's why we're here to-night!'

'You want to earn twenty-five pounds, eh?' Bob asked quietly.

'Cranford does!' Kimber nodded towards his pale-faced companion. 'He's been ill, and he's hard up. If we see the Phantom, he'll collect the twenty-five pounds. I'm only helping him. I'm—'

He broke off, and looked past Bob, his eyes staring.

'What's that?' he gasped.

Bob turned sharply.

Out of the gloom a dim figure was moving, close to the wall. For a moment Bob's heart seemed to stand still. The street was full of shadows and of reflections flung by the rain-wet walls, so that everything appeared strange.

Then he saw that the form was that of a man emerging from a passage a little way along.

'It's all right!' Bob breathed.

Even as he spoke the approaching figure became clearer, and he recognised the red, smiling features of Mr Jolly.

'Bob, I was looking through some old documents at my office this afternoon,' he said. 'I found this. It seems to be part of some notes which a past Warden of the Fields wrote about the Phantom. Have a look at it.'

Bob and the newspapermen bent over the sheet of paper which Mr Jolly held out. It was yellowed and cracked, but the writing on it was plain enough:

'. . . And once again the Phantom revealed itself on this St Barnabas' Night just gone. All beholders were terrified, and many have left the Fields never to return. The dreadful babbling of the spectre rendered one man of the Watch senseless from fear. Alas, that none has power to quiet this Phantom which has so long haunted the Fields!'

The three looked up, while Mr Jolly took back the old document and returned it to his pocket.

'It is supposed to appear along Willow Walk on St Barnabas' Night,' Mr Jolly said quietly. 'That's on your beat, isn't it, Bob?'

'Yes, sir,' Bob answered.

'And do you know what to-nights is?' Mr Jolly asked.

The reporters exchanged glances, then Kimber spoke.

'It's St Barnabas' Night, sir!' he exclaimed.

* * *

At the end of Bankside stood all that was left of old Cursitor Prison—just a section of broken wall and an ugly watch-tower, which was now used as a warehouse.

The darkness was misty, rendering hardly discernible the stalwart figure of Bob Bryan as he stood in a deep, recessed doorway. It was close upon midnight, and with him were the two reporters.

'I've got to go round my beat,' Bob told them, 'but I'll be all right to watch here with you for another ten minutes: then I'll go round my beat and come back again.'

'And if we see the Phantom we'll give it a warm reception,' Kimber said, and reached one hand into his pocket as he spoke.

The three had just left Mr Jolly, and they had been there only a few minutes. Bob peered through the darkness at the newspaper reporter as he saw something flash in his hand.

It was a revolver.

'What's the idea of that?' Bob asked quickly.

'I've got one, too!' Cranford produced a similar weapon while he spoke. 'It's loaded,' he added.

Bob watched them as they examined their weapons. He saw the blunt, leaden noses of bullets in the chambers and the brassy gleam of cartridge cases.

'You don't need revolvers!' Bob exclaimed. 'Have you —'

'If we see this Phantom, we're going to capture it!' Kimber told him grimly. 'It's no ghost at all, my boy; it's some clever fellow playing tricks!'

'You think so?' Bob asked quietly.

'I do.' Kimber weighed the revolver in his hand and smiled a little. 'And a bullet will put a stop to his game — as well as earn twenty-five pounds for Sammy Cranford here!'

It began to rain again with a thin drizzle which made the flagstones of Willow Walk go black and shiny, and then came a strident clangour through the night.

Br-r-r-ring! Br-r-r-ring! Br-r-r-r-ring!

It was the rhythmic sounding of an alarm gong, waking wild echoes through the streets and alleys all around, and at the very first hint of it Bob leaped forward.

The gong was on a wall, fifty yards away, and above the office of Jonas Perkin, solicitor. Bob saw that one of the windows to the office stood open, and he realised that it was a burglar alarm which was sounding.

As he ran towards the building a window on the second floor was flung open, and the head of the solicitor himself appeared. He was an old man, and he lived on the same premises as those in which he did business, just as his father and his grandfather had done before him.

'Police — thieves!' he called hoarsely.

'All right, sir!' Bob shouted to him 'Switch off that alarm!'

Bob heaved himself up on the narrow sill of the window. He slipped inside just as the office door opened and the dressing-gowned figure of old Jonas Perkin appeared.

'I've been robbed!' he gasped through the gloom. 'The burglars set the alarm going, and they — they —'

He broke off. The two newspaper reporters were clambering through the window now, and a nearby street lamp flung a glow into the room. There was enough light to show the white features and the trembling hand of the old man as he pointed to the broken deed-box on the floor.

Clear through the half-darkness glowed a blue streak. It lay across the twisted lid, shining with a ghostly gleam, which seemed to fade while they watched it.

'Look!' Perkin gasped, while he pointed. 'Look! The mark of the Phantom! There it is on the box — the mark that the Phantom always leaves behind it! It's the Phantom that's robbed me!'

'Switch on the lights!' Bob shouted, and himself found the electric light switch.

He touched it and the light came on, to reveal the old solicitor's trembling figure as he examined the box.

Nothing else in the room had been touched, but this big, black-painted steel box had been wrenched and twisted with a force that was almost superhuman. Some of its contents had been spilled on the floor, and old Perkin examined them.

'It's Sir Gordon Murgatroyd's box,' he said. 'It's one of them, at any rate. It's the oldest one — and all the oldest of his papers have been taken. I put them in here myself, and now they're gone!'

'Were they important?' Bob asked quickly.

'There was nothing that he can't do without,' the solicitor answered, and straightened up, relief on his face. 'Seems as though the Phantom's got away with papers that aren't much good,' he added. 'If it was the Phantom!'

Bob knew all about Sir Gordon Murgatroyd. He lived on the edge of the Fields, and was said to be the richest man in the City of London. Bob had never seen him.

'It's a funny kind of Phantom, if it has to force a window to get in here,' Kimber commented.

The newspaperman pointed to the window behind him, and showed where some tool had been used to open it.

'I've said all along that the Phantom of Cursitor Fields is only somebody playing a trick,' he added. 'And if we're quick, we might catch him. He can't have got far away.'

'That's an idea,' Bob agreed, and turned to the solicitor. 'You telephone to the police station and report this,' he said. 'Say that I'm searching the streets around, pursuing the thief.'

'All right.'

The solicitor nodded shakily, and moved towards a telephone on a nearby desk. As he lifted the receiver, Bob followed the newspapermen out through the window to the street.

* * *

For fifteen minutes the running search continued, and the three pulled up when they reached the dark, deserted Willow Walk.

'We're getting out of breath for nothing!' Kimber panted. 'Whoever robbed that office has got away.'

'It's strange that they never took anything worth while,' his companion commented.

Bob pushed his helmet back off his forehead, and wiped his brow. The drizzling rain had stopped. Everything was wet, and mist was in the air.

'Well, here we are at Willow Walk,' Bob went on. 'This is where Phantom should show up, according to that paper Mr Jolly had.'

'We shan't see it,' Kimber said, and he chuckled a little. 'You used to be a bank clerk, didn't you, Bob Bryan?' he asked. 'Well, you must be a sensible sort of chap, and you ought to know from what you've seen to-night that the Phantom is only some thief dressed up, and scaring people to make his thieving more easy.'

'You think so?' Bob asked, and went on quickly: 'I've seen the Phantom. I've heard it babbling, and I've seen its face.'

Silence fell between them, and they began to move slowly up Willow Walk.

On either hand were the black and empty windows of buildings left untenanted for the night. Here and there, between them, courts and passages opened abruptly, lending a glance at dark corners and recesses in which anything might have been hidden.

In the middle of the Walk the three stopped short.

'What's that?'

It was Kimber who spoke. The reporter's stocky figure had become tense.

With straining ears they listened.

They heard water trickling in the gutters and down the drains. They heard the very creaking of the old houses around, and they heard queer, cacling laughter.

It seemed to come from every direction at once. It was a jeering sound, cold-blooded and evil, which made all three quail where they stood.

It came again, and then again, and finally died away.

'That was the Phantom — laughing at us. I've heard it before,' Bob breathed.

He gripped his truncheon resolutely and moved watchfully. They were almost at the top of Willow Walk when all three stopped dead.

Before them was the wall of the old prison in Bankside, with the tarred and shining fence which filled the gap where stones had fallen down — and against this they saw a blue haze appearing!

The haze hardened. Suddenly the three found themselves

looking into the grinning features of the Phantom!

It was glaring straingt at them, its eyes black and terrible. It was rimmed by bluish fire, leering at the three, and while they gazed they heard it mumbling.

Through the quiet came the dreadful, wordless sound as the spectral lips of the ghostly figure muttered. Fear gripped at the hearts of the three who heard it, and they were appalled by the phantom curses which the blue-tinged wraith let fall on the night.

Seconds passed, then Bob recovered himself.

He hurled his truncheon with all his strength, while his companions lifted their revolvers and fired point-blank at the Phantom before them. Flame flashed from the muzzles of the weapons as the men fired shot after shot, but without effect. The bullets went clean through the spectral figure and smashed into the wooden fence behind!

Bob heard his truncheon strike the woodwork and bounce off. He was half deafened by the reports of the revolvers. He saw Kimber empty his chambers, lift the weapon, and fling it full at the spectre; then all three dashed forward, ready to give battle with their bare hands.

And as they moved the Phantom vanished!

The unearthly blueness in which it floated faded out, and the thing was gone!

All that was left was Bob's truncheon rolling on the road, with Kimber's revolver near it. The tarred and shining fence was marked and splintered where a dozen bullets from the weapons had plunged through the Phantom, to bite into the wood behind.

'It's gone!'

Bob jerked up his truncheon as he looked up and down Bankside. Nowhere was there a sign of movement, although the echoes of the shots still rang out.

'We saw it—it was the Phantom!' Kimber exclaimed.

The Phantom's horrific chuckling turned into a snarl of fury

'You'll believe in it now, eh?' Bob asked him grimly.

Bob had switched on his lantern and its white beam flashed on the fence.

'I aimed for the legs at first, then I fired higher!' Kimber said. 'If the Phantom had been human, it must have—'

He broke off.

Something lay on the narrow pavement, shown by the edge of the light from Bob's lamp.

It was a piece of parchment, and on it was lettering, written in a blue that seemed to burn:

'GO—GET THY GOLD!'

In amazement Bob and the others looked at the paper; then the young policeman picked it up. He saw that the writting was already beginning to fade, just as the Phantom's mark in the office had faded a little while before.

'Go—get thy gold!' Kimber read. 'What does that mean?'

'It means that this note is for you!' Bob went on. 'It means that the Phantom knew you wanted to see it. That you'd get twenty-five pounds if you saw it!'

The two gasped. The last of the colour faded from Cranford's face.

'We heard it laughing at us coming up Willow Walk,' he said. 'And it showed itself to us, and left this note, so—' He stared at the paper. 'It's blank now!' he exclaimed.

The blue writing had faded.

Kimber looked at it, then bent and snatched up his revolver from where it lay on the ground.

'A ghost that laughs at you and laughs at bullets!' he exclaimed, and his voice trembled. 'Writing that shines like blue fire and then vanishes!' He gasped. 'I'm going to get out of this! I'm—' He stopped.

Then on the air came the quaking laughter of the Phantom. At the sound of it the two newspapermen started away, for both to break into a run and go racing down Bankside.

They ran until they were clear of Cursitor Fields—and safe.

But they left Bob Bryan behind them. He could not run. He had his duty to do.

On Duty

Bob Bryan stood at one side of the narrow street, watching a group of men talking together on the steps of a building across the way.

They wore rich cloaks of crimson and gold, as well as strange, three-cornered, blue hats. Their garbs marked them as councillors of Cursitor Fields, and they had attended the annual dinner of the warden.

It was half an hour short of midnight, and the warden's guests were now leaving the hall in which the dinner had been given. There was a row of cars waiting along the narrow, cobbled way, their sleek paintwork shining, and their lamps making bright blurs of light in the darkness.

The lamps on one car caught a small notice pasted no the wall near the open doorway. Because the light was bright, and the street not very broad, Bob could read the words printed there:

'£100 REWARD

offered to anyone giving information leading to the arrest or repression of the Phantom of Cursitor Fields.

JOSEPH JOLLY (Warden).'

Notices like this were posted up all around Bob's beat. They were on walls, on the sides of lamp-posts, on fences, and in windows. Through the darkness the little bills looked like so many watchful, pallid faces, looking out for the spectre which haunted the streets and alleys, passages and courts of this old and ancient quarter of the City of London.

But for the cars, and Bob's blue-uniformed figure, the red-and-gold clad councillors might have been figures of two hundred years earlier. They looked like men out of the past as they stood bathed in the glow that came from the heavy, oaken doorway.

It was then that a small, bent figure appeared around the corner, and caught Bob's attention. Bob recognised the form as Old Anne, a poor, grey-haired old flower-woman, who lived in the Fields.

She was struggling along with a great flower-basket, and she moved as though every step were a labour, and the basket itself a burden that she could hardly support.

Frowning, Bob left the doorway and crossed the road, hurrying to meet her.

'You're out late, old lady!' he exclaimed.

He stopped before her as he spoke, lifting one hand towards his helmet in a polite little salute.

She dropped the basket to the broken paving-stones, and looked up at him. Old Anne had a great weight of years, and little wisps of silvery hair had struggled from under her bonnet. Her wrinkled cheeks were unnaturally flushed, and she was breathing heavily.

'Hallo, Bob!' she panted. 'I'm late. And a mortal hard job I've had getting my basket all the way back here from the West End. I ain't sold much—and it's heavy.'

Through the gloom Bob saw that the basket was nearly full of flowers. It meant that she had not sold many during the day.

'I've lost my old pitch,' she said. 'They're putting up a new building, and they've turned me off it. I didn't get many customers, and I—I—'

Her voice seemed to fail her, and Bob jumped forward to catch her as she almost fell across the basket.

Bob carried her as well as the basket along the street. When they neared the open door of the hall where the warden's dinner had been held, he glanced at her again.

Her face showed flushed in the light, and her eyes wer bright and feverish. Bob could see that she was very ill.

Bob soon had the grey-haired old lady stretched out on a rough bed in the corner of her mean little room. The oil-stove was alight, and over it a kettle was beginning to sing. A broken candle provided the only light, and it revealed Bob Bryan as he bent over the bed.

'There'll be a cup of tea for you in a minute,' he said. 'That'll make you feel better.'

It had taken him some time to get Old Anne to her poor home, and he was doing his best to make her comfortable. But he saw, now, that her eyes were closed, and when he shook her shoulder gently she did not rouse.

'She's fainted!' He gasped the words as he straightened up. 'I'd better get help and—'

He broke off.

To one side, the door was slowly opening, and in the utter blackness of the little passage beyond was a chill, blue haze.

It grew stronger, and out of the haze materialised the face of the Phantom of Cursitor Fields.

Its glaring eyes, its grimacing features, its lean lips were lined with cold fire, and through the quiet came the uncanny, wordless mumble which always marked the Phantom's presence.

So sudden was its appearance and so unexpected its visitation that Bob was rooted to the spot. The terrible face seemed to float nearer to him in the blackness, then the spectre vanished as abruptly as it had come!

His heart pounding, his body tense, Bob remained there, while to his nostrils drifted a faint, indefinite and yet pungent smell—the reek of brimstone.

He recovered himself, steadied his momentarily shaken nerves, and leaped for the passage.

He dashed to the little street outside, but there was nothing to be seen save the empty pavement and the blank fronts of the tumble-down buildings opposite.

He turned back, then, and he was on the threshold of Old Anne's room when he almost tripped over something. He bent, and the candlelight showed him a bundle of black cloth.

'The Phantom must have left this behind,' he told himself. He lifted it cautiously and carried it into the room.

The cloth was knotted, and he untied it, letting the ends fall to the floor, and the contents of the bundle made him stare in blank amazement.

He saw delicate grapes in a basket, a cold chicken, ingredients for beef-tea, and all manner of luxuries needed by one who was ill!

Bob Bryan looked from the things which the Phantom had brought to the door to the still figure of the flower-seller on the bed.

The Phantom of Cursitor Fields had been mysterious enough before, but now the mystery was doubled. With his own eyes Bob had seen the spectral form in the doorway, and it was beyond him to guess why the gostly shape should have brough these luxuries.

The kettle hissed and sung on the oil-stove, and the candle flame flickered; then clearly Bob heard quick footsteps outside. They paused near the window; then followed a knock on the outer door.

Before Bob could move in answer, the door was pushed open, and a moment later someone appeared in the passage.

Bob's eyes widened when he saw a nurse standing there, and while he stared she entered, gazing at his uniform.

'Does Old Anne live here?' she asked. 'Oh, is this her?'

She glanced at the quiet form on the bed, while Bob nodded; then the nurse spoke again, and he noticed that she was breathing quickly.

'I'm a private nurse,' she said. 'A little while ago there came a hammering at my door, and I found this note in the letter-box. Look!'

She held out a slip of paper, which crackled like parchment as Bob took it. In black, scrawled handwriting he read:

'Go ye hastilie to ye olde Flower Woman in Bye Street. Remain ye there until ye olde woman is better in her health.'

'There was money in it!' the nurse said. 'Twenty pounds!' She showed the notes in her hand.

'I knew the note referred to Old Anne,' she added. 'So I came at once. But I don't know who sent the message, and—' She broke off and looked at the pile on the floor. 'Did you bring those for her?'

'No,' Bob answered.

He glanced at the strange note which he still held. He knew who had written it.

He had seen a note before like that in the same queer handwriting.

'No,' Bob repeated. 'These things came from the same source as the money and the note to you.'

'D'you know who sent them?' the nurse asked him.

'I can't tell you that,' Bob aanswered evasively.

As he spoke Old Anne stirred, and the nurse moved to her side. After that she forgot the strange way in which she had been brought there, and busied herself with her patient. Bob did what he could to help, then finally shook hands with the nurse and moved out into the open, intending to return to his beat again.

Outside the little house where the flower-seller lived Bob Bryan paused. He buttoned his jacket thoughtfully, then stood for a few moments staring into the darkness.

The night's events made the mystery deeper. How had the Phantom known of Old Anne's illness? And why had the ancient ghost brought luxuries to the grey-haired old woman, and paid a nurse to go and tend her?

Bob realised that if the nurse had known whence that note and those glittering coins had come, she would never have come near Old Anne, for fear that the Phantom might appear again.

Bob drew out his notebook and then and there jotted down details of what had just occurred, so that he could report to the station officer when he came off his beat at dawn.

Orders

Bob Bryan stood stiffly at attention, his clear gaze fixed on the hard, inflexible features of the man who was seated in the worn leather chair placed behind the desk.

At one side stood the inspector in charge of Cursitor Fields Police Station, and at the other stood Sergeant Cobb, second in command. Both were, like Bob, at attention.

'This Phantom is some clever crook who has hoodwinked you all.'

The seated man spoke in a voice that was as cold and as grim as his expression. He was Commissioner Hayes, who had come down from Scotland Yard specially to investigate the Phantom which was terrorising Cursitor Fields.

'It is a peculiar thing that it has never appeared anywhere except on your beat, Constable Bryan.'

His chilly, grey eyes met Bob's steady gaze, and the young policeman felt his heart leap.

'You have seen it,' the commisioner went on. 'You report that you have attacked it,; but you've not caught it. You—'

'No one can catch a ghost, sir!' Bob broke in.

'There are no such things as ghosts,' came the swift retort.

'I've seen bullets go through it, and I've seen a truncheon thrown at it, sir,' Bob said. 'And I know—'

'Nonsense!' The commissioner jerked to his feet, and looked angrily from Bob to the inspector. 'I say that it is some rogue who is frightening you all so much that you're ready to believe anything.'

The three standing men did not move, nor did they answer; but the inspector reddened a little at the scorn expressed by the man from the Yard.

'Do you mean, sir, that you think Bryan is incompetent?' asked the inspector quietly.

'I do!' the commissioner snapped.

'Then you'd better take me off my beat.'

Bob spoke almost without thinking, his voice indignant, his eyes gleaming. The commissioner turned on him, and gazed at him a moment before he spoke.

'That is what I intend to do!' he snapped.

He bent over the desk, and studied a plan which lay there. It was covered with notes, and it had marked on it the various beats patrolled by all the police in Cursitor Fields.

'Inspector,' he said, 'put another man on Bryan's old beat, and put him out here by Swingletree Lane. Do that immediately—to-night!'

'Very good, sir!'

The inspector nodded, but he glanced sympathetically at Bob.

They all knew that the commissioner was a hard man. He believed that the reports he had read about the Phantom were exaggerated, and he had come down from the Yard determined to put an end to the ghost—if it was a ghost—which held all the old Fields in thrall.

There sounded a knock on the door in the silence which followed as the commissioner wrote a note on a slip of paper, ordering the change in Bob's beat. Then the door handle rattled, and a man entered.

He wore evening clothes, and he crossed with outstretched hand to the commissioner.

'You remember me, don't you?' he asked. 'I'm Leonard Snell—Sir Gordon Murgatroyd's nephew.'

'Of course I remember you!' the commissioner exclaimed. 'How are you? How's your uncle?'

'Pretty bad,' Snell answered, and went on: 'I heard that you were down here, and I wondered if you had any clue to this Phantom. My uncle appears to be terrified of it for some reason, and he—'

'The Phantom won't last much longer!' the commissioner broke in. 'I've just started making arrangements which will put that imitation ghost under lock and key in one of the cells here.'

Bob, standing stiffly by the desk, looked at the newcomer. He knew that Leonard Snell was heir to Sir Gordon Murgatroyd.

Snell was lean-faced, and his eyes were narrowed. He had thin lips, and there was something crafty in his expression. But the clothes he wore were perfect, and diamond studs winked with little points of fire in his white shirt fornt.

'I hope you'll keep that Phantom from my uncle's house,' Snell went on. 'If it does come our way, you'll have to give us extra protection.'

'Here's the constable whose beat runs past your uncle's house.' The commissioner nodded towards Bob. 'I'm putting him on the Swingletree Lane beat to-night, and—'

'Then you keep your eyes open, my man!' Snell turned to Bob. 'If you see the Phantom report it at once, so that we can have more police sent out.'

Snell's voice was arrogant and unpleasant. Bob would have answered him, but he remembered in time that he was only a police constable, and under strict discipline.

'All right, you can go, Bryan—and you, sergeant!'

The commissioner waved the two away, and Bob made for the door. Sergeant Cobb followed him out, and he caught Bob's arm when the door closed behind him.

'Don't take any notice of the commissioner,' he advised quietly. 'That's only his way. He doesn't really mean to be nasty.'

'He's taken me off my beat, and—' began Bob.

'You'll get your beat back as soon as he returns to the Yard,' the sergeant cut in. 'And you don't want to take any notice of Leonard Snell, either. He's just an upstart, that's all he is. And I bet if the truth was known his uncle isn't scared of the Phantom! It's him what's frightened!'

'Well, there won't be much chance of the Phantom coming near Swingletree Lane,' Bob said. 'It's never appeared anywhere except on my old beat.'

'You never know,' Sergeant Cobb told him. 'That thing's a mystery. It might show up anywhere.'

'If it shows up—' Bob broke off and looked through the window of the charge room out into the lamp-lit streets of Cursitor Fields, his eyes narrowing. 'If it shows up on my beat to-night,' he repeated, 'I'm just about in the mood to go for it single-handed!'

* * *

With rubber-shod boots Bob Bryan paced quietly down Swingletree Lane.

It was a narrow street, and at the far end of it he could see the ancient house which was the home of Sir Gordon Murgatroyd.

As he neared the end of the lane he saw that straw had been strewn along the private street outside Sir Gordon's big house.

That was because, in daytime, traffic rattled incessantly over the narrow cobbles. The rich man was ill and he needed quiet to restore him to health.

Bob stood looking at the great house before him, and at the yellow-lit windows. He wondered what it would be like to be as rich as Sir Gordon, owning almost half the Fields.

Bob decided that although he might have made use of the wealth he would not have cared to be in Sir Gordon's shoes. He was not much liked. He was said to be mean and grasping. Although he was old, and although all his money would eventually go to his nephew, he still made all the money that he could and drove very hard bargains.

Inside, Sir Gordon Murgatroyd leaned on a heavy ash stick. He had a silken dressing-gown flung about his shoulders as he reached a trembling hand towards the open door of a wall safe.

That hand clutched papers which crackled, because they were yellowed parchments half as old as the very walls around him.

He thrust the papers into the little safe, then closed the thick, rounded steel door, and jerked down the lever which locked it.

It was an effort for Sir Gordon. He was so ill that he could hardly stand, even with his stick, and it was a few moments before he could reach out to a secret spring in the panelled wall before him.

He pressed the spring, and at his touch a panel slid over the front of the safe, completely hiding it, so that no one would have known of the existence of the stout little strong-box.

Sir Gordon did not know that he was being watched. He did not know that a dark eye was gazing through the big keyhole to the massive door, and that his every movement was being noted.

Staggering, he made for his bed, flinging off the gown and dragging himself painfully between the sheets of silk. He pulled them up about his neck, then lay panting from his exertions.

Breathing heavily, ha lay with his head against the silken pillow. He had been cunning to get rid of his attendants, so that he could place the papers in the secret safe, and he was more contented now. He had kept the documents hidden all day beneath his pillow, fearful that they might be discovered through some mischance.

He looked around the room. The rich hangings to the windows had cost enough to keep a poor family in a corner of Cursitor Fields for a year. Everything about him was the best that money could buy, matched only by the other evidences of his wealth in that house.

But he knew that if the contents of those old parchments ever became known, he would lose all his riches.

Presently his breathing grew easier and his eyes closed. A long time passed. No sound came to him from the street outside, where Bob Bryan patiently paced his beat, looking for another sighting of the Phantom, and soon the old man sank to sleep.

The midnight hour was chimed in faint, silvery tones by a small clock in the room, and as the sound died away the handle of the door turned soundlessly, and Leonard Snell slipped in.

There was stealth in his every movement as he closed the door behind him, and paced slowly towards the bed.

'Uncle!'

His voice was barely a whisper, and he repeated the call a little louder.

The old man did not move, and a faint smile of satisfaction creased the lips of the rich man's heir when he saw how soundly the sick man slept. He looked around the room, then slipped his fingers into his waistcoat pocket and brought out a phial.

Its contents were colourless as water, and as dangerous as venom!

Snell's hands were trembling, and he had to grit his teeth to steel himslef to the work before him.

He looked at the sleeping man, and his lips tightened. Sir Gordon was old, and he had wealth, but he would part with none of it to his heir. Leonard Snell was menaced by a mountain of debts, and the contents of that phial could pave the way to his uncle's wealth.

He moved to a small table near the side of the bed. On it were bottles, and in a medicine glass Snell saw a dose already poured out, and he drew the glass stopper of the little phial.

No sound came into the room save that of his own laboured breathing. His heart seemed to beat high up in his throat, almost chokingly under the strain of what he now meant to do.

He poised the tilted phial, then grew rigid.

Something, he knew not what, drew his gaze.

He lifted his eyes, then started back in terror.

Silhouetted against the opening formed by a secret panel showed the Phantom! One gaunt white hand was outstretched, as though to stay the emptying of the poison phial which the young man held, and into the silence of the room came the spectre's wordless mumbling, menace in its notes.

The phial dropped from Snell's nerveless hand, and its contents spilled to the carpet and soaked away.

Spellbound, he saw the Phantom glide into the room. He saw it come towards him, and he could not take his gaze from the blue haze in which the glaring features hung!

The bed was between them, when suddenly the Phantom seemed to rise in the air.

It came towards him, appearing to hurl itself on.

Snell leaped back. His lips parted, and a cry of fear croaked in his throat, then—

The Phantom was on him!

Vapour surged in a haze before Snell's eyes, choking his mouth and nostrils, and bringing blackness to his brain, so that he sank to the floor, inert and unconscious.

The Phantom loomed above him, sable garments brushing the still figure. For a moment the grimacing features bent low, then, with a movement that was incredibly swift, the spectre swept across the room.

It approached the panelled wall, and a section of the panelling opened before it as one pallid hand touched the woodwork.

The huddled figure of the Phantom hunched before the rounded door of the little safe that was revealed. The utter silence of the room was broken by a click as the door flew open, and from the interior of the safe yellow parchments appeared in the Phantom's hands.

They vanished under the folds of the spectre's flowing cloak, then the safe door shut and the panel covered it.

The ghostly visitant glided towards the larger panel, and faded through it, just as a blue-clad figure hurled itself bodily through the bedroom window!

It came in with a wild crashing of broken glass. It was Bob, truncheon in hand!

He flung himself cross the room, only to see the secret panel close in his face!

He smashed on it with his truncheon, while Sir Gordon started up in bed and Leonard Snell stirred against the floor.

The narrow-eyed young man came to his feet, his senses suddenly cleared again, and stared blankly for a moment as Bob hammered on the panel.

The thudding of the truncheon echoed through the room, to be broken by a sudden shout from Snell.

'He's the Phantom! Uncle, ring for help! He knocked me out somehow—he came through a panel in the wall, and it's closed! He can't get back!

Bob spun to face him, staring.

'What are you talking about?' he gasped. 'I saw—'

'Commissioner Hayes said that the Phantom appeared only on your beat—and it's appeared here! You came in to steal —*you're the Phantom!*'

Snell panted the words at him, then leaped for the door, opening it to shout down the passage for help. His wild cries roused servants, and they came running, hurling themselves at the astounded Bob.

* * *

Bob Bryan stood in the charge-room at Cursitor Fields police station, with handcuffs on his wrists, and four constables guarding him.

Commissioner Hayes and the station inspector were facing him, Lionel Snell at their side. He had told how he had gone to see that his uncle was all right, when the Phantom had appeared, and, somehow, momentarily robbed him of his senses.

'When I came round Bryan was in the room, trying to get back through the panel. The window was smashed, but that was broken when I threw something at him when he first appeared, and before he knocked me out!' Snell lied.

'I see!' Commissioner Hayes' smile was very grim as he eyed Bob's manacled figure.

'I tell you that I was in front of the house when I saw the Phantom through the window!' Bob exclaimed. 'It was bending by the wall at one side. I jumped clean through the window at it, and Mr Snell was then lying on the floor!

'The Phantom disappeared through a panel! When I tried to follow, the panel closed, and—'

'You mean that you couldn't open it again!' Snell broke in. As he spoke the telephone bell rang. The inspector answered it, then passed the instrument to the commissioner. He took it and listened to the voice which came over the wire, answering briefly before he replaced the receiver.

He paused a moment, looking at Bob with his eyes half-closed, and his expression very dour.

'Search him!'

He snapped the order to Sergeant Cobb. As the burly police officer moved to obey, the commissioner spoke again.

'That telephone message was to tell me that some very important papers have been stolen from a small safe in Sir Gordon's room!' he said.

The contents of Bob's packets were placed on the desk, but the missing documents were not there.

'He's got rid of them, somehow!' Snell rasped.

'I tell you I jumped through that window into the room!' Bob exclaimed. 'I saw the Phantom! I don't know anything about any papers, and I—'

'Listen, Bryan,' said the commissioner, and he made his voice quiet. 'I suspected you from the moment I came down here! You are the Phantom—and you might as well confess to it and save us a lot of trouble.'

'If I'm the Phantom, then I must have knocked my own father down and got him turned out of the Force!' Bob exclaimed. 'If I—look there!'

His last words came in a shout, as he pointed to the window.

Beyond it was the darkness of the street—and against the darkness showed a blue haze. Through that haze appeared the grimacing features of the Phantom of Cursitor Fields!

It was looking in through the window at the grouped police, and every man of them heard its babbling, muffled by the panes.

Before any of them could move the glass was suddenly broken as if something was hurled through it—and with the breaking of the glass the ghostly figure vanished.

Through the shattered window something pitched to the floor, rolling to the commissioner's feet.

'Heavens, that was the Phantom!' he gasped. 'Outside—catch it!'

The sergeant led a rush to the doorway. He looked up and down the street with the others. They saw nothing. They made a swift search, only to return.

'If the Phantom was there, it's gone now', said the sergeant.

The commissioner stared at him, then stooped above the object which had fallen to the floor. It was a slip of parchment wprapped about a stone, and he smoothed the parchment out.

Strange blue lettering glowed against the yellowed strip:

'There is but one Phantom—not thy prisoner. Hys accuser would have taken the life of hys uncle. Y stayed hys hand. Seek ye poison phial by ye bed.'

While the commissioner was reading the words the lettering faded, and before his eyes the parchment grew blank.

He looked up, first at Bob, then at Leonard Snell. The commissioner was some time before he spoke.

'Take those handcuffs off Bryan,' he said at last. 'And, Mr Snell, will you wait a little while in the inspector's room?'

He moved to the door as he spoke coldly, and opened it. Snell unsuspectingly walked into the room, and the door closed behind him. The commissioner turned to the inspector.

'Come with me to Sir Gordon's house,' he said. 'Bryan, you will stay here.'

Fifteen minutes later, the commissioner was standing by Sir Gordon's bed with the glass phial in his hand.

After that he searched Leonard Snell's room, and there he found all the evidence that he wanted, to prove what Snell had attempted to do.

* * *

Dawn crept up from the east, up along the River Thames, and tinted London's rooftops.

The growing daylight lit the figure of Leonard Snell as he hurried through the streets with a bag in his hand. Sir Gordon had decided not to prosecute him, but he had turned his nephew out, and Snell was hurrying away for fear that the police might yet arrest him.

In the inspector's room at the station, Bob stood sriffly at attention before the commissioner.

'I'm sorry I ever doubted you, Bryan,' the man from the Yard was saying. 'You will go back on your old beat to-night!'

'Thank you, sir!' Bob answered.

'The Phantom is a greater mystery than ever,' the commissioner went on. 'It came back here to clear you—but it stole papers which Sir Gordon appeared to value. And ghosts don't steal documents!'

'This one does,' Bob said steadily.

'Then you stil believe it is a ghost?' asked the commissioner.

'I do,' Bob answered. 'I shall go on believing it—until I find out how bullets can be fired at it without hurting it!'

By the Ebony Door

All London and half England now knew of the terror which stalked by night through the centuries-old streets. Every paper in the country told of each fresh visitation and such few folk as actually lived in half-forgotten dwellings tucked away amongst the office buildings were careful to remain behind locked and barred doors when darkness had fallen.

But even Bob was uncertain whether the spectral form was a ghost or a rogue, although he had seen it many more times than anyone else had.

He stood now by the side door of Cursitor Museum. It was a big, black door made from solid ebony, and had come from the tropics as a present from some past councillor of the Fields.

At Bob's side was the night watchman from the museum, and the door stood open behind them. A nearby street lamp, clamped high on the face of a building, cast a pale light on a paper which Bob held.

'I thought this would interes you, Bob', the old watchman was saying. 'I was prowling about in the library after I came on duty, and I found it in there tucked away inside one of those old books piled up at the end. Somebody made the museum a present of 'em last week!'

Bob did not answer. The paper that he held was actually a parchment, and it bore a date of nearly three hundred years earlier. The parchment was yellow, but it was well preserved and the peculiar writing on it was plain enough, although it was a little difficult to read.

'We've got some old papers like this at the station,' Bob said, after a moment. 'I think I can read it!'

'It's about the Phantom, anyway!' said the museum watchman, as he pushed his peaked cap to the back of his head. 'That's as much as I could make out! So I kept it for you, your eyes being younger than mine!'

Bob raised his glance from the sheet, and looked up and down the narrow street. It was not far from Four Ways and the Cursitor Fields Police Station, and he did not fail to mark the fact that faint mist was drifting up.

His rugged, resolute features set grimly.

'Geting misty now,' he commented.

'Ay! Just the night for the Phantom to come again!' the old watchman answered comfortably, and he chuckled.

He knew that he would be safe behind locked doors, and he did not fear the spectre there.

'I wouldn't care to be you, out in the streets wi' that thing likely to pounce on ye! It's lucky you've got strong nerves, Bob!'

'It's shaken my nerves a few times,' Bob said, and tilted the parchment towards the light. He began to spell out the writing on it, word by word:

'Ye Freemen of Cursitor Fields—take Warning. There be about ye Fyldes a very dreadfulle spectre which do appeare before ye goode men and ye rogues alike. Some does it touch and upon them it leaves ye marke like unto a blue finger. Such as he so touched straitway wither and do pine, and no prayers be of avail. Take heede, guard well thy doores and shutter thy wyndows in ye dark hours and go not abroad in ye night.'

Bob looked up at the watchman. He had read the words aloud, and the man was staring at it.

'That's something new!' he breathed. 'I've heard that it leaves ghost writing, and now if it touches you——'

'There's no need to take any notice of an old paper like this!' Bob broke in grimly. 'It's probably just a yarn which got about at that time!'

He peered at the lettering again, but in that weak light he could not make out any more.

'I'll take this to the station with me and hand it in when I go off duty,' he said. 'I'll——'

Bob broke off.

Suddenly every nerve in his body went taut.

On the uncanny silence of the night he heard a sound and he met the watchman's gaze. They stared at one another, their eyes widening.

The sound was a strange, wordless mumbling—the weird murmuring of the Phantom of Cursitor Fields as it shifted through the night!

The sound came from behind them, and both turned.

In the passage beyond the heavy ebony door, there was a hazy blue glow out of the heart of which the face of the Phantom itself grimaced at them.

It was inside the museum, glaring at them, with its dark eyes glinting as they reflected the shimmering blue fire which marked out its terrible visage.

Bob jerked his policc whistle from his pocket and placed it to his lips. Its stirring call echoed again and again down the street, shrilling clearly on a strident note that reached the ears of the curious people who stood in the chilly darkness watching the Fields.

The blasts of the whistle set them all agog, craning to see what was going on, but not daring to set so much as a foot over the boundary of the Fields.

The answer to Bob's call for aid was immediate. The echoes were still dying away when a blue-clad figure appeared at one end of the street and came racing towards him, truncheon out.

Two more policemen appeared from the other end, and a fourth man darted from the gloom of a nearby alley. In a matter of seconds six of Bob's alert comrades were racing to the spot.

'The Phantom's got inside the museum somehow!' Bob exclaimed. 'One of you get help from the station. Two of you go around to the front and see that the Phantom doesn't get out that way. The rest of you help me—come on!'

He hurled his weight on the door, while three of his companions ran off to obey his quick orders. The three who were left joined with the watchman in charging at the door.

Dust and splinters flew upwards in a cloud, and Bob pitched headlong forward, all but falling. The three police with him stumbled and went down, while he jumped into the corridor beyond, and then pulled up.

Ahead of him was darkness, lit only by thin moonbeams which came through the leaded windows of the old museum.

Those beams made hazy white patches on the polished floor, and they vanished when he switched on the electric bulls-eye at his belt.

It sent a broad swathe of light down the corridor in front, gleaming on the metal of armoured figures at one side and on showcases full of curios.

He went forward slowly, truncheon in hand. He heard the policemen behind him get up, and the light of their torches came to join his own.

From the cobbled street outside now came the thud of booted feet, and then the hoarse voice of Sergeant Cobb, who had rushed up from the station.

'Spread out there—put a circle right around the place! Let nobody pass you!' Other shouts answered him, then the sergeant called: 'Where's Bob Bryan?'

'In here!' Bob checked and turned.

'All right, Bob!' The sergeant appeared in the smashed doorway. 'Can you see anything?'

'No, sergeant!' Bob replied.

'Six more men in here!' the sergeant ordered, and police crowded in at his heels. 'Four of you others stand guard at the door.'

He came forward to join Bob. Now the passage was full of police, while their torches made the place as bright as day.

'What happened?' asked Sergeant Cobb as he came to Bob's side.

Bob told him quickly what had occurred and he saw that the sergeant's face was grim.

'All right, then we'll search the whole museum. Lead the way, Bob, and the rest of you search every corner as you come to it—and don't forget to look inside those old suits of armour.'

Bob went on, leading the men, who came close at his heels. There was nothing in the passage in front, and the whole museum was strangely quiet, so that the shouts of the constables outside, as they took up position, sounded peculiarly loud.

They went on down the corridor until they came to the big hall behind the main entrance. From this, passages opened off and stairs led upwards.

'Wait a minute!' the sergeant called grimly. 'Now then, split up—search everywhere!'

Bob made for a short passage at one side. It was dark and his torch-beam split its gloom, revealing double doors at the far end, beyond which was the library.

He strode towards them and pushed them open—to see a blue haze in the darkness beyond. He stopped short.

Pallid moonbeams came down through a window at one side, and they caught the figure of the Phantom. It had turned as the library doors swung softly shut behind Bob.

He saw its sombre eyes, its stark-white features and grinning lips. He saw the sable shroud which cloaked it, and lean, bloodless hands which were pawing at the pile of old books from which the night watchman had obtained the parchment about the spectre.

The Phantom had turned at Bob's entry.

The young policeman saw that one hand gripped a little sheaf of papers which appeared to have been torn from inside the cover of one old tome, as though they had been secreted there.

Bob drew in his breath, and his grip tightened on his truncheon.

At last he was face to face with the spectre which had ruined his father. It could not escape him now. He moved forward, and as he did so the Phantom came to meet him.

Bent and crooked limbs appeared to trail over the floor as, with a sudden rush, it started towards Bob.

From its distorted lips there wakened that strange babbling, evil and menacing. It made no other sound as it slid though the moonbeams, mis-shapen and ugly—swooping at Bob.

His truncheon went back, and he braced his every muscle to meet its attack.

'Man or ghost, I'm not afraid of you!' Bob challenged, and brought the truncheon smashing down towards the evil head.

Even as he struck, the Phantom was on him.

He felt his descending arm seized in a clutch which was cold and clammy—and as strong as tensed steel!

His blow was stayed, and he felt the truncheon wrenched from his hand; then he was bent backwards as a second grip came at his neck.

The face of the Phantom loomed above him. Its wild mumbling drummed in his ears, while he struggled impotently against its superhuman clutch.

He was helpless, utterly at the spectre's mercy, and his nostrils were filled with the acrid reek of brimstone.

He strove to break free, but the spectre's grip tightened. The dark eyes blazed into his own, and he felt his senses reeling. He struck out with his hands, but they met only thin air.

There came a drumming in his ears, and through that he heard Sergeant Cobb's voice!

The sergeant had heard Bob's challenging cry, and three policemen came with him in a rush towards the library. They saw Bob bent, with the Phantom rearing above him, and at the sight of the wraith the sergeant hurled his truncheon.

It whizzed through the air, aimed full at the Phantom—but all that followed was the shattering of glass, as the weapon smashed a bookcase at the far side of the library!

The rushing police saw the Phantom rear up. They saw Bob slump to the ground, and then the spectre of the Fields was retreating from its victim, gliding across the floor to the darkness beneath a balcony which bulked from one wall.

The sergeant's companions hurled their truncheons—three weapons sang purposefully through the air as they whirled at the glowing, blue head!

The truncheons only struck the wall. The glass of a picture smashed, then came the haunting, cackling laugh of the Phantom as it vanished.

Every electric globe in the library was blazing light when Bob recovered. The sergeant helped him to his feet.

The library was full of police. The smashed bookcase and the shattered picture showed, with the fallen truncheons, where they had attacked.

On the floor near Bob were sheets of parchment, and he stared at them, his eyes widening.

'The Phantom dropped these!' he exclaimed. 'I saw it taking them out of one of those old books—they must have been dropped in the fight!'

'Are you sure you're all right?' the sergeant asked him. You had a nasty turn that time, and—look at your wrist!'

He pointed suddenly, his eyes dilated, and Bob looked at his wrist. Where the Phantom had gripped him there was a blue mark!

'The mark of the Phantom!'

The quavering voice of the museum watchman rose as he saw the imprint.

'Look—it's a blue finger-mark!'

Bob stared at the impress on his skin, and he remembered the words that he had read: 'Such as be so touched strait-way wither and do pine, and no prayers be of avail.'

He had to grit his teeth to check the sudden panic which rose within him. Supposing there should be something in what that old document said!

'You'd better get along to the station,' the sergeant said. 'I'll send a couple of men with you, and you'd better take these papers as well.'

He gathered them up, while Bob still gazed at the mark on his wrist. He pulled himself together when the sergeant turned and began to speak to him again.

'Here you are, Bob! Now, you get along and report all this, and then have a rest. I'll put another man on your beat.'

Bob moved for the door as the sergeant detailed two men to go with him, and soon the three were moving slowly down the street outside, walking through the tendrils of mist which twisted and broke before them.

In a little while, Bob saw the lights of the Cursitor Fields police station with two lorries outside, which had brought up a force of police reserves.

He entered the building and went straight to the inspector's room. He saluted the man at the desk as he entered, then standing at attention, made a swift report.

'The sergeant and the others came in time to rescue me,' Bob ended. 'But the Phantom left a mark on my wrist!'

'A mark?' The inspector leaned forward. 'Let's have a look at it.'

Bob pulled back the cuff of his tuncic, and held his arm forward. The inspector peered at it.

'Where's the mark?' he asked.

The blue imprint was no longer there!

Just for a moment, Bob said nothing as he gazed down at his wrist. When he did speak, his voice shook a little.

'There was a mark there, sir!' he said. 'The Phantom touched me—and it's supposed to put a blight on anyone it touched.'

He drew out the document which the night watchman had given him, and held it out. The inspector took it and read it slowly, then looked up.

'Don't take any notice of this, Bob', he said. 'It's only a yarn that was going about at the time this parchment was written.' He added: 'What's that you've got there?'

'Oh, these are the papers that the Phantom was trying to steal,' Bob replied. 'It dropped them in the struggle.'

He placed them on the desk, and the inspector glanced

quickly at the document, then smiled slowly.

'Well, my boy,' he said, 'you've had a nasty experience, but I think you've settled once and for all that the Phantom is not a ghost—but a criminal as solid as you or me!'

'What makes you think that, sir?' Bob asked :quietly.

'Well, if it's a ghost—it's the first ghost I've ever heard of that could shut a door in a policeman's face!'

The inspector chuckled a little, his gaze on Bob.

'And no ghost could master a strong young fellow like you!' the station-officer added. 'You're pretty fit, you know, and can give a good account of yourself!'

'Then why did the Phantom want the old papers he was trying to get? They were hidden in one of the old books there—and he must have known that!'

'Let's see what the papers are, first,' the inspector said.

Together they bent over them.

All were stiff parchments, so tightly folded that at first it was difficult to open them.

When at last the first one was opened and spread on the desk, they saw that it had a heavy red seal at one end.

The writing on it was black, and written in so crabbed a hand that they could barely make it out.

'Know all men by these presents that ye lands and all ye buildings bounded by ye Foure Ways and ye prison wall, unto ye Abbeye are in reality owned not by ye man who now controls them—but by a pauper called . . .' And at that point the ancient scrawl became even less distinct.

'Looks like something to do with some land!' the inspector exclaimed.

'It does, sir,' Bob agreed. 'Doesn't it strike you as queer that the Phantom has been trying to get hold of a lot of these old papers? Didn't take some from the Guildhall the other night—and from Mr Jolly, the warden of the Fields?'

'That only goes to prove what I've been saying.' The

inspector turned to him. 'The Phantom's a crook who's after something. A ghost wouldn't be interested in a lot of fusty old papers and—and—and——'

His voice trailed away as he saw Bob step back, his jaw dropping while he stared at the desk.

The inspector followed his gaze, then started from his chair.

Through the solid wall behind the desk had come a gnarled and pallid hand, hazed by faint blue fire.

Lean fingers were clutching the parchments which lay there; and while the two gazed the hand was withdrawn, vanishing through the wall and taking the documents with it.

'The hand of the Phantom!' Bob gasped.

Awed, rooted to the spot by sheer amazement, the two looked at the wall as solid now as it had been before the clutching fingers appeared.

'Heavens!' the inspector breathed.

'It came through the wall!' Bob panted. 'It—'

He broke off and leaped for the door, to plunge across the charge-room and gain the darkened street outside.

The window of the inspector's room flung a yellow glow across the cobbles, and its blank wall flanked the empty street.

While Bob gazed the inspector come out after him.

'There's nothing here!' Bob said.

'You're right; but that hand came through the wall!' the inspector gasped shakily. 'It took those paper—the Phantom took them!'

They looked at the wall. It was built from massive blocks of stone, enduring and solid, yet that ghostly hand had penetrated them, taking what it sought and vanishing again.

'Will you—will you believe that it's a ghost now?' Bob asked.

The inspector paused, and gave Bob a knowing glance.

'Nothing human could have done that!' the inspector replied.

The Rack Room

A single electric bulb glowed in the old library of Cursitor Museum, but it was enough for the work that Bob Bryan had to do.

It was close upon nine o'clock, and in a little while he would have to report to the police station for night duty. In the meantime, he was seeking for something which would give him a clue to the nature of the uncanny spectre and what it was searching for.

The library was fairly large, and it looked larger still, because the single light flung corners and walls itno shadow, so that it was hard to tell just how large the room might be.

Bob was working in a corner, his broad shoulders hunched a little. He looked very trim and smart in his police uniform, and his rugged features were set.

On a shelf before him were a dozen old books. They were bound in musty, scarred leather, and their pages were printed in very heavy, awkward type. All the books were ancient tomes, and Bob was examining them very closely.

The last tome was bigger than the others, and its leather-padded covers were very thick. He opened the book, gazing at the black type on the pages, then looked closely at the cover.

He drew out a penknife and raised the canvas at one corner. Beneath he saw a clear gap, and in this gap he just sighted a yellowed corner of a parchment.

'Bob's heart leaped. He had been hoping to discover something like this, and his knife blade went to work to strip off the canvas, laying the whole gap bare. It was then that he found that the book cover was actually padded by a long, folded sheet of parchment.

Carefully he drew out the parchment. It crackled as he unfolded it gently, then straightened it out. It had been well preserved when it was hidden away in the covers of the old book, and the writing on it was clear.

The document had been written with a quill pen, which made odd, heavy letters. But Bob could read them easily enough:

'Since I, Thomas Strongi'th'arm, am nigh to my last long rest, I have sett downe what is known to me of ye Phantom, which I did see many times, and of which I was betimes mightily afeared.'

Bob drew a deep breath as he read that first paragraph, and he tilted the sheet so that the light fell more strongly on it.

'Since I have belief that ghostes and such cannot be, I, meeting ye Phantom by chance, did dare tarry after it, following it from ye Foure Ways.

'That which I founde, I have set down and hidden secretly away in a certain place, for th' knowledge is very dreadfulle.

'Anny who read this and desire to learne of ye Phantom of ye Fyldes should go to ye Dower House, and to ye upper floor and ye Rack Room.

'There in ye Rack Room is a very secret place in ye empty walle. It is revealed if——'

Bob read no more than that. He had been intent upon the strange paper, concentrated on it, but now his very heart seemed to stand still as a hand came over his shoulder.

It was a pallid, dead-white hand, with gnarled and bony fingers!

That hand gleamed with a very faint blue, and the fingers clutched at the document and snatched it clear.

Bob spun in his seat.

The Phantom was towering behind him!

He saw its livid face and smouldering eyes. He saw filmy, black garments which appeared to merge with the shadows, and he heard the mumbling of the grinning lips.

He saw the document clutched in the spectre's hand, while it backed away across the library floor.

Rooted to the spot Bob stared, watching the bent and shambling shape with staring eyes. He saw the Phantom near the opposite wall and only then did Bob recover himself.

He slid off his chair and fairly hurled himself across the polished floor. He saw the Phantom against the wall, its blue-tinged features glowering at him—and, fearlessly, the young policeman dashed at it.

His hands were outstretched to grip it—when the Phantom vanished and Bob dashed into the solid wall of the room!

He reeled back, half stunned, shouting for help. While he still staggered the voice of the night watchman answered him, and a moment later the man ran into the room, switching on all the lights.

A little dazed, breathless from his headlong contact with the wall, Bob stared at the place where the Phantom had disappeared.

There was no longer anything to be seen, save the solid stone wall through which the spectre had gone.

Bob drew his truncheon and hammered on it, searching for some hollow place which would hint at a secret entrance. He found nothing.

The Phantom of Cursitor Fields had come out of thin air and had faded away through a wall that was as unyielding as living rock. And it had taken with it a document which, had Bob read all, might have taken him far to learning the secret of the spectre.

Bob did not remain long in the library. He was still a little dizzy and shaken while he examined the wall, but by the time he came to the conclusion that it held no secret exit, he had recovered himself.

He stood, thinking quickly and trying to remember the words that he had read in the strange black writing.

'Dower House—the Rack Room—on the upper floor!' he reminded himself and turned to the night watchman.

'Where's the Dower House?' he asked.

'Never 'eard of it!' the man answered.

'Then how can I find out?' Bob said tensely. 'I've got to—'

He broke off.

He remembered then that at the Cursitor Fields Police Station there was a whole pile of old plans and papers. They had been gathered by detectives, who were following up a theory that the Phantom was nothing more than some clever crook.

With a hasty word to the watchman Bob hurried out of the library, running down a corridor to a side exit, which took him out to a narrow street.

He wondered what the document meant by 'ye empty walle', but that was a lesser problem which would probably be solved if he could find the Dower House first.

That place held some great secret about the Phantom, and it offered the biggest chance Bob had yet had of getting a real clue to the great mystery.

He slid around a corner and raced on into a narrow alley. He tore down it, to burts out into a street which led him direct to Four Ways, and from there he could see the blue lamp of the police station.

Less than thirty seconds later he was leaping up the steps into the charge-room. Already some of the night-duty constables were there; they and the sergeant-in-charge stared blankly as Bob hurled himself across the floor and rapped on the inspector's door.

He did not wait for permission to enter, but thrust the door open and crossed the threshold, slamming the door behind him.

From his desk the inspector looked up in astonishment, then jerked to his feet as he saw Bob's face and his flashing eyes.

'I've just seen the Phantom again, sir!' Bob exclaimed, as he saluted. 'It was in the museum library!'

Words jerked from his lips, while he still panted for breath, telling his story of what had occurred.

'So if we can locate the Dower House and the Rack Room,' Bob ended, 'we may learn something useful, sir. I thought it might be marked on the plans here!'

'Have a look at them.'

The inspector slipped out of his chair and reached for a thick sheaf of plans which lay on a shelf near at hand. All were old; some showed details of houses and others showed open spaces which had since been built over. On some were marked little streams which had once burbled through the fields on their way to the Thames; now those streams ran through pipes underground and reached the great river unnoticed.

For minutes the two searched the plans, finding nothing about the Dower House; then the inspector suddenly gripped Bob's arm.

'What about old Harry Shore?' he asked suddenly. 'He'll know that house, if anybody does. I'll send a man for him!'

The inspector dashed from the room and some ten minutes later there came a gentle tap on the door and an old man entered. He had a grey beard and very kindly eyes, which were almost china-blue. His clothes were old, and he had the bent shoulders of a student.

He bowed to the inspector, then to Bob.

'I had a message asking me to come,' he said.

His voice was clear and quiet, and Bob smiled when he saw the man. He knew that old Harry Shore lived in a funny little house, which consisted of but two rooms. It was jammed away in the angle of a court, and very few had ever been inside the house.

The old man knew more about London than anyone living. All his life he had studied it, until the very cobbles in the roads had stories to tell him of peoples and events long past.

'We want your help, Mr Shore,' the inspector said. 'Have you ever heard of the Dower House?'

'And the Rack Room?' Bob cut in.

'The Rack Room?' the old man repeated. 'Why, yes, I have heard of it. That's where they used to make racks in the old days; they used to put prisoners on them to make them talk! In the Tower dungeons, they show you the marks left where a rack was screwed to the floor, and that very rack was made in the Rack Room!'

'And you know Dower House?' the inspector asked.

'Yes, but it isn't called by that name now,' came the reply. 'It must be close on five hundred years old, that houes. It's got solid stone foundations, but the rest of it is timber. A fine old house, inspector—one of the oldest in all London, and it—'

'Where is it?' Bob asked.

'It's in Vine Walk,' old Harry Shore replied. 'You know where the Warden's House is? Well, it runs behind that, does Vine Walk, and the Dower House is right there in the middle! But now they call it Rack House, and—'

'Rack House!' Bob exclaimed. 'Why didn't we guess it, inspector? If they make racks there, that's what it would be called, and——'

He broke off.

Into the room came the clanging, stirring sound of a fire-engine's bell, rapidly rushing towards them. And like an echo to it came the sound of other engines, speeding through the narrow streets.

'There's a fire somewhere!' the inspector exclaimed.

While Bob gazed from the window the telephone bell jangled, and the inspector snatched at the receiver.

'Yes?' he called. 'What? What's that you say? Rack House in Vine Walk is on fire?'

He slammed the receiver down, and stared at Bob.

'Did you hear that?' the inspector gasped. 'That house is on fire—burning like tinder!'

'And the Phantom is the one who set it alight!'

Bob panted the words, and went for the door in a single leap. The Phantom had forestalled him again! He had set the building ablaze that the secret which it contained might never be revealed.

Bob made straight for the street, just as a fire-engine hurtled past. He ran as he had never run before. Soon he could see the old Dower House. It was broad fronted, and from every window of the lower floors, flame licked and fumed.

Bob ran on. He saw firemen dragging lengths of hose and others braced on the pavement of Vine Walk, while they sent solid founts of water in through windows from which the glass had long since vanished.

He could see that it was impossible to get into the place. The lower floors had already collapsed, and the stairs would be an inferno of flame.

While he ran, he saw a scaling-ladder which had been tossed off an engine. It was fairly long, and as he saw it an idea came to him. If he could carry it to the top of the fire-escape, he might be able to use it as a kind of bridge from the escape to a window of the Rack Room!

If he could to that, he might yet defeat the Phantom's purpose—because Bob was certain that the fire had been started by the spectre of the Fields.

With no thought of the risk, Bob snatched up the ladder and ran on. He was close behind the group of firemen when they stopped the escape, and the heat from the burning building came at him like something solid.

Up and up the escape he went, gasping under the strain. The slender escape shook and shuddered under his feet, while two firemen raced after him from below, shouting.

Bob neared the top of the escape, and now he could look into the Rack Room. It was immediately beneath the roof, which was already alight farther along.

The door to the room was open, and he saw that the chamber was utterly bare. Light from the fire within the house lit the apartment, and smoke was streaking through the old, broken floor-boards.

With a last effort, Bob hauled himself to the topmost rung of the escape, then lifted the scalling-ladder. It needed all his strength to thrust in forward through mid-air until its farther end rested against a sill of one of the windows of the big Rack Room.

He dropped the nearer end of the ladder to the head of the quivering escape, thus forming a bridge to the ancient house.

He felt the escape shuddering as the two firemen dashed up it in an effort to stop him, because they could read his intention.

But Bob was on the scaling-ladder by the time that the leading fireman gained the top, and the man could then do no more than steady the frail bridge for the intrepid young policeman.

Half-crawling, Bob moved forward. Faces were upturned below as firemen watched him, half-hidden by flames and smoke which surged upwards in great swirling clouds.

Bob felt the ladder quaking beneath him, and he went forward at half a crawl. He was midway over the bridge when he looked ahead and saw something which almost made him lose his balance.

From the smoke-shrouded window of the burning building the Phantom itself was leaning, gesticulating for Bob to go back. Bob stared at the livid, evilly-grinning face of the spectre; then he went on, half-running over the slender bridge, daring everything in his eagerness to come to grips with the terror of the Fields!

The ladder shook and trembled under Bob's feet. He saw

No 'Phantom' would stop Bob Bryan now

the Phantom draw back as he came; then with a last, reckless leap, Bob hurled himself in through the open window—just as the scaling-ladder slid off the sill and went crashing into the smoky depths below.

Bob landed on the floor, and as he slithered, he saw the Phantom leap at him. The room was choked with smoke, the wild crackling of burning woodwork filled it with sound, but above all this he heard the spectre's wordless babbling.

He ducked aside, only for a steely grip to fasten on one shoulder. Bob was jerked around. He saw the awful face leering at him; then came a blow which numbed his very brain and sent him slumping to the floor.

Half senseless, he lay there. He was conscious of acrid smoke in his eyes and nostrils, but his brain was spinning and it was some moments before he could make any effort to get up.

When he did come to his knees, he saw the Phantom bending close against the floor. In a glance Bob saw that at one side was a door, apposite was a window, and behind him was the fire-grate—and that the Phantom was bent by a blank wall. The 'empty wall' of the old document!

It was the hiding place of the secret!

Thought of that lent Bob strength, and he forced himself to his feet, then lurched across the room in a staggering run.

The Phantom straightened. In his hand Bob glimpsed a square of paper which might have been an envelope bearing a purple seal. The spectre had taken it from a hole at the bottom of the wall, and Bob heard the black-garbed wraith snarl as it faced him.

It seemed to rise above him. Bob saw a pallid hand swooping down, bearing some weapon; then a second smashing blow caught him.

Bob crumbled up, pitching backwards to the floor.

The firemen on the escape saw the Phantom move away.

It merged with the smoke that was flooding the room—and vanished. They were just in time to see the floor of the Rack Room collapse!

It dropped in a smother of fire. Sparks volleyed outwards in furious clouds, and while the sound of the falling floor still roared on the night—while the two firemen imagined that Bob had gone to his doom in the heart of the blaze—there came a cheer from below.

The cheer grew. A dozen hands pointed out a figure on the roof. It was climbing over the slates, through which the smoke spurted and flames licked, making for safety—and bearing a form in police uniform with it.

Firemen stared. Those on adjoining buildings rigged scaling and hook ladders and in a very few moments the two were safe.

Only then did anyone recognise Bob—and Mr Jolly, the Warden of the Fields. Bob was still unconscious, and the warden had rescued him!

'My house is at the back,' Mr Jolly panted—'I saw the fire—and I saw the Phantom! It was moving along the roof at the back, and I followed it. The fire wasn't at the top of the house then, and I saw it get down through a skylight.

'When I looked through, I saw it in that room, attacking Bob. I saw Bob fall, and I ran down to his aid. But when I got to the room the Phantom had gone. The room was afire then, and all I could do was to carry Bob up through the skylight. Where the Phantom went to, I don't know!'

Bob was borne to the ground on the shoulders of one of the fire-fighters. In a little while he came round. He was scorched, but not much hurt, and when he discovered how he had been rescued he grasped the warden's hand.

'Don't try to thank me, Bob,' the warden said.

'But for you, I might have been—in that!'

Bob looked to where the burnt-out hulk of the old house

showed. The firemen had kept the blaze from spreading, but hoses were still working.

'The Phantom started it,' Bob added.

'I guessed as much!' the warden said.

'The Phantom wanted to hide a secret that was there,' Bob went on. 'It has beaten us again. If we listen, we'll hear it laughing at us. It always does!'

They listened. But no cackling laughter came.

'Do you think that the Phantom was caught in the fire?' Mr Jolly asked slowly.

'No.' Bob shook his head. 'If bullets can't hurt it, and if it can get through stone walls, fire will make no difference to it, sir.'

He stared at the burnt-out building. When he spoke again his voice was tense.

'But I won't give up until I've caught it, sir! Some day I'll get my chance, and then we'll know whether the Phantom is human, or really a ghost!'

The Phantom Laughs Again

'We've got to set a trap for the Phantom!'

The inspector in charge of the Cursitor Fields Police Station intoned the words grimly as he leaned across his desk.

'I don't see how it is possible to lay a trap for a ghost!'

It was the Warden of the Fields who spoke then, Mr Joseph Jolly.

'That is, if it is a ghost!' Mr Jolly added.

'I shouldn't like to say what it is,' observed Bob, glancing at Sergeant Cobb, standing at his side.

'You can set all the traps you like, but you won't catch it!' the sergeant growled. 'The Phantom seems to know what we're going to do as soon as we know it ourselves. It wouldn't surprise me if it was listenin' to us now!'

He glanced uneasily around him as he spoke.

The inspector had called Bob and the sergeant to the station that afternoon to talk things over. Detectives from Scotland Yard, special investigators and men from great ghost-hunting societies had all failed to catch the ghost.

Bob smiled a little, and glanced at Mr Jolly.

'You'd better keep indoors then tonight, sir,' he said.

'I've got to be out at a dinner party,' the warden said. 'But I'll be all right, Bob—not that I want to meet the Phantom, though!'

After a moment, he turned to the inspector. 'Well, you've got us all here for something, haven't you?' he adked. 'Bob and the sergeant ought to be asleep at home, getting ready for night duty instead of——'

'I wanted them here,' the inspector cut in, 'because we've unearthed another of these documents about the Phantom. This was found among the foundations of those old places on Sir Gordon Murgatroyd's ground.'

He lifted from his desk a big, creased square of vellum, yellowed from age. It was covered with spidery writing, the letters of which seemed to run into one another.

'This was written a couple of hundred years ago,' the inspector went on. 'It's difficult to read, but, fortunately the museum people made a transcription of it, and I've got a typewritten copy here.'

He raised a second sheet, on which were close-set words.

'That ought to be interesting,' Mr Jolly commented as he bent forward.

'It's this that put the idea of a trap into my head,' the inspector daid. 'I'll read it to you!'

He laid the vellum adide and lifted the typescript. He was a few moments before he started to read, then his words came clearly:

'This is set down by Peterkin Marr, volunteer of the watch which guards the Fields at nights against the Phantom.

'Many have been made much afeared by this wicked ghost, and we did try to catch it with nets. Twenty men with five nets did hide themselves at Four Ways against the coming of the Phantom.

'Twice did we hide, and on the night of St John's Eve, it did come again and we ensnared it with our nets. It did struggle and did scream and did fight dreadfully, but the Phantom could not escape.

'When we could approach and it was still, we did see that within the nets lay one Mark Tralee, a cobbler, whom all men then believed to have dressed as the Phantom that he might steal.

'Tralee was put on trial and sentenced, and at noon the next day he went to the gallows tree, and did hang there in chains. And all folk made merry, believing that the Phantom was ended.

'Before he died, Tralee said he knew naught, and that he had been peacefully in bed, but awakened to find himself in the net, carried there by some mystery of the Phantom. But the judges scoffed at him.

'The folk made merry after dark and stayed abroad in the streets and danced about the gallows tree. Mist came up from the river, and out of the mist the Phantom did appear again.

'It mumbled and laughed, and the folk were afraid, and ran to their houses.

'So men now believe that Mark Tralee spoke truly, and nore dare attempt to catch the Phantom for dread it steal some other poor man from his bed, to suffer for the crimes of the spectre.

'The Phantom comes still and all are much afeared.'

When he had finished reading the typescript, the inspector

looked up at the three before him, then spoke quietly:

'So, from that we see that an attempt was once made to catch the Phantom with nets. When caught, in some mysterious way, it placed an innocent man in its stead, and then appeared again after the man had been hung.'

'That's just an old legend!' Mr Jolly exclaimed. 'It's not much good taking any notice of that, inspector!'

'I think it is,' the police officer answered slowly. 'You see, all the Yard men insist that the Phantom is some crook playing tricks on us, and that we ought to catch him. I propose to use nets, and try to trap the ghost—if ghost it be! If it swings a trick on us like the Phantom is said to have done in this document, we shall be able to investigate further. And if the nets actually trap the Phantom, we shall then——'

'But the Phantom will only vanish out of the nets,' Mr Jolly exclaimed.

'I've seen it vanish!' Sergeant Cobb said.

'So have I!' Bob added quietly.

'If it's really the Phantom, it will probably vanish—and then we'll know we're dealing with a real ghost,' said the inspector. 'But if we do actually catch it, then we'll know that it isn't a ghost, but a crook, as the Yard people insist.'

'Well, I'll admit it may be worth trying,' Mr Jolly observed, after a moment. 'When are you going to do it?'

'On St John's Eve,' the inspector said.

'When is that?' asked Bob.

The inspector glanced at him, a faint smile playing around his lips.

'St John's Eve is to-night,' he said.

* * *

Moonbeams struck down from a clear sky, flinging black shadows from the buildings in Cursitor Fields, tinting the roofs to silver, and flooding the streets with misted light.

Thin fog was rolling up from the Thames. It ran through the streets in wavering streamers, or curled and twisted on the air, clinging to the cobbled roadways and sweeping along the house fronts.

In the market place thirty police were on duty. Some stood hidden in doorways, and some were crouched on roofs, clinging to the gables and keeping in the shadows.

Here and there the moonlight caught wires strung through the air; as slender as the threads in a spider's web, they seemed. Some of those wires ran from the ground to roofs, others crossed over the entrance to courts and alleys which opened off the square.

Sometimes on the roof, sometimes in the deep shadow at the foot of a building were long rolled bundles. They were stout nets, rushed up from the mouth of the Thames to Cursitor Fields. The wires were a clever system by which the nets could be opened and spread in a twinkling, covering all exits from the square.

Bob stood in the Guildhall doorway, his police whistle ready to his hand. On a roof opposite the inspector was hidden and at another side of the one-time market place Sergeant Cobb watched.

When either of their whistles sounded, all nets were to come into action. If all went well, and if the Phantom showed on this square so near to Four Ways—then the spectre was caught. Nothing living could escape those nets when they were opened and held in position by a score and a half of special duty policemen.

Midnight chimed. Bob heard the cracked bell in the nearby church toll the strokes, and silence settled again as the last note died away.

In a few moments that silence was broken again by a murmuring which seemed to come from the roof above, and, in an instant, Bob felt a change in the atmosphere in the square; it became tense, electric.

Then he saw a figure sidle into the square from a court quite near him.

'The Phantom!'

Bob heard a choking gasp come from a constable who stood near him.

Across the breadth of the square, clear to the ears of the waiting police, came the mumbling which always marked the presence of the uncanny visitant to Cursitor Fields. Bob heard it as a wordless jabbering, and he saw the spectre's flaccid lips move.

Its eyes were dark and blazing, seeming to reflect the unnatural fire which rimmed them. The spectre shambled clear of the court entrance—then came the shrill blast of the superintendent's whistle.

It wakened wild echoes on the night, sounding again and again. It made the very air strum, and in all directions hiding men leaped into visibility.

The great close-meshed nets sung as they streaked along the jerking wires. Massive bundles pitched off roofs and unrolled as they fell, and in a moment the Phantom was surrounded, while from the roof above where he stood, a great mass of netting swooped outwards to envelop him.

The spectre's retreat was cut off. From everywhere police were running, closing in and dragging nets with them.

The Phantom was trapped. It could not escape.

Bob jumped from the doorway. For a moment he thought that the dropping net would catch the Phantom squarely, then the weird figure slid sideways, missing the meshes as they fell.

With incredible swiftness the spectre darted towards the Guildhall, making for where Bob himself stood. He jumped out drawing his truncheon and rushing to meet it.

Whistles were sounding now, and men were shouting above the sound of rushing feet.—Through all this Bob heard the Phantom's babbling. It was almost an angry screech.

Careless of what might happen, he hurled himself forward—only for the Phantom to sweep aside. It missed a trailing end of net, and then travelled in a floating leap at the front of the Guildhall.

To Bob's amazed eyes the very stones opened to receive it. He saw the ancient masonry part, to make an opening through which the spectre slid.

Bob spun as the Phantom stepped into the orifice, then fairly flung himself towards the gap. Reckless of the result, the young policeman plunged through—only to miss his footing and go headlong down steps which lay beyond.

He landed on stone flooring and came to a slithering halt. There was a light in his eyes, and he saw that it came from an old lamp hanging from the roof. All about were arches, and he realized that he was in a vault of the Guildhall, entered by a secret panel above.

Then he saw the Phantom again. It was crouched and glaring at him from a couple of paces away, while beyond it was a great wooden door leading to the steps down which Bob had just fallen.

Bob heaved himself upright, but before he could get to his feet, the spectre appeared to rear up. Its babbling rose to a fiendish scream, then came a blow which felled Bob again.

His very brain seemed to split, his head was reeling and he fell. But for all his hurt, he heard footsteps on the stairs outside.

Police were coming to his aid, and as they leaped down the Phantom jumped at the wooden door, flinging it shut; but not before brawny shoulders came at it from the other side.

Babbling fiendishly, the Phantom strove to close the door, while stalwart policemen charged it again and again in an effort to force an entrance and come to Bob's aid.

More police came to the help of those who had first arrived, and suddenly the Phantom leaped back.

Bob saw it floating up the steps and he was the first to pursue it.

He saw the Phantom dart through the opening in the wall above, making for the square again, only to run full tilt into a net which had been stretched out over the cavity.

'It's caught!'

The wild shout came from outside. Bob saw the Phantom running forward, clawing at the net with its hands, striving it seemed to tear the meshes away.

Then a second net swooped down and after that came a third.

They fell squarely over the struggling, babbling figure. Then came more and more nets, hauled taut by men in blue until the form of the Phantom was lost in a mass of netting, until the mad struggling and the uncanny babbling checked and the mass lay still.

'Got it at last!'

Bob heard the inspector's voice. The officer was pale, and at his heels was Sergeant Cobb who had also lost his colour.

'Some of you stand by with fresh nets!' the inspector called. 'The rest of you start to unroll those, and go steadily. Start now!'

The nets were dragged carefully away, while every man watched tensely, his heart almost standing still. Net after net was cleared, but still there came no struggle from the Phantom.

Bob saw a dark mass wrapped in the heart of the last net, and he moved closer with the rest as the meshes were pulled away.

'He's knocked out!' the inspector muttered, and bent with Bob over the figure.

At the same moment, the policemen flung themselves at the Phantom

Moonlight flooded clearly down, catching the mist as it wreathed quietly over the scene. Tendrils of it were wafted on the night air across the prostrate form as the two bent yet closer.

The inspector started back.

'It's Mr Jolly!' he gasped.

It was the warden who lay there, clad in evening clothes, and with an opera hat on his head. The old-fashioned cloak which he always wore revealed his white shirt front—as white almost as his face.

'He's the Phantom!' the inspector exclaimed.

'He hasn't got the face of the Phantom,' Bob answered. 'And remember what that document said: When it was caught, the Phantom made a man take its place in the net.'

* * *

Mr Jolly sat on a chair against the wall in the inspector's room at the police station.

His normally ruddy face was still pale, and his hands shook, while he gazed around him in a bewildered way.

Bob and the inspector and Sergeant Cobb were facing him, and the room behind was full of police, while others were out in the charge-room.

Somehow the news had spread that the Phantom had been caught. Reporters were on the scene, and they had taken pictures of the warden as he sat there.

'I tell you you're making a terrible mistake!' Mr Jolly breathed.

'Mistake or not, you'll have to stay here, sir, until we get detectives down from the Yard,' the inspector told him. 'Then you can explain things to them. They're coming in a Flying Squad car, and they'll be here shortly.'

'But I have explained,' Mr Jolly answered. 'I was at home.

Then I found myself in the market place, coming round, with you all saying that I was the Phantom. It's absolutely ridiculous!'

'All I know is that we flung nets over the Phantom and caught you,' the inspector told him grimly.

'Inspector—' Bob stepped forward—'you haven't forgotten what you read from that paper this afternoon, have you? Two hundred years ago they hanged a man in chains bacause he was caught like this, only to find out that they'd made a mistake!'

'I haven't forgotten,' the inspector answered quietly. 'But this has got to be investigated. If it had been the real Phantom it could have vanished down in that crypt. But it didn't. It tried to get away, and we caught Mr Jolly.'

Silence followed his words. The warden looked around the room, bewilderment still in his eyes.

'I don't understand,' he muttered. 'I got home tired, and I may have dozed off in the chair by my desk. They'd left some coffee for me, and I'd been drinking it. Then—then all this happened.'

Quiet fell on the room, save for the buzz of excited comment from the special duty police packed in the charge-room outside.

'What's happened to the lights?' somebody suddenly yelled.

Every light in the station was growing dim, and as they faded to sudden darkness Bob saw a blue glow come from where Mr Jolly sat. It hardened, and in its heart grimacing features appeared.

'The Phantom!' Bob yelled.

He saw the face; he saw the glaring eyes; and he heard its babbling grow loud, to be succeeded by a cackling, jeering laugh.

'Get a light! Somebody switch on a torch!'

The superintendent roared the words and his voice was almost drowned by the laughter of the Phantom; then its face began to fade.

'Catch it!' the inspector shouted wildly.

'At it, Bob!'

Sergeant Cobb bellowed the order; and Bob flung himself forward at his side. Several policemen charged over the floor at the same moment, as the Phantom's laughter died.

They all hurled themselves through the darkness to where the wraith had been but a moment before—and their groping hands came into contact only with the solid stone wall which formed the side of the room.

While they floundered there, the lights began to come on again, rising swiftly to their old brilliance.

The Phantom had gone!

The chair in which Mr Jolly had sat was empty. The warden had vanished, too!

'The windows! Get outside—search the street!' The superintendent snapped crisp orders. 'Jolly can't have got far away!'

'He's vanished, sir!' Bob turned on him. 'We've seen the Phantom in this room before! It's—'

'Rot!' the superintendent half snarled, while constables rushed to obey his orders. 'He can't have got away!'

'You don't know what's been happening here!' Bob snatched the typewritten sheet, which still lay on the inspector's desk. 'Read that, sir!'

He thrust the paper into the superintendent's hand; and, in spite of himself, the high official glanced at the words and then read them.

'Do you seriously mean to suggest that the Phantom put this man in his place, and has now spirited him away again!' he demanded. 'That's nonsense!'

'When you've been working around Four Ways and have

seen the Phantom as often as I have, you won't say it's nonsense,' Bob answered. 'And if you want to know where Mr Jolly is, I can tell you.'

'What do you mean?' the superintendent glared at him.

'The Phantom's put him back where he got him from—in his home!' Bob said.

'What!'

The superintendent, the inspector and Sergeant Cobb all stared at him.

'Well, the warden isn't here, is he?' Bob asked. 'And he couldn't have got out. And who turned off the electric lights? How did that happen?'

'A momentary failure at the power station,' the superindendent said.

'It was funny that it should come just when the Phantom showed himself, wasn't it?' Bob exclaimed. 'It came to get Mr Jolly back, because it didn't want him accused. I've seen the Phantom do some good deeds as well as bad ones, sir.'

The superintendent drew in his breath, then turned as the inspector spoke.

'There may be something in what Bryan says, sir,' the station officer observed. 'It can't do any harm to go to Mr Jolly's place and find out.'

At that moment one of the detectives returned.

'There's nothing to be seen outside, sir,' he reported. 'All the windows are shut and locked, and nobody could have got out of the door with all the men in the way.'

'There's no one in the street?' the official asked.

'Not a soul, except our own men, sir,' came the answer.

'Well, this is a mystery if you like!' the superintendent said. 'All right, inspector,we'll take six men and go to the warden's house and see what we can find there. Hurry up!'

Half a minute later Bob marched out of the police station,

heading a file of six constables. With him came the three detectives, the superintendent and the inspector, as well as Sergeant Cobb.

Of all the things which had happened in the Fields since the appearance of the Phantom, it seemed to Bob that this was the most amazing.

He had seen bullets pass harmlessly through the spectre, but he had not thought it possible that the Phantom could change itself at will into the form of a living man.

Yet that was what it had done. And it had faded from a room before his very eyes—taking with it the form of its victim!

Bob hurried with the rest until they turned the corner into a broad passage which had no roadway. It was the thoroughfare in which Mr Jolly lived.

Steps led up to Mr Jolly's doorway, and against the door at the top, something glowed with a faint, luminous blue.

'It's the Phantom again!' one of the detectives shouted.

'It isn't!' Bob answered and jumped ahead of the rest, peering through the darkness. 'It's ghost-writing—on the door!'

The rest crowded forward at his heels . . . and now they saw the lettering clearly. Through the gloom glowed the fiery message from the Phantom:

'I see all
I know all
I laugh at thy snares!'

'It's been here!' Bob exclaimed, then leaped up the steps. He drew out his torch as he searched for the handle of the door and flung it open.

The light from the torch showed him the little office which the warden used, and Bob sought the electric light switch, pressing it, and flooding the room with the glow of electric bulbs.

There was nothing to be seen, and no sign of Mr Jolly.

'He's not here!' the superintendent said.

'There's another door opposite.'

Bob pointed and crossed the floor. He knew that this other door led to the warden's own rooms, and he thrust the door open. He felt for the switch near the door-post and clicked it down. The lights came on, and the men crowding behind Bob caught their breath.

In a chair by a little table was slumped the unconscious figure of Mr Jolly.

His chin was on his chest, and his eyes were closed. In front of him were sandwiches on a plate and a cup of coffee half-filled.

'There he is!'

Bob breathed the words as he leaped to the warden's side. The rest came after him, gathering around the chair.

'Mr Jolly!' Bob shook the unconscious man; and Mr. Jolly's head rolled against his shoulders. 'We'd better try to lay him on that couch over there,' Bob went on. 'Get some water, somebody!'

The warden was raised and stretched out on the couch. Water was splashed into his face, and after a little while his eyes opened.

He looked around him, then slowly recognised Bob.

'Hallo!' he said, and smiled faintly. 'What's the matter? Where—where is——' He jerked upright against Bob's arm and gazed wildly around him. 'Where's the Phantom?'

His eyes were almost starting from his head and he caught at Bob's hand.

'What's been happening?' Mr Jolly asked. 'What are you all doing here?'

He passed his hand across his eyes, then spoke again, his voice puzzled.

'I—I've had a nightmare or something. It's queer, but

I dreamed that I was at the police station, and that the—the Phantom came there and—and—'

His words trailed away.

'It took him away—and it brought him back!' Bob whispered to the superintendent, crouching at his side. 'Now will you believe it, sir? It brought him back, and it left that message in ghost-writing outside!'

'What are you talking about?' Mr Jolly asked faintly. 'Am I still dreaming?'

No one answered him.

Later they told the warden what had happened. But for the moment, every man there was too astounded at the unnatural power of the Phantom to speak.

Each man was wondering what would happen next.

By the Broken Wall

The cracked bell in the clock-tower of old Cursitor Church marked the hour with eleven jangling notes. The sound of its tolling went scuttling away over the moon-bathed roof-tops, just as it had always done since the massive old clock was put in a hundred years before.

Bob Bryan paused on a corner of his beat as he heard the hour, and drew out his watch. He tilted its shiny face to the moon in order to see the position of the hands, and he nodded as he saw that it was exactly eleven.

'That clock may be old,' he told himself, 'but it keeps good time.'

Bob replaced his watch and buttoned up his policeman's tunic, then his athletic broad-shouldered figure moved slowly on, his rubber-soled boots making no sound against the broken stones of the pavement.

In a few yards he came to a stretch of rusted railings which, here and there, were broken down. Beyond these a large, open space was flanked by buildings, and at one side the front of the old church looked quietly down.

This open ground had once been occupied by ancient buildings upon which the hand of time had rested very heavily. They had become unsafe, their foundations had given way, and the places had been pulled down.

There were holes in the ground, like pits. There were other places where grass had begun to grow, and broken walls jutted up like ruins. Until recently, in the daytime, children had played over this old site.

The walls and what was left of the cellars of the vanished buildings had formed a wonderful playground for their games, and on the level parts boys had played cricket, or had kicked about old football cases stuffed with paper.

But now the entrance gate in the railings was closed and heavily padlocked. Children who came there to play had gone elsewhere, disappointed. Bob Bryan paused by the gate and peered at a poster stuck at one side.

'£75,000 required to secure this site as a Children's Playground,' the poster said, and it went on to give details of the efforts which were being made to raise the money and make this stretch of ground a place where children could play for all time.

Over this appeal a brief notice was posted: 'Closed—By Order.'

Bob nodded grimly as he saw it, then suddenly turned when he heard footsteps approaching the corner from which he had just come.

Footsteps were rare at night in the Fields, because the Phantom was abroad, and all men feared him. Some of the police, even, who were normally on night duty had been changed over to day work, that their places might be taken by constables with stronger nerves.

Bob watched the corner and a few moments later, a tall figure swung around it. It was a man who wore a dark coat over his evening clothes, and Bob recognised the cheery, red features of Mr Jolly, the Warden of the Fields.

'Good night, sir!' Bob exclaimed as he saluted, and the warden paused.

'Hallo, Bob!' he greeted. 'How's your father?'

'Quite well, thank you, sir,' Bob answered.

'Good.' Mr Jolly glanced past Bob to the notice on the railings and he frowned. 'Hm! I see that has been closed to the kiddies now,' he commented.

'Yes, and it's a rotten shame,' Bob exclaimed.

'Well, seventy-five thousand pounds is a lot of money to pay for a bit of land like this,' the Warden told him. 'I tried to persuade Sir Gordon Murgatroyd to lower his price, but he wouldn't budge, the old skinflint!'

'Is he the one who owns this ground then?' Bob asked.

'He is, and the Children's Society have been weeks trying to raise enough to buy it from him, but they can't manage it,' Mr Jolly said. 'Sir Gordon says times are bad, and he can't afford to sell for less.'

'I always thought he'd got plenty of money,' Bob replied. 'He's Mayor of the Fields, and they seal the scroll for him tomorrow.'

'It wouldn't hurt him to give the place to the children!' Mr Jolly exclaimed. 'Those who live around here haven't got many places to play in. The society would have had most of it levelled off, and have sown grass and—but what's the good of talking about it? Sir Gordon's closed the place now, and he'll sell it to some builder.'

He turned from the rusted railings and gazed down the street at the thin mist which was creeping up it.

'See that, Bob?' he asked. 'Mist coming up from the river! This is the kind of night for the Phantom, isn't it?'

'It only comes when there's mist about,' Bob told him.

'Then I'll get along home,' the Warden answered. 'I don't want to meet it again.'

'Some night I'll run it down,' Bob answered. 'Good night, sir!'

'Good night, Bob! Remember me to your dad!'

'I will, sir—thank you!' Bob answered.

Bob listened until Mr Jolly's footsteps died away, and he was about to move on along his beat when a new sound came to his ears.

It was the quick clicking of iron-shod hoofs against the cobbles and through it he heard the soft rumble of rubber-tyred wheels.

A moment later, a mounted police inspector rode into the street, while behind him rolled a coach, piloted by a postilion and drawn by two white horses. At the rear of this marched four policemen, and Bob suddenly remembered that this was a rehearsal for the ceremony of the Gilded Scroll, which took place the next night.

That ceremony had its beginnings in the past. Every year the mayor of the Fields was elected and was given a Gilded Scroll. At the end of his term of office, if he had served his people honourably and well, the scroll was sealed at midnight, marking him as a man worthy and true.

And on the night before the sealing of the scroll, the coach was taken on a practice run through the streets in order that everything might pass without a hitch when the real ceremony was held.

The coach was now passing during its rehearsal; the postilion wore his ordinary clothes, and the coach was empty. But the vehicle looked like something which had slipped out of the past as it came around the corner between the timbered buildings, its wheels jumping against the cobbles.

Bob saluted the inspector, and the police officer nodded.

'Everything all right, Bryan?' he called.

'Everything quiet, sir!' Bob answered.

The coach passed him, rocking on its springs. It rolled away down the street and around a bend out of sight.

Bob hitched his electric bulls-eye lantern more comfortably on his belt, then started slowly after it. As he moved, he glanced through the railings at the ground beyond.

He stopped short.

Crossing a moonlit patch of level ground making for the shadow flung by a broken wall, Bob saw the dark, shambling shape of the Phantom.

It was shrouded by the thin mist which drifted over the ground where, a little earlier, innocent children had played. Bob saw the Phantom's grinning features, blue-lined and hazy. He saw its dragging limbs below its dark, filmy cloak, and his heart leaped at the sight.

For a fraction of a second he considered blowing his whistle and summoning aid, then he changed his ming and jumped for the gate in the fence.

He gripped the rusted iron bars and swung himself up. He was quick-moving and agile, and a moment later he was dropping to the ground on the other side, picking his way forward.

He dashed on, reaching for his truncheon. The leather thong had slipped over his hand and the stout wood was pressing against his palm as he drew the weapon—when the Phantom backed from him.

It glided into the shadow, slipping around the end of the broken wall.

Fiercely, Bob flung himself on. His breath was noisy in his throat as, truncheon uplifted, he leaped around the wall to see—nothing. The Phantom had vanished.

He ran down the length of the wall, but there was nothing to be seen.

The spectral visitant had disappeared as completely as though it had never been. Except that, on the air, there hung the faint, acrid reek of brimstone.

* * *

'This is the map you wanted. We borrowed it from the museum.'

The sergeant in the charge-room at Cursitor Fields police station spoke as Bob entered to report for duty the following night.

On the sergeant's desk lay a map. It was very old, and it showed the buildings which had stood in the open space where the Phantom had appeared the night before.

Bob had reported the occurrence. Police had searched over the ground, but had found nothing. Bob had asked for the map that he might examine it and, possibly, find some clue to the Phantom's haunting of the place where ancient buildings had once stood.

'The curator at the museum brought it in,' the sergeant went on. 'He told me all about it.'

Bob bent over the map and examined the lines which indicated where houses had once stood. Carefully, he calculated the spot where he had seen the Phantom, and where it had disappeared.

He used the end of a penholder from the sergeant's desk to indicate the spot.

'I saw the Phantom about here,' he said.

'Was that the place?' The sergeant bent closer. 'That would be just where the biggest house stood on that site. There's the name of it written down. Can you read it?'

'Yes—"Knight's House"!' Bob answered.

'The Knight's House, eh?' The sergeant whistled softly to himself. 'You saw the Phantom prowling about the foundations of where the old Knight's House used to stand!' he added. 'The curator told me all about that—there was treasure supposed to be hidden in that house!'

'Treasure!' repeated Bob.

'Yes. When the workmen pulled it down, they had orders to examine every stone in the place in case they found something—but they never discovered anything worthwhile.

'There used to be a City knight living there, Bob, and they say he was supposed to have hidden a lot of gold. Maybe the Phantom was looking for it!'

The sergeant chuckled.

'He was after something,' Bob said, and looked at the map again. 'I just wanted to know what house stood there, sergeant, in case it offered a clue. I'll keep my eyes open again tonight.'

'And if you see the Phantom walkin' off with that gold, you take him in charge!' the sergeant grinned, as he slipped the map inside his desk again.

Bob moved away, and a few minutes later, he paraded with the other constables for night duty; in addition, there were eight men detailed for special duty for the ceremony of the Gilded Scroll.

These eight had to escort Sir Gordon Murgatroyd's coach from his great house to the Cursitor Fields Guildhall, in the old market place.

'There's no special order for tonight,' the inspector said, after he had read out the usual description of men wanted by the police. 'You all know that Bryan saw the Phantom last night, so keep a sharp watch out, because it's misty again tonight—worse than last night. And the Phantom usually shows up when there's anything like fog in the air!

'And don't forget that every man along whose beat Sir Gordon's coach passes is to salute and remain at attention until he has gone by. That's all, Sergeant. Take over!'

Bob took over at Four Ways just as the clock in the old

church was chiming ten, and he set off at once on his first tour of his beat, making sure that all doors and windows were closed in the buildings which he had to guard.

In the old days the sealing of the scroll had been the highest honour which the councillors of the Fields could pay to any man. Bob could not see that Sir Gordon Murgatroyd deserved such an honour.

He thought of all this as he moved on around his beat, and he thought of the man who was to ride through the Fields at midnight in the old mayoral coach. Sir Gordon would be dressed in robes, police would salute him, and at the banquet held at midnight, according to tradition, speeches would be made in his honour.

But those honours would fade, and all the money he got for the sale of his land could never bring him so much happiness as the sight of little children playing in the summer sunshine.

As eleven o'clock was striking, Bob returned to the rusted railings and took up his position in a patch of shadow. He watched the open stretch of ground and the clinging mist which swept over it, and he listened for the hoof-beats which would mark the approach of the coach.

Suddenly, as his gaze searched the mist, he sighted a movement near the broken stone wall which marked where the Knight's House had once stood.

Bob tensed, straining his eyes to pierce the murky gloom. He was not sure, but he thought he saw something dark in the motion by the wall. Half a minute passed, and he saw it again, dim in the mist.

That was enough! He gripped the top of the railings and swung clean over them in a single leap, landing lightly at the other side.

Quietly he moved forward, watching the wall.

He was twenty yards from it when against its darkness he made out a shimmering blue glow. It was the Phantom!

Bob's hand dropped to his truncheon, and he whipped the weapon from its long pocket. He could now see the Phantom crouching low against the wall, and to Bob's ears came the scraping of something heavy against the stonework.

Nearer he approached and nearer still. Then suddenly he saw the Phantom turn, and once again he was conscious of its glaring eyes, and yet again he heard its uncanny babbling.

But now its unnatural mumbling was shrill and angered. He saw one dead-white hand come out and strike the air as though, had it the power, this spectre of the night would have annihilated him with that vicious gesture.

Bob saw the Phantom rise from the ground and for and instant it stood with the thin mist wreathing around its black garments. Then, on shambling limbs, it shifted sideways with amazing speed, and Bob jumped in pursuit, determined that it should not escape.

He was four yards behind the Phantom when it reached the end of the wall, and Bob remembered how it had disappeared before!

He slipped the thong of the truncheon from his wrist and hurled the weapon with all the strength of his arm full at the Phantom. In the instant that the truncheon left his hand, the spectre merged with the shadow of the wall and disappeared.

Bob heard the weapon strike stones on the ground far beyond; then he reached the end of the wall and turned.

Twenty yards away he saw the Phantom again, gliding over the ground, its bent limbs shifting beneath the black cloak which floated out on the foggy air.

And Bob saw that in one hand the Phantom swung some burden.

Bob drew in his breath and dashed in pursuit. He was fast on his feet, but even his pace was no match for that of the wraith which slid ahead of him.

Bob saw broken ground where old bricks lay piled, and as the Phantom passed over them the thing which it held struck the bricks. Bob saw that the spectre carried a leather bag caught up at the neck.

The bag swung as the wraith glided on, soundless save that from its flaccid, blue-tinged lips its babbling came back in a snarl which would have daunted one with nerves less steady than Bob's.

It was making for the grey wall of old Cursitor Church and it gained this while Bob still sped in pursuit. The Phantom slipped around a massive buttress which jutted from the wall, and again the leather bag struck the stones.

Bob heard a tinkling, as though something had fallen; then the spectre was lost to him in the darkness around the buttress.

Three seconds later he himself was at the wall, and he switched on the torch at his belt as he jumped into the shadow.

The torch flung a clear beam for thirty yards along the side of the church, but in all that distance there was no sign of the Phantom. It had eluded him again.

But the edge of his beam caught something which glittered against the stone flags of a path around the hoary old edifice. Bob tilted the torch.

The light showed four coins, which could have fallen only from the Phantom's leather bag when it struck the buttress. Four large, old coins which glittered with the yellow hue of gold!

* * *

Bob scoured the ground all about the church. He examined the moss-grown stones which formed its walls in the place where the Phantom had disappeared. He found nothing.

He was giving up the search when he heard the clatter of

horses' hoofs, and across the open space he sighted the passing of Sir Gordon Murgatroyd's coach, with eight policemen marching behind, and with a uniformed postilion on the saddle of one of the two white horses.

'I'd better report this to the station,' Bob told himself.

He was still clutching the four coins which he had picked up, and he slipped them into his pocket, then hurried over the site of the old Knight's House to the street.

He knew that the old coach was going to the Guildhall, and that he would have to pass this on his way to the station. But he did not follow the coach. Instead, he cut through the numberless alleys and passages which intersected the houses of the Fields.

As he hurried he suddenly remembered the plan he had seen—and that he had caught the Phantom where the Knight's House had once stood!

'That bag must have contained the Knight's Treasure!' Bob exclaimed to himself. 'That's it! That's what he was after!'

He slowed his pace as the thought came to him, then stopped and pulled out the four coins, examining them closely. They were two-guinea pieces, each at least two centuries old.

'The Phantom's found the treasure; it was in that leather bag!'

Bob slipped the coins into his pocket, then hurried on.

He was half-running when he reached the end of an alley, which opened out into the market place where stood the Guildhall.

The door was opening, and in the moment that the robed figure of Sir Gordon started to alight there came a shout and a whinny of fear from one of the horses.

Leaping from the alley, Bob saw the horses rearing up—in front of them had appeared the figure of the Phantom, wreathed in the trailing mist! One pale hand was outstretched, pointing at Sir Gordon Murgatroyd as the Mayor of Cursitor Fields cowered back, craven fear and terror on his face.

Bob saw the Phantom glide forward. The horses plunged from its approach, and Sir Gordon was like a man transfixed as the terrible figure came towards him.

The watching policemen were stricken by stark astonishment, and Bob saw the Phantom snatch from Sir Gordon's hand the scroll which he had brought to be stamped with the Seal of Honour.

Brandishing the scroll, the Phantom turned and slid away, shambling around the corner of a near-by court. Bob was the first to recover.

He ducked away as the startled horses, rearing and plunging in their fear, almost trampled him down. Then he leaped past their tossing heads and glittering hoofs, making for the corner.

He darted around it, to see the Phantom in front of him. Its misted figure was vanishing in the thin fog and gloom of the court. But now Bob ran as he had never run before, drawing on all his strength and speed to overtake the floating figure ahead.

It turned the corner at the end, and when he reached it, the Phantom was across the road beyond, vanishing into another turning.

Bob sped after it. When he gained the other street, he saw the Phantom already half-way down it, almost lost in the trailing mist—and it had paused.

It was looking back at him and on the night air Bob heard its jeering laugh.

The cackling sound came to him, and with the laugh the mist seemed to thicken, cloaking the spectral form so that it merged with the mist and faded from view.

Two seconds later Bob was at the spot, but of the Phantom there was no sign!

Bob ran on. Behind him the other police were running up, and their whistles were sounding for help, asking constables on nearby beats to come up and cut the Phantom off.

Bob gained the end of the street, where it opened into a square. Mist drifted across its emptiness, but nothing moved except the blue-clad figure of two policemen, who came running into the square from the other side, answering the call of the whistle.

The two ran towards him, while the police caught up behind as Bob stopped. He turned to them.

'It vanished back there, about the middle of the street!' he exclaimed. 'Hurry up and search the doorways!'

More police came on the scene. In what appeared to be a matter of seconds, the narrow street was full of them, and with them came the robed figure of Sir Gordon Murgatroyd, supported by the inspector.

'Did you catch it?' he gasped.

'No; it got away!' Bob answered.

'You fool!' Sir Gordon Murgatroyd half-snarled the words, his eyes glaring under their shaggy brows, and his hooked nose showing like a beak against his face. 'What do you think you're paid for? The Phantom is only some crook! You let him slip through your fingers!'

He turned on the inspectors and raged anew.

'You're incompetent, the whole parcel of you!' he rasped. 'You should have caught the Phantom when it went for me and took the scroll from my hand. I could have caught him myself, but I was hampered by the door of the coach!'

Bob's face set as he looked at the angry man. Bob remembered that Sir Gordon had been scared half out of his wits when he had seen the Phantom, and there had been no question of his trying to catch the spectre!

'You're all afraid of it!' Sir Gordon barked. 'You're—you—'

His voice faded out, then he vented a sudden shout of fear. 'Look!' He pointed.

On the door at one side was something faintly blue. For a moment Bob thought that the Phantom was coming back, then he saw the blue glow take the form of lettering—of the Phantom's 'ghost-writing'!

Swiftly the glow grew stronger and across the door they read these words:

'Thy Scrolle shall never be
sealed, for thou art
without honoure.
'To ye children Y do give gold
to buy ye Land whych
thou would deny
them.'

The astounded policemen gazed at the words written in tenuous blue fire, while Bob stepped forward and looked at something which lay on the step below the door. It was the leather sack.

Its neck was opened and from this had spilled a fount of gold pieces—the Knight's Treasure which the Phantom had unearthed!

It had found the gold and was offering it as a gift with which to purchase the ground which Sir Gordon denied the children!

Only then did Bob see that the doorway was the entrance to the offices of the Children's Society, who had appealed in vain to the grasping mayor.

But that was not all.

Scattered over the step and the bag of guineas were fragments of gilded parchment—the remnants of Sir Gordon's Scroll of Honour, justly destroyed by the Phantom!

Day of Reckoning

The mid-morning sun beamed through the high, cell-like windows of Cursitor Fields police station. But the atmosphere inside that time-worn building was anything but sunny. Five uniformed policemen stood in the inspector's office, and among them was an ashen-faced Bob. These policemen were the ones most involved in the previous night's chase of the Phantom. Two newspaper reporters stood by the door, looking as though they were about to run. Behind the great desk stood three more men—the superintendent, looking every bit like a trapped Bengal tiger; the inspector, biting his lower lip and staring uncomfortably at the ground; and Sir Gordon Murgatroyd. It was the latter who held the attention of all in the room.

He was shaking from head to toe in rage. Streams of invective poured from between his tight, mean lips. The police were fools, bungling idiots who should be in jail for their incompetence, he told them. He had been made to look a complete, utter fool by the mysterious Phantom, and now he was after blood; it didn't matter whose.

Sir Gordon was a little wary of the man from the Yard, but any saving of temper he made by not raging at the superintendent he more than expended in his efforts against that lonely constable called Bob Bryan.

'You blithering ass!' he screamed. 'This must be the hundredth time you've let this cheap crook slip through your fingers. Pah! Phantom!' So far, Murgatroyd seemed to be repeating everything he had said the night before, thought Bob. He could understand the baronet being annoyed at his loss of face, but Murgatroyd's rage seemed to suggest more than simple annoyance—it seemed to suggest *fear.* But fear of what?

'But, sir . . .' began Bob.

'Don't answer me back, you ingorant fool! It wouldn't surprise me if *you* were this crook who calls himself the Phantom. You've bluffed the police before, but you can't bluff *me*, you jumped-up bank clerk!'

Bob let that pass.

'And if you're not the Phantom, then you're a coward. You hear me, a miserable, sniffling little coward . . .' Murgatroyd stared up at Bob's six-foot frame, '. . . who takes after his father. Yes, you make a nice pair, you two do, both as yellow as each other!'

Bob *couldn't* let that pass.

'Listen, Murgatroyd,' he yelled, no longer caring that he was just an ordinary police constable, 'my father was many things, but he was never a coward. And one day I'll prove that to you—to everybody—and then I'll be waiting for an apology, you fat toad!'

Murgatroyd stood rigid with shock. All his life he had blustered and talked down to all around him, and he couldn't believe his hearing when an ordinary constable talked to him in this way. The superintendent gazed at Bob open mouthed. The four other policemen watched with barely-concealed admiration. The two reporters grinned openly and scribbled in their note-pads furiously. *This* was the stuff which their readers wanted to read!

'It seems to me,' Bob was making a good job of it, 'that this Phantom makes a ten-times better person than you'll ever make, Murgatroyd. At least the children have got their playground now—and they never would have done if it had been left up to you. The way that you go on, nobody would ever dream that you're a baronet at all, you greedy miser!'

And that last sentence seemed to snap something in Sir Gordon's mind. He erupted into violent life.

'Out!' he roared. 'You're fired!'

'You haven't got the power to fire me,' said Bob quietly.

'But there's no need to worry, I'm going anyway. You will recieve a formal notice of resignation tomorrow, sir,' he added to the inspector. 'Good morning.' And with that, he walked calmly out.

The two reporters scuttled out a few minutes after him, note-pads full and front-page stories already being worked out in their minds. Their editors would be more than pleased at this latest development. For with Bob's resignation, they had found a *hero*—someone their readers would love to sympathise with and read about . . . 'LONE POLICEMAN RESIGNS TO CLEAR HIS FATHER'S NAME' would sing the headlines that afternoon.

* * *

All the national papers sent armies of reporters to Cursitor Fields the next day, all of them briefed to dig up new facts and to be the first to solve the great mystery which had now caught the country's imagination to such an extent.

Sir Gordon, meanwhile, raged at their interference.

'The fools are just encouraging this crooked "Phantom",' he snarled at the inspector one morning. 'They know that the thing is after me, and they're leading it on. Get rid of them, man—throw them out of Cursitor Fields!'

The inspector looked wearily up at Sir Gordon. He was growing rather tired of this miserly little man who had caused him to lose one of the best constables at the station—but as long as he remained a policeman he had to stay reasonably polite.

'You seem to forget, sir, that this is a free country. You can't throw the press out of a sizeable part of London just because they're annoying you. Besides, from what I saw of this morning's paper, these reporters are talking sense. They seem to think that the only reason that the Phantom exists is to fight some sort of injustice that happened several hundred years ago. The fact that he has been rushing around Cursitor Fields for the last few months suggests that that injustice took place around here and is at last about to be righted. But I can't imagine why he should be carrying out some sort of vendetta against you in order to settle a miscarriage of justice. Can you, Sir Gordon?'

He looked up at the baronet and saw two fear-stricken eyes staring back at him. Sir Gordon was shocked; his eyes and blanched face showed that clearly enough.

'Why, is something the matter, sir?' said the inspector, rising to his feet.

'N-no—nothing. Nothing at all,' replied Sir Gordon, walking quickly from the room, leaving a thoughtful inspector staring after him.

What had caused the baronet to act in that peculiar way, thought the inspector. Why had he been so shocked when he repeated the theory of the newspapers that the Phantom was seeking to right an age-old crime? Was Sir Gordon trying to hide something? It certainly seemed so.

The Phantom's continued robbery of his most private papers looked very much like a case of proof-collecting to the inspector. Anyway, with over a hundred newspaper reporters sifting carefully though the facts at that very moment, it certainly looked as though something was going to happen very soon. One final question. Why did the Phantom always make a point of appearing on young Bob Bryan's beat? Was there some link-up between Phantom and policemen?

Those same questions were whirling around in Bob's mind at the very same moment, as he sat staring into the fire in the tiny kitchen of his home. But neither the inspector nor Bob realised just how soon and how incredible would be the hour when those questions would be answered.

It was two weeks to the day after Bob's resignation from the force when BBC television put on an hour-long documentary about the Phantom of Cursitor Fields.

There were recorded interviews with all the people who had seen it; Bob, most of the other policemen at the station, several bystanders, Mr Jolly, and of course, Sir Gordon Murgatroyd, who was in the studio. Sir Gordon was the last person to speak. He felt that that was most important position on the programme to be in.

'What I myself think,' he began pompously, and Bob lit one of his rare cigarettes to steady his temper as he watched the programme at home, 'is that this "Phantom" is just a common criminal determined, for some reason or other, to discredit me. Others have been frightened by it, but I can assure you that a Murgatroyd couldn't be frightened by such a thing. Oh, no—*we're* not cowards!'

And as Sir Gordon finished the last syllable of that last word, the screen went blank.

'Blast!' grunted Bob, as he rose from his fireside seat. 'The tube would go *now!*'

But the tube hadn't gone, for in the top right-hand corner of the screen appeared a soft, pulsating glow, which lit up the studio scaffolding in an eerie, unreal was. Bob stood transfixed in the middle of the carpet, his father clutching his shoulder.

'The Phantom!' they breathed as one.

Gently, the incandescent light grew, filling the studio whith light and showing Sir Gordon and the interviewer sitting paralysed with fear in their seats.

Then, from the very depths of the blinding glare, a shape began to form, and the cackling laugh and mumbling intonations which all who had met the Phantom knew so well could be heard.

The Phantom drifted across the studio floor, and came to a halt in front of Sir Gordon, standing between him and the slightly shaking camera. And then, the most incredible thing of all happened—the Phantom *spoke!*

Clutching a sheath of ancient papers in one hand, it turned to the camera and said to the watching millions in cackling tones: 'Hear ye! Hear ye! For hundreds of years gone by, I have been kept from my grave by ye great injustice. But now my imprisonment from ye everlasting sleep is nigh over.' Bob could imagine the breathless silence reigning in the living-rooms of Britain as countless families gazed at the mysterious Phantom explaining his mystery before their very eyes.

'For here,' the Phantom waved the papers above his head, 'I have proof of ye incredible fraud of many moons gone by. My name is really Gerald Murgatroyd—proud son of Sir Henry Murgatroyd. At the age of five, I was turned out on the streets by my dying father's valet—a man called Benjamin Bryan. This man Bryan had a son the same age as myself, and when my beloved father finally died he told the world that his son was really me, and that son became known by my name—Sir Gerald Murgatroyd. I grew up under the name Bryan and had a family. My great-great-great-great-great grandson is known as John Bryan, father of the constable who has seen me so often lurking about Cursitor Fields. Just before I died so many moons ago, it came to my notice who I really was, and the shock was so great that I found myself unable to die a *complete* death, and I have lived these hundreds of years as a ghost—hovering between life and death, called the "Phantom" by all who came across me. But now my task is done, all the proof has been gathered, and I can go at last to ye everlasting sleep—secure in the knowledge that the world now knows that this greedy and evil man,' the Phantom indicated the perspiring Sir Gordon, 'is not entitled to the wealth and position he has claimed, but is just an ordinary commoner. The real baronet is John Bryan, of Cursitor Fields. And so my work is done. Now I bid you farewell and leave you forever, leaving behind only these . . .'

And as the sheath of papers proving the Phantom's tale fluttered to the floor, the glowing Phantom disappeared into nothingness.

Five miles away in Cursitor Fields, two men stood together in their tiny home. They were Sir John Bryan and his son and heir, Bob Bryan . . . Justice had been done at last.

The Black Cat

by EDGAR ALLAN POE

For the most wild yet most homely narrative which I am about to pen, I neither expect nor solicit belief. Mad indeed would I be to expect it, in a case where my very senses reject their own evidence. But tomorrow I die, and today I unburden my soul. My immediate purpose is to place before the world, plainly, and without comment, a series of mere household events. In their consequences, these events have destroyed me. Yet I will not attempt to expound them.

From my infancy I was noted for my kindly disposition. I was especially fond of animals, and was indulged by my parents with a great variety of pets. With these I spent most of my time, and never was so happy as when feeding and caressing them. This peculiarity of character grew with my growth, and, in my manhood, I derived from it one of my principal sources of pleasure.

I married early, and was happy to find in my wife a disposition not uncongenial with my own. Observing my partiality for domestic pets, she lost no opportunity of procuring those of the most agreeable kind. We had birds, goldfish, a fine dog, rabbits, a small monkey, and a *cat.*

This latter was a remarkably large and beautiful animal, entirely black, and sagacious to an astonishing degree.

Pluto—this was the cat's name—was my favourite pet and playmate. I alone fed him, and he attended me wherever

I went about the house. It was even with difficulty that I could prevent him from following me through the streets.

Our friendship lasted, in this manner, for several years, during which my general temperament and character—through the instrumentality of the Fiend Intemperance—had (I blush to confess it) experienced a radical alteration for the worse. I grew, day by day, more moody, more irritable, more regardless of the feelings of others. I suffered myself to use intemperate language to my wife. At length, I even offered her personal violence. My pets, of course, were made to feel the change in my disposition. I not only neglected, but ill-used them. For Pluto, however, I still retained sufficient regard to restrain me from maltreating him. But my disease grew upon me and at length even Pluto began to experience the effects of my ill temper.

One night, returning home, much intoxicated, from one of my haunts about town, I fancied that the cat avoided my presence. I seized him; when, in his fright at my violence, he inflicted a slight wound upon my hand with his teeth, the fury of a demon instantly possessed me. I knew myself no longer. My original soul seemed, at once, to take its flight from my body; and a more than fiendish malevolence, gin-nurtured, thrilled every fibre of my frame. I took from my waistcoat pocket a penknife, and cut one of its eyes from the socket! I blush, I burn, I shudder, while I pen the damnable atrocity.

In the meantime the cat slowly recovered. The socket of the lost eye presented, it is true, a frightful appearance, but he no longer appeared to suffer any pain. He went about the house as usual, but, as might be expected, fled in extreme terror at my approach. I had so much of my old heart left, as to be at first grieved by this evident dislike on the part of a creature which had once so loved me. But this feeling soon gave place to irritation. And then came, as if to my final and irrevocable overthrow, the spirit of Perverseness. Of this spirit philosophy takes no account. Yet I am no more sure that my soul lives than I am that perverseness is one of the primitive impulses of the human heart—one of the indivisible primary faculties, or sentiments, which give direction to the character of Man. Who has not, a hundred times, found himself committing a stupid action, for no other reason than because he knows he should *not?* This spirit of perverseness, I say, came to my final overthrow. One morning, in cold blood, I slipped a noose about the unoffending cat's neck and hung it to the limb of a tree; hung it with the tears streaming from my eyes, and with the bitterest remorse at my heart; hung it *because* I knew that it had loved me, and *because* I felt it had given me no reason of offence; hung it *because* I knew that in so doing I was committing a sin even beyond the reach of the mercy of God.

On the night of the day on which this most cruel deed was done, I was aroused from sleep by the cry of fire. The curtains of my bed were in flames. The whole house was blazing. It was with great difficulty that my wife, a servant, and myself, made our escape from the conflagration. The destruction was complete. My entire worldly wealth was swallowed up, and I resigned myself thenceforward to despair.

On the day succeeding the fire, I visited the ruins. The walls, with one exception had fallen in. This exception was found in a compartment wall, not very thick, which stood about the middle of the house, and against which had rested the head of my bed. The plastering had here, in great measure, resisted the action of the fire—a fact which I attributed to its having been recently spread. About this wall a dense crowd were collected, and many persons seemed to be examining a particular portion of it with very minute and eager attention. The words 'strange!' 'singular!' and other similar expressions, excited my curiosity. I approached and saw, as if graven in *bas-relief* upon the white surface, the figure of a gigantic *cat*.

The impression was given with an accuracy truly marvellous. There was a rope about the animal's neck.

When I first beheld the apparition—for I could scarcely regard it as less—my wonder and my terror were extreme.

For months I could not rid myself of the phantasm of the cat; and, during this period, there came back into my spirit a half sentiment that seemed, but was not, remorse. I went so far as to regret the loss of the animal, and to look about me, among the vile haunts which I now habitually frequented, for another pet of the same species, and of somewhat similar appearance, with which to supply its place.

One night as I sat, half stupefied, in a club, my attention was suddenly drawn to some black object, reposing upon the head of an immense hogshead of gin. I had been looking steadily at the top of this hogshead for some minutes, and what now caused me surprise was the fact that I had not sooner perceived the object. I approached it, and touched it with my hand. It was a black cat—a very large one—fully as large as Pluto, and closely resembling him in every respect but one. Pluto had not a white hair upon any portion of his body; but this cat had a large, although indefinite, splotch of white, covering nearly the whole region of the breast.

Upon my touching him, he immediately arose, purred loudly, rubbed against my hand, and appeared delighted with my notice. This, then, was the very creature of which I was in search. I at once offered to purchase it of the landlord; but this person made no claim to it—knew nothing of it—had never seen it before.

I continued my caresses, and when I prepared to go home, the animal evinced a disposition to accompany me. I permitted it to do so, occasionally stooping and patting it as I proceeded. When it reached the house it domesticated itself at once, and became immediately a great favourite with my wife.

For my own part, I soon found a dislike to it arising within me.

This was just the reverse of what I had anticipated; but—I know not how or why it was—its evident fondness for myself rather disgusted and annoyed me. By slow degrees these feelings of disgust and annoyance rose into the bitterness of hatred.

What added, no doubt, to my hatred of the beast, was the discovery, on the morning after I brought it home, that, like Pluto, it also had been deprived of one of its eyes. This circumstance, however, only endeared it to my wife, who, as I have already said, possessed, in a high degree, that humanity of feeling which had once been my distinguishing trait.

I was yet withheld from destroying it with a blow partly by a memory of my former crime, but chiefly—let me confess it at once—by absolute *dread* of the beast.

This dread was not exactly a dread of physical evil—and yet I should be at a loss how otherwise to define it. I am almost ashamed to own that the terror and horror with which the animal inspired me had been heightened by one of the strangest situations it would be possible to conceive. My wife had called my attention, more than once, to the mark of white hair which constituted the sole visible difference between the strange beast and the one I had destroyed. The reader will remember that this mark, although large, had been originally very indefinite; but, by slow degrees—degrees nearly imperceptible, and which for a long time my reason struggled to reject as fanciful—it had, at length, assumed a rigorous distinctness of outline. It was now the representation of an object that I shudder to mention: the image of a hideous GALLOWS!

And now was I indeed wretched beyond the wretchedness of mere Humanity. Alas! neither by day nor by night knew I the blessing of rest any more! During the former the creature left me no moment alone, and in the latter I started hourly from dreams of unutterable fear to find the hot breath of *the thing* upon my face, and its vast weight—an incarnate nightmare that I had no power to shake off—incumbent eternally upon my *heart!*

Beneath the pressure of these torments the feeble remnant of the good within me succumbed. Evil thoughts became my sole intimates—the darkest and most evil of thoughts.

One day my wife accompanied me, upon some household errand, into the cellar of the old building which our poverty compelled us to inhabit. The cat followed me down the steep stairs, and, nearly tripping me headlong, exasperated me to madness. Uplifting an axe, and forgetting in my wrath the childish dread which had hitherto stayed my hand, I aimed a blow at the animal. But this blow was arrested by the hand of my wife. Goaded by the interference into a rage more than demoniacal, I withdrew my arm from her grasp and lunged at her with the axe. She fell dead upon the spot.

This hideous murder accomplished, I set myself to the task of concealing the body. I knew that I could not remove it from the house, either by day or by night, without the risk of being observed by the neighbours. Many projects entered my mind. Finally I determined to wall her body up in the cellar, as the monks of the Middle Ages are recorded to have walled up their victims.

For a purpose such as this the cellar was well adapted. Its walls were loosely constructed, and had lately been plastered throughout with a rough plaster, which the dampness of the atmosphere had prevented from hardening. Moreover, in one of the walls was a projection, caused by a false chimney, or fireplace, that had been filled up and made to resemble the rest of the cellar. I had no doubt that I could readily displace the bricks at this point, insert the corpse, and wall the whole up as before, so that no eye could detect anything suspicious.

And in this calculation I was not deceived. By means of a crowbar I easily dislodged the bricks, and, having carefully deposited the body against the inner wall, I propped it in that position, while with little trouble I relaid the whole structure as it originally stood. When I had finished, I felt satisfied that all was right. The wall did not present the slightest appearance of having been disturbed. The rubbish on the floor was picked up with the minutest care.

My next step was to look for the beast which had been the cause of so much wretchedness; for I had, at length, firmly resolved to put it to death. Had I been able to meet with it at the moment, there could have been no doubt of its fate; but it appeared that the crafty animal had been alarmed at the violence of my previous anger, and had disappeared. It is impossible to describe or to imagine the deep, the blissful sense of relief which the absence of the detested creature occasioned in my bosom. It did not make its appearance during the night; and thus one night, at least, since its introduction into the house, I soundly and tranquilly slept; aye, *slept* even with the burden of murder upon my soul.

The second and the third day passed, and still my tormentor came not. Once again I breathed as a free man. The monster, in terror, had fled the premises for ever! I should behold it no more! My happiness was supreme! The guilt of my dark deed disturbed me but little. Some few inquiries had been made, but these had been readily answered. Even a search had been instituted—but of course nothing was to be discovered. I looked upon my future felicity as secured.

Upon the fourth day of the assassination, a party of the police came, very unexpectedly, into the house, and proceeded again to make rigorous investigation of the premises. Secure, however, in the inscrutability of my place of concealment, I felt no embarrassment whatever. The officers left no nook or corner unexplored. At length, for the third or fourth time, they descended into the cellar. I quivered not in a muscle. My heart beat calmly as that of one who slumbers in innocence. I walked the cellar from end to end. The police were thoroughly satisfied and prepared to depart. The glee at my heart was too strong to be restrained. I burned to say if but one word, by way of triumph, and to render doubly sure their assurance of my guiltlessness.

'Gentlemen,' I said at last, as the party ascended the steps, 'I delight to have allayed your suspicions. I wish you all health and a little more courtesy. By the by, gentlemen, this—this is a very well-constructed house,'— (in the rabid desire to say something easily, I scarcely knew what I uttered at all) —'I may say an *excellently* well-constructed house. These walls—are you going, gentlemen?—these walls are solidly put together'; and here, through the mere frenzy of bravado, I rapped heavily with a cane which I held in my hand, upon that very portion of the brickwork behind which stood the corpse of my wife.

No sooner had the reverberation of my blows sunk into silence, than I was answered by a voice from within the tomb!—by a cry, at first muffled and broken, like the sobbing of a child, and then quickly swelling into one long, loud, and continuous scream, utterly inhuman—a howl—a wailing shriek, half of horror and half of triumph, such as might have arisen only out of hell, conjointly from the throats of the damned in their agony and of the demons that exult in the damnation.

Of my own thoughts it is folly to speak. Swooning, I staggered to the opposite wall. For one instant the party on the stairs remained motionless, through extremity of terror and awe. In the next a dozen stout arms were toiling at the wall. It fell bodily. The corpse stood erect before the eyes of the spectators. Upon its head, with red extended mouth and solitary eye of fire, sat the hideous beast whose craft had seduced me into murder, and whose informing voice had consigned me to the hangman. I had walled the monster up within the tomb.

One Foggy Night

by DAN WALLIS

The mighty ship ploughed steadily forward, while the last dark traces of land fell away astern, lost in the gloom of night.

The bright lights from the Southern Heritage's portholes lit the heaving waves of the Atlantic as they rushed along her towering sides, and the night wind carried thin smoke backwards from her funnels.

The smoke spun and writhed upon the air, seeming to loom above the liner as if it embodied the phantoms and spectres said to haunt her decks at night.

It was as though ghostly shapes hovered above the vessel, waiting for the lights to dim, when those weird forms might drift down the corridors and creep past the cabin doors.

The shadows about the decks had a strange quality. It appeared as though their velvety blackness constantly cloaked hidden things. Men said that the Southern Heritage was haunted and drama-doomed—so that every voyage she made witnessed some strange event!

From the depths of the mighty vessel came a rhythmic thudding as her great engines forced her on.

Thrump—thrump—thrump!

The sound was sullen at times, but in the silence of the night it rang clearly, as if the very engines of the haunted ship voiced warning with a thousand metal tongues.

Thrump—thrump—thrump!

The sound drummed in the ears of a girl who stood near the bow. The collar of her warm coat was upturned against the night wind, and it provided a frame for regular, beautifully formed, oval features. Her dark eyes were gazing straight out to sea, where the night-cloaked horizon was lost in faint mistiness—as if the ocean itself was veiled by mystery.

Unmoving, she stood, staring as though her deep eyes saw something through that veil.

A little distance from her, against the ship's rail, stood Simon Light, the purser. His hands were clasped behind his back, and the shoulders of his gaunt frame drooped. He had grey-green eyes, which invariably stared straight ahead, appearing to notice little, yet missing nothing.

With him was Jonathan Hyde, the broad-shouldered detective of the Southern Heritage. He was drawing upon a pipe, and, with every puff, the glowing tobacco lit his rugged features redly. His glance was upon the girl, whom he knew was travelling alone.

She was a first-class passenger, and this was her first appearance since they had left Liverpool some fifteen hours before. The detective also knew that she was named Miss Doreen Carter, but he knew no more than that.

Watching her, Jonathan Hyde wondered what it was that she seemed to perceive in the misty distance. Presently, she turned slowly, and her eyes appeared to be alight with some strange fire as she glanced at the purser.

'The sea is very misty to-night,' she said.

Her voice was rich and clear, and Simon Light's thin tones came in answer as he bowed.

'Such a mist hides many things,' he said.

His reply was a little unusual, and Jonathan Hyde glanced at him sharply, but he had long since discovered that Light was a peculiar man, gifted with equally peculiar knowledge.

'Yes, the mist can hide many things,' the girl agreed, and

her rich voice quickened. 'It may hide the ghosts of dead ships!'

She faced the gaunt purser, who continued to stare straight before him, while his lean lips moved.

'The ocean is full of the ghosts of ships,' he said slowly.

'And there is one that I would wish to see!' the girl replied.

With those words, she stepped to the purser's side, and her eyes seemed to burn as she lifted a hand and pointed into the murky night through which the Southern Heritage was steaming.

'It would come as a great ship, voyaging out of the dark,' the girl breathed. 'A ghost-ship—with the spectre of a dead captain upon her bridge!'

For long moments she stood pointing with a quivering finger. Then, suddenly, she covered her face with her hands, and turned away, stumbling along the deck—leaving Simon Light still staring straight ahead, while Jonathan Hyde gazed with amazement after the strange girl.

The ship's detective knew, for a fact, that Simon Light had never spoken to Doreen Carter before. Yet the purser seemed to understand, somehow, what was going on in her mind! And she must have been thinking very strange things to speak of a ghost-ship and a spectral captain!

Jonathan Hyde came to the conclusion that the girl was out of her mind in some way or other. He remained with his pipe poised in his hand as he watched the girl go, making for steps which led to the upper deck. It was as she entered the circle of light flung by a lamp poised above the stairs that a man descended them, and the girl stopped short.

For a fraction of a second the detective had a glimpse of her features silhouetted against the light, and never in all his life had he seen such an expression as now showed upon them. They were already pale, but they became set, and her beautiful, dark eyes seemed to grow small as they fixed the man with a glance that was full of hate.

The passenger came on down the steps. He was richly clad in a fur-lined coat, and everything about him suggested wealth. His face was round, with pasty, flabby cheeks, and he had watery, blue eyes which widened as he saw the girl standing there.

He stopped short, and for some moments the two stood looking at one another—the hate-filled glance of the beautiful girl meeting the amazed, aghast stare of the passenger in the fur-lined coat.

Then, abruptly, she mounted the steps, moving up them lightly, and yet with such speed that she seemed eager to leave the staring man behind her. She had vanished before he turned away, sighting the uniformed figure of the purser, and stepping quickly towards him.

'Who is that girl?' he demanded.

His voice was trembling, and Jonathan Hyde could see that he was ashen pale. His manner was curt, as if he had such great wealth that he could address his fellows without the formality of being courteous. Simon Light continued to gaze into the mistiness ahead of the ship's heaving bow, and when he spoke his voice was toneless and brief.

'I could not tell you,' he said.

'You are the purser,' the man replied. 'You know everyone aboard the ship—and you know that I am Vincent Hale, the steel millionaire!'

'I am aware of that, Mr Hale,' Simon Light replied.

'Well, is that girl—Doreen Carter?' the millionaire demanded.

Simon Light turned slowly. His grey-green eyes appeared to look straight through the man in the fur-lined coat.

'There is a young lady of that name aboard the ship,' the purser replied coldly.

Vincent Hale gasped. He appeared hardly to notice the detective, and now his gaze went to the mist that hung above the sea. He stared across the heaving waste of the Atlantic, then spoke in a voice which seemed strangled and afraid.

'Purser, have you ever seen a—a ghost-ship?' he asked. There was a silence, during which Simon Light made no reply, and the millionaire turned to him, clutching him by the arm.

'You heard what I said!' he gasped. 'Have you ever seen—a ghost-ship!'

'I have seen many things while I have been aboard the Southern Heritage,' Simon Light answered.

There was a long silence between them, while the ship's engines grew louder, full of sudden warning.

Thrump, thrump, thrump!

They hammered insistently through the quiet—and above them a strange cry rang out abruptly!

It appeared to come from the bows, yet it seemed to be in the air above the ship's prow!

It rang thinly and eerily through the misted gloom, and such was the sound that Jonathan Hyde started upright where he leaned against the railings, while a shiver ran down his spine. 'What was that?' Vincent Hale gasped.

A second time the cry sounded, echoing with ghostly unreality out of the night, seeming to be aboard the ship—and yet to come from the air above!

'What is it—what is it?' the millionaire panted.

'I have heard that cry before,' Simon Light replied. 'It is the voice of the man who built this hip—the man who died in the hour that the Southern Heritage was launched!'

'Nonsense!' the millionaire panted. 'It can't be!'

'It can be—and it is!' Simon Light replied in slow and measured tones. 'We always hear the cry before the ship runs into a storm!'

He paused, still seeming to stare straight through the passenger.

'We shall have a storm before daylight,' the purser said.

As if in response to his words, that eerie voice sounded a third time, and, as it thrilled upon the air, the millionaire rammed his fingers into his ears, stumbling from the spot.

The two heard the thud of his footsteps dying away along the deck, while the weird voice from the dark trailed slowly and uncannily to silence.

As quiet dropped again, Jonathan Hyde found himself gripping the rail tensely. Simon Light turned slowly to him, and uttered words almost as startling as those he had spoken before.

'This will be a strange voyage, my friend,' he murmured. 'But something—always—happens aboard the Southern Heritage!'

The Lost Liner

The Southern Heritage was in the grip of a storm into which she had run just before dawn—as Simon Light had predicted.

Despite her enormous size, the vessel was heaving and rolling. Her engines had been reduced to half speed, or the ship might have damaged her plating against the great seas.

The thrump—thrump—thrump of the engines now came more slowly, more sonorously, like a steady echo of the thunder which followed the lightning flashes that seared the storm-swept clouds.

The decks were flooded with water, and hatches had been battened down. Most of the passengers kept to their cabins, watching the green seas as they smashed across the portholes.

Again and again the Southern Heritage dipped her mighty bow through some mountain of water, which broke across it and went spuming amongst the superstructure, showering in cascades through the rails and down the ship's sides.

Jonathan Hyde was in the first-class saloon, seated in his

favourite corner and smoking his pipe. Only a few yards from him was Vincent Hale, and the millionaire seemed terrified.

Never had the ship's detective seen a man's face so pale. Hale was huddled in the corner of a leather settee, cringing every time some wave thundered against the porthole above him.

Again and again he glanced at the thick glass, as if he feared that the angry gods of the sea might reach through and claim him.

Then, as he sat there, Hyde saw the millionaire's glance become fixed, and Doreen Carter walked into the saloon. She moved with balanced ease across the carpeted floor, pausing when she saw the millionaire, then turning to him.

She paused before him. Her dark eyes were blazing, while her features once again showed that hate-filled expression which Jonathan Hyde had seen the night before.

'You're afraid—and you have reason to be!' she exclaimed, as she addressed the man.

He cringed from her, clutching at the arm of the settee with shaking hands, while a mighty wave crashed upon the deck above and made the whole ship shudder.

'But it was not a storm that sent my father to the bottom of the sea!' the girl cried, above the thunder of waters overhead. 'It was—you!'

Vincent Hale tried to speak, but no words would pass his pallid lips. He dragged himself to his feet, staggering as the floor heaved underfoot, the expression of terror heightened upon his face.

'I know why you're afraid,' the girl said. 'You fear that my father may come back!'

She leaned towards him, words falling swiftly from her lips, her eyes burning as they bored into the man's pale orbs.

'That's why you've always been afraid to cross the Atlantic!' she exclaimed. 'And you are going to the States now, only so that you can ruin my brother! But you won't succeed.'

The millionaire staggered back, raising both hands before him as if to defend himself from the steady glance of her accusing eyes.

'If there is any justice, the sea itself will demand vengeance!' she exclaimed.

By this time Jonathan Hyde was upon his feet, and he saw the millionaire reel out of the saloon, with the girl turning to watch him go. Not until the door had crashed behind him did she relax, then she swayed, and the detective saw her turn pale. She looked as if she were about to fall, and he jumped towards her, catching her arm and leading her to the settee, vacated a few minutes before by the man who appeared to be her enemy.

She recovered rapidly, looking about the saloon and seeing that they were the only occupants.

'Thank you for helping me,' she breathed. 'I might have fainted!'

'The worst of the storm is over,' Hyde told her. 'There is nothing to fear.'

'I know—and I am not afraid,' she said, then looked at him suddenly. 'You're the ship's detective, aren't you? she asked.

'I am,' Jonathan Hyde said. 'Is there any way in which I can help you? Has that man—Vincent Hale—been bothering you?'

'No—but his conscience is troubling him!' she replied, and her eyes blazed again. 'He is the man who killed my father! He killed him as surely as if he had struck him down with his own hand!'

'Your father?' Hyde repeated.

'Yes, he was captain of a liner,' Doreen Carter replied. 'He had been master of the ship for twenty years, and the owners decided that it must be broken up, as it was no longer fit for service.

'Vincent Hale bought that ship, and my father sailed it on its last voyage across the Atlantic, with only a skeleton crew and no passengers. Vincent Hale arranged for the ship to be scuttled in mid-ocean, and as it went down the crew got away—but my father remained upon the deck!

'He was still on the bridge when the ship sank—sank because Vincent Hale had planned to get the value of it from the insurance company! Since then Hale has always been afraid to cross the ocean, for fear that my father should appear to him during the voyage—and I have a feeling that he will!'

Her eyes made Jonathan Hyde's heart leap as he met her glance, her stare was so strange, as if she could see things that were invisible to others.

'Hale is crossing the ocean so that he can ruin my brother!' she said. 'Vincent Hale is a steel millionaire, and my brother Dick owns a little struggling firm which has invented a new metal process. If Hale lands he will force my brother to sell his factory—and he'll ruin him, because he's been working for this for over a year. He has a strangle-hold on Dick, and nothing can save him once Hale sets to work.'

While she was speaking she came to her feet, turning to face Jonathan Hyde as he rose with her. Her voice sounded tremulously above the roaring of the storm through which the Southern Heritage was battling her way.

'But Hale shan't ruin my brother!' she said. 'My father will stop him somehow.'

She turned to the door, and the ship's detective followed. When she emerged to the corridor she ran to the swaying steps that led to the watery deck above and mounted them. He shouted to her, but she paid no heed, and he saw her release the catches on the door at the top of the steps, jumping out to the streaming deck.

The storm-wind caught at her as she appeared, and the water of a wave washed about her feet, while Jonathan Hyde plunged up the steps, to stop short. She was standing in the centre of the deck, both arms upraised as she faced the storm, while she lifted her voice, crying to her father.

'If you can hear me—save Dick from this man!' she called. 'Save him!'

In that moment, all the fury of the storm died, and a strange and sudden silence fell. It was as if the very elements were listening, but only for a moment did the quiet endure.

Next instant the ship heaved, and the storm in all its might battered at the Southern Heritage again, while the girl turned, stumbling to where Hyde stood by the doors at the top of the steps. He caught her arm, dragging her clear and locking the door, while she spoke breathlessly.

'My father will come; he heard me!' she said. 'I know he'll come!'

Jonathan Hyde stared at her, wondering if her agony of mind had deranged her brain. But he saw only the blazing light in her eyes, and the burning desire for vengeance which lay deep in them.

She sank her voice almost to a whisper, leaning towards him and speaking tensely.

'To-morrow night we shall be crossing the very spot where his ship went down,' she said. 'We shall be there at midnight'.

With these words she laughed suddenly, her eyes gleaming.

'I must tell Vincent Hale that!' she added.

She leaped down the steps, and Hyde saw her running towards the millionaire's state-room. When she reached it she tried the handle, only to find that the door was locked.

Hyde saw her beat upon the panel with her hands, then her voice came clearly above the battering of the waves and the howling of the wind along the ship's sides.

'You can hear me, Vincent Hale!' she called. 'At midnight tomorrow we shall pass the very spot where father's ship went down! And do you know what will happen then?'

She paused, and her voice struck clearly, ringing into the millionaire's ears as he crouched in a corner of his state-room.

'Then my father will come for you!' she cried. 'He'll come for you—on the ship which you sank!'

She laughed wildly, speaking once again.

'You'll see a dead captain on a spectral ship—coming to take you as a passenger!' she cried.

The storm had passed. The Southern Heritage's engines were moving at full speed again.

The ship was in mid-ocean, on the third night of her voyage—but it was not a normal night.

A warm breeze had swept across the chill waters of the Atlantic, filling the air with thick fog. The mist wreathed about the deck lights and filled it with shadows; it trailed like phantom arms past the portholes, and it seemed to dim the music of a band in one of the saloons, so that the strains were unearthly and unreal.

It wanted but half an hour to midnight.

Simon Light and Jonathan Hyde were taking their accustomed stroll around the deck. The purser walked with his hands clasped behind his back, his eyes staring straight before him, while his thin, clear voice came to his copmanion's ears.

'I remember Captain Carter, the father of that girl,' he said. 'He was a fine man, proud of his ship. But I did not know that his vessel had been scuttled by the orders of Vincent Hale.'

The detective had told him all that he had learnt from Doreen Carter, and the shadow of a smile now curved the purser's lips.

'But I did know that Hale was the captain's enemy,' he said. 'I can tell you, Jonathan, that the captain was the millionaire's rival in love. The woman who became the captain's bride preferred him to Vincent Hale and his wealth—and the milionaire has never forgiven it.

'He took his revenge when he sent Doreen's father and the ship to the bottom—and evidently he's now pursuing his evil designs in attempting to bring ruin to her brother.'

Simon Light said no more as they moved steadily on. Everything was unnatural in the mist, shadowy and spectral. The sea itself was oily, and there was an uncanny silence, through which the engines thudded steadily.

Thrump, thrump, thrump!

More than ever on this night that sound held a warning. It was as if the engines of the eerie ship knew that they were driving the great craft remorselessly nearer the spot which had been the setting for an ocean tragedy.

When Hyde and his companion turned towards the bows, after walking around the deck for some little time, they saw Doreen standing there, gazing ahead into the mist which veiled the face of the ocean. She heard the two approach and turned.

Hyde caught his breath, because never had he seen her looking so lovely as she did now. She wore a beautiful evening gown, and there was a bright light in her eyes as she faced them.

'How long is it before midnight?' she asked.

'Hardly ten minutes now,' Jonathan Hyde replied, glancing at his watch.

'Only ten minutes more!' she whispered, then suddenly drew open the cloak that she wore, and her voice changed. 'Do I look beautiful tonight?' she asked, and there was a plaintive note in her tones. 'I want to look lovely for my father; he was always so proud of me!'

'You think your father will come?' Simon Light asked her slowly.

'I am sure he will!' she said. 'He'll come—with his ship!'

'Yes, I think we shall see him,' Simon Light answered.

Jonathan Hyde stared at the two, hardly daring to breathe, quite chilled by their strange, cold speech. He felt as though both Simon Light and this girl knew of uncanny things which were beyond his own comprehension. He saw them looking at one another; then Simon Light bowed and moved on, while Jonathan Hyde fell into step at his side.

'What d'you mean?' the detective gasped. 'D'you really think you're going to see a ghost-ship to-night?'

'I know only that it is a strange night,' Simon Light replied gently. 'On such a night strange things may happen—and the Southern Heritage seems always to draw strange events with it!'

He said no more, and they made another round of the deck, to see a figure creeping before them as they turned back towards the bow. It was Vincent Hale, and the millionaire peered through the mist, his face a pallid oval.

'I can't stay below!' he muttered, as they drew level. 'I must have air!'

He began to walk along the deck with them, his voice quavering while he spoke eagerly, as if he were anxious for their company.

'It's a queer night—and it's nearly midnight!' he said. 'Something seems to be drawing me up on deck—and I'm frightened!'

Neither made any reply, and it was as they neared the bow that all heard a bell chiming from the bridge, indicating the midnight hour.

In that moment the Southern Heritage's siren shrieked wailingly, and the vibrant sound seemed to echo from the mist ahead of the ship.

All three stopped, staring before them. A gasp broke from Vincent Hale's lips as they heard a siren sound again from the murk in front. This time they knew that it was no echo!

'There's—there's a ship out there!' the millionaire panted.

The watched tensely, and it seemed as if the mist was parted by impalpable hands, and through this a ship became visible—steaming towards them! Steaming relentlessly on.

It was white and ghostly in the darkness, and on the spectral liner's mighty shape showed a single figure, visible on her bridge.

Steadily, silently, the weird ship came on and a cry broke from Vincent Hale's lips.

'She has three funnels!' he cried. 'Captain Carter's ship had—three funnels!'

'It is my father's ship!' the voice of Doreen cried ringingly from behind them.

She leaped forward, pointing across the waters.

'It's my father's ship!' she repeated, her voice full and piercing.

The millionaire stood rooted to the spot, his eyes wide and staring, his whole body trembling from fear.

The ghost-ship was coming straight towards them, looming out of the mist, travelling without lights—and with only that lone figure visible!

'It's coming for me!' Vincent Hale gasped.

He reeled, raising his hands, striving impotently to fend off the vision before him.

'It's the ghost-ship—she is coming for me!' he repeated.

He staggered, then collapsed where he stood.

In the moment that he fell the vessel in the mist changed its direction, sheering off. The girl remained staring after it, her eyes shining and a strange expression upon her face.

Simon Light and Jonathan Hyde stood side by side above the prostrate figure of the senseless millionaire, and neither moved until the spectral shape became invisible, as the cloaking mist veiled in once again.

'It was my father!' they heard the girl saying.

She glanced to the deck where Vincent Hale lay, then she spoke again.

'I always knew that my father would come,' she said.

'It's my father's ship,' cried Doreen.

She turned, and began to walk quietly away, while Jonathan Hyde and Simon Light bent over the man who lay at their feet, and from the purser's lips came whispered words.

'Something—always—happens aboard the Southern Heritage!' he breathed.

* * *

The Southern Heritage was near New York, but the mighty liner had been stopped.

Close against her side lay the dark-painted pilot's boat, and the pilot himself was climbing a ladder which fell sheer down the side of the ship.

Hardly more than a cable's length distant, another liner had heaved-to, and this craft was headed back across the Atlantic bound for England.

It had been halted by a wireless message sent from the Southern Heritage, and Vincent Hale's luggage was being lowered to the pilot's boat.

On the deck stood Jonathan Hyde and the purser, and with them was Doreen Carter.

All the fire had gone out of the girl's eyes now, and there was an expression of content upon her face as she saw the millionaire appear. Hurriedly he stepped on to the ladder, descending to the boat that waited beneath.

Vincent Hale was going back to England. The events of that dramatic midnight had forced him to abandon his vengeful plan, and Doreen's brother was saved.

As the Southern Heritage drew away, they saw the millionare climb aboard the other ship, and soon that vessel, too, was steaming full-speed ahead.

As it went, the girl made her way towards the stern, and the two men moved with her. They stood looking across the heaving water, gazing towards the misted distance into which the liner was gradually receding, carrying with it the frightened millionaire.

'My brother is saved,' Doreen murmured at last. 'He was saved—by my father! Vincent Hale dare not carry out his plan!'

She remained there until the last vestige of the England-bound ship had vanished, then she turned slowly away, moving to her cabin and making ready for the hour when the Southern Heritage would dock in New York and she could hurry to the brother whom she loved.

'He was saved—by the ghost of a sunken ship!' Jonathan Hyde exclaimed, when she had gone. 'Was it really a ghost-liner, Simon?'

The gaunt purser turned to him, and the stare of his grey-green eyes appeared to look through the ship's detective. A slowly smile curved his lips.

'I do not know,' he said. It may have been another liner, travelling through the night to be broken up in some distant shipyard, or it may have been a spectral vessel from the bottom of the sea!'

He paused, then spoke again.

'The sea is full of lost phantoms, Jonathan—and this is a ship which will draw them from their hiding-places!' he said.

The Green Feather

by SYDNEY PHILIPS

As the train drew out of Liverpool Street Station, Bob Peters sank back in his seat by the window, and smiled at his friend Jack Winter, who sat in the opposite corner.

'Well, we're off at last,' he said with a grin.

'And not before time either,' replied Jack. 'August the second it is, couldn't have waited another day.' He took a bag of chocolate toffees out of his windjammer-pocket.

'Have one?' he asked, holding them out.

Bob took two, and for a time both boys chewed in a companionable silence, each thinking his own thoughts, watching the grey, drab houses with their television aerials, and the great towering blocks of flats sliding-past the train window.

The boys had been friends since primary school, gone to the comprehensive together, fought side by side in playground battles, and, as they grew older had worked solidly for their 'O' levels. Bob, thick-set, short with yellow curly hair, was always cheerful, a grin never far away. He talked steadily all day, and never kept still for a moment. Jack was quite the opposite — a fellow of few words, dark, tall and thin. He practised with a chest expander every morning but it never seemed to make any difference. He did forty push-ups every night, but that never made any difference either, except the kitchen ceiling creaked ominously.

Jack's gaze shifted from the scenery to the luggage rack

above. He hoped he'd packed everything in his rucksack — he'd had to put his foot inside and stamp on the contents before he could get the drawstring closed. In his mind he ran over the list, checking, re-checking until at last he could stand it no longer. He stood up. Bob looked at him and kicked him gently on the ankle.

'Stop worrying, mate. If you've left it behind, whatever it is, it's too late now.'

Jack shrugged his shoulders, took out his wallet and began to count his money. Bob sighed. Jack was a real old worrit, sometimes he was like an old hen, he thought. Then he dismissed it from his mind — Jack was a good friend, a tower of strength when there was trouble around. He packed a surprising left hook.

As the train left the London suburbs and the green fields came into view both boys felt excited. They had camped and sailed with the Sea Scouts every summer since they were eleven, but this was their first trip on their own. Bob felt it was a real expedition, a journey into the unknown. Nobody knew what adventure they might stumble into. He and Jack had saved up for a year for this holiday. Ploughing round the grimy streets on his paper round, through snowy slush up to his ankles in the middle of January, Bob had thought of the summer holiday after the 'O' levels were over. Freedom for a fortnight! Every penny he could spare, all his Christmas tips and his birthday money went into a cocoa tin stashed underneath his shirts in his chest of drawers.

Jack had a Saturday job in a shoe shop, and when customers were being difficult, asking to try on every pair of shoes on the premises, he, too, had thought of the summer holiday — and thinking of it helped him to keep his temper.

Here, at last, the great day had dawned and they were on their way! At Sheldon they changed trains for the little branch line, and a couple of stations farther on, had their first glimpse of the river. In the distance, the Thames estuary glistened in the afternoon sun.

'Turnham! Turnham!' came the porter's shout, and the two friends clambered out, shouldering their rucksacks. Soon they turned off the main road and were trudging along a muddy lane to Mr Bladgett's house. Bill Bladgett had served in the Navy with Jack's father during the war, and afterwards he'd turned to farming. When they arrived, he was hosing down the yard.

'There you are, lads,' he said, pointing to a field about half a mile away with a woodland copse in the corner, quiet near to the river. 'Make yourselves at home. Water from this tap, here in the yard. Got your water carrier?' Jack nodded. 'Right then, fill it.' Jack did as he was bid. 'Eggs and milk from the back door in the morning. All the rest of your grub you can get from the village shop, mile up the road.' He jerked his thumb over his shoulder. 'O.K. for now?' Jack nodded again. Bill Bladgett grunted, then grinned.

'Off you go then,' he said, taking up the hose again.

'Hasn't got much time for chat, has he?' commented Bob as they were crossing the fields.

'You should hear my Dad talk about him, though,' said Jack. 'He never batted an eyelid when they were in action.'

'Weren't they stationed hereabouts?'

'Yep. M.T.B.s. Mr Bladgett liked the countryside so much, he swore if he came through alive, he'd settle down here.'

Bob looked at the river flowing peacefully along, a light breeze ruffing the surface of the water, and hundreds of boats sailing quietly at their moorings. It seemed impossible to believe that it had been the scene of wartime activities.

'They got to know the district pretty well,' Jack went on. 'Some very weird stories used to go around — you know — queer noises at night and cr ies that couldn'tbe accounted for.' Bob glanced at him.

'You don't believe all that stuff about *ghosts*, do you?' he asked incredulously.

'H'm, there's lots of things we don't really know about,' said Jack seriously. Bob let out a great bellow of laughter.

'Jack Winter,' he roared, 'I'm surprised at you.' Jack said nothing.

'Glad I've got my old jeans on,' Bob said to change the subject, as they climbed over a stile. 'I've just ripped my pants.'

They soon reached the copse of trees, and threw down their rucksacks, easing their aching shoulders.

'What about a brew-up?' suggested Bob.

'No sooner said than done.' Jack whisked out the Primus stove, primed it, turned it up to full pressure, set the billycan on top and watched for the water to boil. As soon as it was ready, he threw in a handful of tea, then carefully poured the brew into two mugs. Bob added some condensed milk. The two friends sat on a little hillock and drank the tea slowly, looking at the river.

'This is the only way to make tea. Learnt it from a night-watchman. All that fuss with kettles and teapots and cream-jugs — I don't go for that,' Jack muttered as he sipped the scalding liquid.

'Right — now for some action.' Bob sprang up, refreshed by the rest and the drink.

They were seasoned campers, and within an hour had set up their camp in a workmanlike fashion. The tent was pitched on a slight incline, fly sheet carefully in place, tent pegs at the right angle, guy lines taut. The ground sheet was smoothed out and an old blanket laid on top. Sleeping bags rolled at the far end. At the front, the flaps had been pegged out to give shelter from the wind when the boys were cooking. On the tentpole, Jack strapped a torch, pointing inwards. All the gear was stowed away neatly. Just inside the tent opening, they stacked the provisions and cooking utensils. The water carrier had been sunk in a neat hole outside, to keep the water cool.

Jack went round, testing the tent pegs with his foot, and tugging the guy ropes with his fingers.

'I'm glad we bought a big enough tent,' he said. 'A small one's O.K. for a weekend, but on a long trip you need something you can move around in.'

Both boys looked at their handiwork with satisfaction.

'I think it'd even pass old Scoutmaster Bluenose's inspection', Jack laughed. 'What about grub?' he asked. 'I'm famished.'

'Just one small job to do before we eat.' Bob disappeared into the tent. A moment later he came out wearing his swimming trunks, his jeans in one hand, needle and thread in the other. He sat down and carefully mended the three-cornered tear. Jack watched the pattern of the needle as it stabbed in and out of the blue material.

'Y'know, you'd never believe it, but Mr Bladgett was marvellous at embroidery.' Bob looked up, eyes round with surprise.

'Well, there's not much room on an M.T.B. Off watch they all had their hobbies. Mr Bladgett used to embroider coats of arms and badges. We've got a Royal Naval coat of arms that he did at home as a firescreen.'

'What did your Dad do?' asked Bob.

'He carved chess sets out of driftwood. And other blokes used to make wooden toys.'

Bob bit the thread off.

'There we are,' he said, 'it wouldn't pass my mother's eagle eye, but it'll do.' By the time he was fully clothed again, Jack had the Primus going and sausages sizzling in the frying pan.

'Sausages, cocoa, bread and jam and tinned peaches. O.K.?' he asked. Bob cut four enormous doorsteps of bread, smeared them thickly with raspberry jam. He began to wave his arms above his head.

'Wasps?'

'You're telling me,' grunted Bob, swishing all round him in vicious swipes. After supper, they washed up and tidied the camp.

The sun began to set, and the wind freshened a little. Bob shivered and pulled on an extra sweater. The shadows lengthened rapidly, and the copse of trees turned silvery grey and mysterious in the dusky gloom. Somewhere, a long way off, an owl hooted. Across the river, the moon, like a great yellow plate, began to rise over the horizon. They could hear nothing but the slap of the water on the mud, the rustle of the wind in the trees, and tiny noises in the undergrowth where small animals were making ready for a night's hunting.

Bob had a fleeting thought that perhaps there might be something in the weird stories Jack had hinted at, but it went out of his mind almost as soon as it had come in.

'Stir your stumps. A stroll along the sea-wall on to the hard, into Turnham and back again before we turn in. Get our suppers down,' he said.

The dawn woke Jack next morning. The sun rose slowly into a sky full of clouds, the wind had stiffened during the night into a fresh breeze.

'Good,' Jack thought looking out of the tent flap, 'we'll get a smashing day's sailing.' 'Oi', he shouted, 'hup yer get!'

Bob groaned and turned over.

'Whassamarrer?' he mumbled thickly.

'Get up, you lazy oaf, it's your turn to get the eggs and stuff.' Bob groaned again, but managed to open his eyes. He looked at his watch. Six o'clock? Still grumbling he crawled out of his sleeping bag, and didn't really 'come to' until he was halfway across the field with the water carrier in one hand, and an egg box in the other.

When he got back, Jack had dragged the sleeping bags outside and brailed up the edges of the tent to let the air circulate. The Primus roared. Bob breathed in the fresh salty air, and thumped his chest.

'Nothing like an early start!'

'Come on, Tarzan, muck in . . .'

'All right, all right, just doing my daily dozen,' wheezed Bob.

'Give us a hand and stop yapping,' bawled his friend.

Bob fell back. 'I'm bursting,' he croaked. 'I couldn't sink another thing.'

'If we eat at this rate, we'll run out of money,' said Jack in a worried tone.

'Jack Winter,' said Bob with as much severity as he could muster: 'Shut up!'

It was still only eight thirty when the boys had finished the daily chores, let down the tent brailings, and tidied up the tent. They put on extra jerseys, oilskin sailing jackets, and old tennis shoes. Jack felt in his jeans pocket — knife, spare bootlace for emergency lashing, a two inch nail and some small change.

'What's the nail for,' asked Bob as they walked along the hard.

'An old sailor gave me that tip — useful for undoing rusty shackles.' Bob chuckled to himself. Jack was always thinking of the worst that might happen. For himself, he was content to muddle through. The duffle bag with the day's provisions bumped against his leg as he walked. As usual, Jack had thought of everything — he had to give him that much credit.

By nine o'clock they were at the boatyard. A brisk blue-eyed man in a navy seaman's jersey and enormous black rubber boots came out of the office. His battered old peaked cap was stuck on the back of his greying head.

'You'll be Jack Winter and Bob Peters? The guvnor told me to expect you. There's your boat.' He pointed out to the mooring lines where rows of sailing dinghies bobbed on the tide. 'See, she's called Jago, to the right of that green scow.' The boys followed his finger and nodded.

'Good fresh breeze; you'll have a fine sail today. Here's a couple of lifejackets — it's regulations,' he added.

'I feel like the fat lady in the circus,' giggled Bob, lacing his up. 'You look it too!' retorted his companion.

'The guvnor said you could borrow this pram to get out to Jago.' Bob took the oars with Jack in the stern. The 'pram' was so small that there was no room to stretch their legs. The boatman hurled a dunnage bag with a suit of sails into the bows, and then shoved them off with his foot.

'Tide's ebbing!' he shouted. 'Turns about half-twelve. Wind'll veer a bit, I shouldn't wonder. Good luck!'

They were afloat! Bob's eyes sparkled as he leant on the oars, pulling strongly with the tide against him. Jack trailed one hand idly in the water, looking up and down the river. The houses looked like toys on the bank.

They bumped against Jago's side. While Jack held on to the dinghy, Bob nipped nimbly over the stern.

'Painter coming aboard,' Jack sang out as he threw the rope from the pram.

'Aboard and made fast,' echoed Bob, making a double clove hitch round the mooring rope.

Jack unshipped the oars inboard and secured them, transferred the duffle bag, then the sail bag. He looked round to see that all was shipshape in the pram, and hopped into the dinghy himself.

Ten minutes had passed when Bob cast a final eye over the dinghy. Everything was ready.

'Stand by to slip moorings.' He took the tiller in his left hand, and the mainsheet in his right. Jack was in the bows untying the mooring rope. He held it firmly in the bow cleat with his left hand, and the buoy in his right. On the word, he slipped the moorings and they were sailing!

'Up the jib,' came Bob's voice. Jack heaved with all his might, and made fast. Bob steered skilfully in and out of the moored craft. The sails filled and they were off on their first tack, against the tide and with a following wind, veering slightly.

The sun shone down and the fresh wind blew the clouds scudding across the sky. Bob kept his eye on the triangle of sail made by the boom and the mast, that was where the main force of the wind showed. Jack hauled on the jib sheet.

'Ready to go about!' shouted the skipper as the seawall came up ahead.

'Ready — leeo-h!' He pushed the tiller hard away. The boom swung over with a thump. Jack slackened the port runner, and tightened the starboard one, let go the port jib sheet, scrambled over to starboard, hauled taut the starboard sheet all in one easy movement. At least, it looked easy, but it had taken many voyages, and many painful tumbles before he had mastered the knack.

Bob was content. He had a good crew who knew what he was doing, a brisk wind, just enough lop on the water and the warmth of the sun on the back of his neck. Classroom, school, home and the paper round seemed very far away.

Jack was at peace, too. There was nothing like sailing to forget all one's worries. His particular worry at the moment was his 'O' level results, but he put in firmly out of his mind. He watched the water creaming around the bow, then turned his head.

'Can't we save up for a boat of our own next year; then we won't have to hire one,' he said.

'Good idea — we could probably pick one up second-hand at the end of the season.'

After a couple of miles, Jack pointed out a timber ship moored at the other bank.

'Let's go over and look at her,' he said.

The timber ship was half unloaded, great baulks of softwood were stacked on the quayside, and the sound of fork-lift trucks busy shifting it came floating over the water. They could see a Russian flag fluttering.

Jago crept round the ship's bows at a safe distance.

'She's Russian all right,' said Bob, craning his neck. A big sailor was leaning over the bowrail. Bob waved.

'Strazvitche,' he called. The sailor's face split into a grin.

'Dosvidanya,' he shouted back, giving the thumbs up sign.

'Just shows you, school subjects do come in handy. Glad I took Russian instead of French.' Bob turned the dinghy away up the river again.

'What'd he say?' queried Jack.

'Just said "Cheerio".'

At slack water, about eight miles up the river, they hove to for lunch, in a small inlet. The tiller was lashed and the sails pulled down. Jack flung out the anchor. The dinghy swayed gently on the end of the rope. Bob unpacked the provisions, which they ate ravenously. Soon, with the heat of the noonday sun, they slept, lulled by the rocking of the boat.

When Bob woke, the tide had turned. He shook his companion.

'Make ready to sail' he said. Then he went on: 'Let's go up this creek and explore. We've got plenty of time; now the tide's on the make we can't go aground.' The little boat nosed her way upstream, Bob picking his way up the narrow channel between the mud banks.

Suddenly, at a bend in the river, they saw an old hulk aground on the mud, the rising tide lapping at her stern. She was well and truly stuck. Without a word, the boys worked their way over to the wreck.

'Come on, Jack,' cried Bob, eager for adventure. They made fast, and scrambled up the rough wooden side. The timbers in the bow were split and warped, giving good foot-holds.

'She must have been here for years,' said Jack, kicking an old tin can overboard. Bob stood amidships, staring about him.

'Seems odd, doesn't it, that aft it's in such a terrible state, but forward the condition's quite good . . .'

Jack looked and said slowly: 'Yes, it's strange all right—this deck planking looks almost new, and it's been freshly caulked.' He reached the forward hatch.

'Come on,' he said, 'I've got a torch, let's go down below.' He checked his watch. Two-thirty.

Between them, they pulled up the heavy hatch cover, peered inside and shone the torch down into the gloom. Only it *wasn't* dark or gloomy down there. An old-fashioned oil lantern swung from the bulkhead, and an old sailor with white hair and white moustaches sat on one of the lower bunks. He glanced up and grinned, his tobacco-stained teeth showing as brown stumps. A green parrot sat on his shoulder.

'Come on down, boys, Tom Pegleg's glad to see yer.' The old man was dressed in a rough navy seaman's jersey with a red-spotted handkerchief knotted round his neck. On one foot he had a big sea-boot, the other leg ended at the knee, a wooden peg sticking out in front of him. In his left ear was a gold ring. His gnarled old fingers moved dexterously in and out, over and under, splicing a rope.

The lantern cast shifting shadows over the old man's face, and the light shone eerily on the bulkhead walls. What *was* this place? It must have been the fo'c's'le, where the crew lived and slept.

The upper and lower bunks were covered with neatly folded blankets. Below were the seamen's chests — the crew's chests.

Above the bunks were faded brown photographs of mothers and girl friends in old-fashioned clothes, ships in full sail — the sailors themselves, forearms bent showing off their tattoo marks and muscles. Jack leant forward to look at one of the photographs which bore a date. It said 1902. He looked again. 1902? That was the year his grandfather was born . . .

Jack looked round uneasily. Something was wrong somewhere. If this *was* the fo'c's'le and the crew lived down here, where were they? Why were the photographs on the walls so faded? Did Tom Pegleg live here on his own? Why was he so terribly old, and still at sea?

The old man seemed to sense his doubts and his unspoken questions. As soon as he spoke, all Jack's misgivings vanished, he seemed to fall under the spell of the old sailor's burning gaze. That was what Jack remembered most afterwards — those bright, fevered eyes.

'I'm off watch!' said Tom. 'Hark!'

Above them on the deck, they could hear the hoarse shouts of a crew working, the mast creaking, the slap of the sails, the rushing of the water past the bows. Sharp commands and answering cries of 'Aye aye sir!' Above all, the howling of the wind, and the alarming rocking of the ship as she heeled to-and-fro.

'Sit ye down, lads, and let's have a yarn,' said the old sailor. So, for what seemed like hours they sat entranced while the old man told them stories of the Australian run, the West Indies, and battling round the Horn in the teeth of terrible gales. All the time he talked, the old man went on splicing the rope.

The light from the lantern reflected softly in his brown eyes and showed up the lines in his weatherbeaten face.

'That's a very fine parrot you've got there,' said Jack politely.

'Ar, t'is that,' said the owner. 'I got' er in the East Indies

They were entranced while the old man told them stories.

when I were a youngster, not much older than yourself. Been with me ever since. There's many a crew-mate tried to buy 'er from me, ay, and steal 'er from me, too.' The parrot, as if to reassure her master, rubbed her head against the stubbly chin, and pecked the old man's ear gently.

'Can she talk?' asked Bob.

'I'll say she can. Go on Poll, me old beauty.' And the old sailor gave a peculiar whistle. The parrot started off on its repertoire. Great strings of words came flooding out of its beak. Oaths, nursery rhymes, snatches of songs long since forgotten. The boys chuckled.

Jack stroked the sleek head. The parrot looked at him with his beady eye and croaked: 'One a penny, two a penny, hot cross buns.' Bob laughed and turned to see the spliced rope neatly coiled on the bunk top. Suddenly the sound of a ship's bell split the air.

'Six bells,' cried the storyteller. 'Time for me to go on deck. Off you go, lads.' He held out his hand and as each boy shook it, he felt the hardened horny palm covered with callouses, and the *coldness* of it. The man's touch was like ice.

Bob shivered and went up the ladder as fast as he could, Jack following close behind. Once on deck, they stared about them, bewildered. There was no howling gale, no crew working, no ship's bell. The old hulk was firmly stuck in the mud, not giving an inch of movement either way. All was quiet. The afternoon sun burnt orange, and just above the level of the deck they could see Jago's mast bobbing up and down. Bob's brow creased up, perplexed.

'Funny . . I could have sworn . . . what's happened?'

'Never mind, let's get out of here!' cried Jack, bounding away. He was over the side and into the dinghy, running with trembling legs, Bob at his heels. Together, they panted and worked with fumbling fingers to cast off, away from the hulk, away from the mystery of it, away from the coldness.

On the journey home in midstream, Bob began to laugh and joke, pouring scorn on his fears.

'It was just a trick of the light,' he said.

Jack sat silent, looking at the water with troubled eyes, working the jib sheet automatically. He looked ashore; everything was the same as on the morning's sail, and yet it all looked different at the same time.

'Bob,' he said quietly, 'Bob, I checked my watch when we went down that hatch, and it was two-thirty, remember?'

Bob nodded.

'Well, I checked it again when we came up, and it was two-thirty-two.'

'But we were down there for hours. Your watch must have stopped.'

Jack shook his head. 'You know it's never given a moment's trouble since I had it.' He shifted the rope in his hands.

'Somehow, in a way I don't understand, that old man made time stand still.'

'Rubbish!' Bob moved the tiller a couple of points. 'You're imagining things.'

'No.' Jack shook his head and fell silent again.

As they were rowing the pram back to the boatyard, Bob looked at his friend's white face.

'We've had a long day' he said, 'and a tiring one. I vote we have fish and chips for supper. I noticed a fish bar in the town last night. We won't bother to cook.'

They made their way to the other end of the town and joined the queue outside the fish shop. At seven o'clock it opened and an appetising smell of frying floated out to their nostrils. Six or seven youngsters had just come out of the cinema first-house, laughing and pushing one another about. They went off clutching their fish and chips wrapped in newspapers, and telling each other what a smashing film it had been.

Bob stepped up to the counter, and ordered double portions for each of them.

The man behind the counter laughed.

'Been out on the water, have you?' he asked. 'Then you're bound to have an appetite. How far did you go today?' He swished the chips up and down in the boiling fat. The fish was ready, draining on a piece of white paper. Bob hesitated, but before he could speak, Jack started to talk. It seemed as though his words were like an avalanche. He told the shop owner about the old sailor, Tom Pegleg, the hulk and the strangeness of it all. Of how his watch had shown only two minutes to have passed, and yet it seemed as though the old sailor had talked for hours. It had all seemed so real, and yet . . .

The man behind the counter gave the chips a final thump and scooped them out on to the paper. He wrapped them up in separate portions, and said:

'That'll be four shillings, please.' Then he added quietly:

'I wouldn't go visiting that hulk again if I were you, boys. There's not many as'll go near 'er nowadays. Old Tom Pegleg's been dead these sixty years. He were killed in a knife fight one August the third. One of his mates got drunk, and wanted Tom's parrot. At least, that's how the tale goes. I've never believed it before. Thought it were a lot of foolish old talk. But now you wouldn't get me to go up there for all the tea in China.'

Jack's hand outstretched to take the paper bundles, stayed still, his fingers curved in mid-air.

His face was ashen.

'You mean . .?'

'That I do. 'Tis said old Tom comes back every August the third to fetch his parrot.'

Bob blew out his breath in a long sigh. He laughed and then turned to Jack and scoffed:

'Come on Jack, I've never heard such rubbish in all my life.'

Then the man behind the counter noticed something.

'What's that?' he asked, pointing.

Bob looked down at his windjammer. Nothing unusual, hc thought. He moved his arm. He looked at his hands, turning them over. As he twisted his right wrist he noticed the inside of his sleeve. His eyes bulged and he felt cold tremors down his back. Inside the sleeve quite close to the elbow, stuck by a daub of tar was a long green parrot's feather. A green parrot, such as you might find in the East Indies.